Stories That Move Mountains

Stories That Move Mountains

Storytelling and Visual Design
for PERSUASIVE PRESENTATIONS

Martin Sykes, A. Nicklas Malik and Mark D. West

WILEY

A John Wiley and Sons, Ltd, Publication

This edition first published 2013

© 2013 Martin Sykes, A. Nicklas Malik, and Mark D. West

Registered office

John Wiley & Sons Ltd, The Atrium, Southern Gate, Chichester, West Sussex, PO19 8SQ, United Kingdom

For details of our global editorial offices, for customer services and for information about how to apply for permission to reuse the copyright material in this book please see our website at www.wiley.com.

The right of the author to be identified as the author of this work has been asserted in accordance with the Copyright, Designs and Patents Act 1988.

Reprinted Jan 2013

A catalogue record for this book is available from the British Library.

ISBN 978-1-118-42399-8 (paperback); ISBN 978-1-118-42400-1 (e-PDF)

Set in Centaur MT Std Regular 10/13 and Minion Pro 11/13 by Indianapolis Composition Services

Printed in Italy by Printer Trento S.r.l.

We are lonesome animals. We spend all our life trying to be less lonesome. One of our ancient methods is to tell a story begging the listener to say — and to feel — "Yes, that's the way it is, or at least that's the way I feel it. You're not as alone as you thought."
—John Steinbeck

There have been great societies that did not use the wheel, but there have been no societies that did not tell stories.
—Ursula K. LeGuin

Storytelling is the most powerful way to put ideas into the world today.
—Robert McKee

The most effective way to improve a presentation is to get better content
—Edward Tufte

Publisher's Acknowledgements

Some of the people who helped bring this book to market include the following:

Editorial and Production
VP Consumer and Technology Publishing Director: Michelle Leete
Associate Director–Book Content Management: Martin Tribe
Associate Publisher: Chris Webb
Executive Commissioning Editor: Birgit Gruber
Assistant Editor: Ellie Scott
Senior Project Editor: Sara Shlaer
Copy Editor: Melba Hopper
Technical Editor: David Stewart
Editorial Manager: Jodi Jensen
Editorial Assistant: Leslie Saxman

Marketing
Associate Marketing Director: Louise Breinholt
Marketing Manager: Lorna Mein
Senior Marketing Executive: Kate Parrett

Composition Services
Compositor: Indianapolis Composition Services
Page Design and Layout: Jennifer Mayberry
Proofreader: Wordsmith Editorial
Indexer: BIM Indexing & Proofreading Services

Authors' Acknowledgements

Much of what we include in this book has been known and written about for the last 50 years, with some parts going all the way back to Aristotle. We have tried to bring all that knowledge, insight and wisdom together into an actionable approach, but this would not have been possible without a lot of input, guidance and support from many people.

We would like to thank the people that directly helped with the creation of this book, those who have been involved in the evolution of the approach over the last 12 years, whether they knew it or not, and those who trod this path before us from whom we have been able to learn.

Thinking about writing a book and actually doing it are worlds apart. A very big thank you has to go to the team at John Wiley & Sons for making our vision a reality, and especially to our editor Sara Shlaer. Sally Tickner and David Stewart also deserve a mention for helping to build a book proposal that would land a publishing deal.

The look and feel of the book was as important to us as the content. We wanted it to be interesting and memorable, and without Mark as a co-author much of this would not have been possible. Mark specifically wants to acknowledge Farouk Seif, Faculty Emeritus at Antioch University Seattle, for fuelling an early addiction to infographics and the "wholistic" systems view of complex problem solving, and Erik Knutson, CEO of Design Laboratory, Inc, for the continued mentoring, the priceless meetings, and recognizing Mark's true potential—"how I define 'amazing' is all because of you."

Thank You

Al Noel. Alistair Lowe-Norris. Aristotle. Bob Anderson. Brad Clayton. Brian Burke. Chandru Shankar. Chris Haynes. Edward Tufte. Fabio Salvador. Gabriel Morgan. J.D. Meier. Jeremy Hall. John Hearn. Prof. Joe Peppard. John Dalton. Harvey Webb. Kim Schulze. Mike Manisty. Oskar Göschl. Parker Lee. Philip French. Rick Maguire. Rob Lambert. Robert Fritz. Robin Ray-Howett. Robert McKee. Sally Bean. Sally Buswell. Scott Adams. Steve Fletcher. Steve Metcalfe. Steve Thomas. Tim Linsdell. Tom Farmer. Warwick Holder. William Barry. Every student Mark ever had and all of the attendees at Martin's storytelling workshops.

Contents

About the Authors

Martin

Martin Sykes started writing software 31 years ago and has spent the last 24 years working in IT organizations in the public and private sector. Since 1999 he has focused on IT Strategy and Enterprise Architecture. While developing the process and templates for visual storytelling he has worked in organizations from GlaxoSmithKline to Her Majesty's Prison Service to Microsoft, on projects from product lifecycle management to offender management systems. He has personally seen the difference a visual story can make in gaining commitment and has trained many people in the related techniques. After joining Microsoft Services in 2006 Martin began to develop many of the methods and practices now used by Microsoft Enterprise Architects around the world.

Martin lives near Cambridge in the UK with his wife Jules, cats Solo and Tom, and an ever increasing collection of robots.

Martin is an amazing speaker and storyteller. Like anyone who has practiced his art, Martin makes storytelling look easy, but don't fool yourself. He has worked harder to understand the underlying methods and mechanisms of communication than anyone I know. He's a pretty good photographer as well, and this book has some of his photos scattered throughout. I consider myself both fortunate and blessed to know him and work with him on this grand effort.

—Nick

Martin
- Developing robotic systems
- Enterprise Architect at GlaxoWellcome (later GSK)
- Learned how to sell
- CTO for Her Majesty's Prison Service
- Microsoft Services Enterprise Strategy Architect
- Storytelling training for Microsoft IT EA team

Visual Story #1

Nick
- Software Architecture, using wall-charts to describe software architecture
- Started process modeling
- Cofounder and CTO of Acadio.com Began to use one-page descriptions for communications
- Enterprise Architect for Microsoft IT

Mark
- Started Lizard Tracks Art Studio
- Teaching design at the Art Institute
- Teaching at IADT. Began to focus on telling a narrative
- Teaching logo, symbol, and icon design, with an understanding of culture, meaning, and symbology.

We should write a book about this !

1990

2010

Nick

A. Nicklas Malik is a leader in the Enterprise Architecture community at Micrsoft, a role that is all about making change happen. Most people don't understand the role of the Enterprise Architect, so when Nick met Martin and learned about his remarkable approach to storytelling, he realized the opportunity was right in front of him to leverage these ideas. Some of the visual stories Nick has developed have been used to build support for consistent governance, approaches to design, and plans for building a completely integrated approach to complex business problems. In addition to being a 32-year veteran of high tech, Nick is an amateur actor and vocalist, and a full-time father to Maxwell, Andrew, and Katrina. He loves to take nature walks, breathe fresh air, read well-written stories, and hold hands with his sweetheart for the past 22 years, Marina.

*One of the things I love most about Nick is his laughter. It's a real joy to know I am inspired to say whatever it takes to get a laugh — but even more inspiring to know I design for that same effect. Although this is sometimes a dangerous approach, I find his jovial attitude **energizing** and supportive — to this day I still don't fully understand his role within Microsoft, but hopefully they know they're lucky to have him!*

—Mark

Mark

Mark D. West has a background in art, design, music, education, and training. He started working for Microsoft in 1997, executing graphic design and production solutions for MSN as an independent vendor. After many other contracts and companies, he found himself working on presentation design and data visualization for the Microsoft Services Enterprise Strategy team in 2010, where he ran into Martin. Mark has an M.A. in Whole Systems Design and ten years of experience directing art, teaching, advising, training, and developing curriculum for design programs at five different colleges. He has been awarded Distinguished Educator of the Year at International Academy of Design and technology (IADT)-Seattle and appointed to the Professional Advisory Committee for the Art Institute of Seattle.

Currently, he's engaged in training projects with Microsoft retail stores, helping to create the stories and experiences we wish to share for store customers. Around the time of the publishing of this book, he's enjoying his one-year wedding anniversary—YAY! Mark is also obsessed with ways to get on board with the latest charting rock band, but if that doesn't work out, he's going to solidify plans for illustrating a children's book.

Mark has a very understated and relaxed manner, which makes it all the more amazing when you see his design work and his ability to teach others how to do it. He's also able to inject humor and fun into the work to keep everyone interested.

—Martin

To my loving wife, Jules, for her support and patience during the development of this book.

To my parents, John and Janice, who gave me my first computer in 1982. They had no idea what it could do or where the journey would take me as a result.

—Martin

To my wife Marina, for her patience and steadfast love,

To my son Max, my son Andy, and my daughter Katrina, for their enthusiasm, joy, and inspiration.

And to my parents who have always amazed and inspired me with art, infused me with reason, and taught me with love.

—Nick

To Chrissy, my patient wife... for her support and tolerance for all the Sunday morning author conference calls after busy Saturday nights, and believing and recognizing my potential to make this book happen.

To my parents Joan and Hubert: for cultivating my creative outlets from an early age. Enduring my drumming from the basement for hours at a time was above and beyond anything I would expect of anyone—in retrospect.

—Mark

I had been developing and using the ideas in this book for five years before I presented them for the first time in public at the seventh annual Enterprise Architecture Europe Conference in 2006. Between that first public showing and the writing of this book, the content has been refined, tested, and used to train hundreds of Microsoft employees and people in other major organizations around the world.

In 2010, Nick offered to work on the book with me, and we soon invited Mark to join us. Even at that point, this project almost didn't happen. As we were conducting the market research, I found enough books with similar content that I almost gave up. However, after talking with people who had participated in my training courses I realized we had two very strong reasons to write a book. Many books had a narrow focus on a particular skill set, with very few covering the breadth of techniques, or explaining how to bring all of these skills together in a repeatable process. Hardly any of the books focused on the practical aspect, with worked examples to show how to apply the concepts. Our aim is to keep the theory to a minimum and focus on the practical. Eventually you may need those other books that dive deeper into the details and the theory, but when the presentation needs doing and your career is on the line, we believed a "get the job done" guide was needed.

Stories That Move Mountains is focused on one of the most common reasons for presentations — the need to gain commitment from other people for a change, proposal, or decision. Many presentations and communications are made each day simply to educate the audience, but I know from many years of trying to influence people that when you want the audience to make a decision, or want to change their behavior, you have to work a lot harder.

This is a handbook for people who are ready to go beyond the usual approach of presentation slides covered in bullet lists. This book is about content, focusing on just what the audience needs to understand. It's about understanding your audience, and the reasons why they will be willing to act on your proposal. It's about using stories to wrap your message in a way that has influence and impact. And it's about creating your content in the right format for the situation.

From senior managers tasked with making decisions to call center operators to the followers of 24-hour news shows, people today are constantly overwhelmed with the data and information pushed at them. More and more, we see that people do not have the time to read long text documents and are bored with typical presentations. At the same time, we see too many projects fail because the people involved have not committed to the changes the project requires. In this book, we introduce you to a process that focuses your message onto a single page, and from there build out to the appropriate mix of formats to deliver a compelling visual story.

I know this process has worked for many hundreds of people already, and from all three authors we hope you will find it useful and interesting. If you have any questions, feedback, or examples you would like to share with us we can be contacted through the book website or on our Facebook page.

—*Martin Sykes*

www.storiesthatmovemountains.com
www.facebook.com/storiesthatmovemountains

The Power of Stories

Which is worse: repeatedly performing a flawed process, learning about it without question, or teaching it to others?

In business, and in life, we often repeat the same pattern: We learn flawed ideas, we use them, and then we teach them to others. Usually, this is because our underlying assumptions are incorrect, and since we don't like to question our assumptions, we often repeat our mistakes.

What follows is a true story showing how a good idea can be killed by poor communication and how tenaciously people can fight to reject a good idea.

In the nineteenth century, free or low-cost maternity clinics were set up across Europe to reduce infanticide and improve the practice of medicine. This greatly appealed to poor women. In one unique institution, the Vienna General Hospital, there were not one but two clinics for childbirth. Clinic One used doctors, and Clinic Two used midwives. In the midwife clinic, on average, about four percent of mothers died during labor. In the physician's clinic, the number was at least *twice as high*, and in some years, the death rate topped ten percent. Something was amiss.

Dr. Ignaz Semmelweis, a young resident at the time, compared the practices at the two clinics and, in 1847, suggested a reason for the difference between the two. The doctors in Clinic One were studying anatomy by dissecting decaying corpses and then walking directly into labor clinics to deliver babies *without washing their hands.* The midwives in Clinic Two were not. He theorized that something was being carried on the hands of the doctors. To prove his theory, this young doctor introduced antiseptic hand washing in Clinic One. The results: Infection rates dropped dramatically. Death rates dropped dramatically.

Semmelweis's colleagues started to share his results with the medical community, hoping to save thousands of lives. After all, this was great news! The medical community responded by ridiculing his ideas or misunderstanding him. After all, it couldn't be the *doctors* who were making the women sick!

Historians have concluded that Semmelweis thought his ideas would be obvious to others and they would catch on quickly. Because of this Semmelweis didn't write a paper on his ideas until 1858 and didn't write the book on his findings until 1861. Competing papers and textbooks dismissed his ideas. Bad practices were propagated, and good ideas were dismissed. It was simply inconceivable that doctors were making healthy people sick.

After his book earned bad reviews in 1861, he wrote harsh letters to medical leaders around Europe, infuriating his peers. In 1865, two of his peers conspired to commit

FL WED A COMMUNICATION METHOD

him to a mental institution, where he was beaten and then, ironically, died of an infection within two weeks of arriving at the institution. After his death, his replacement as the head of the obstetric hospital of Pest, Hungary eliminated hand washing. Death rates climbed tenfold. No one protested.

Practicing physicians continued to resist the idea that doctors should wash their hands before performing a procedure *for another 75 years!* The evidence was there, yet change was slow to come. What was missing?

Some scholars have suggested that Semmelweis was a good scientist, but a poor communicator. Perhaps if Semmelweis had used a simple and clear way to communicate the effectiveness of hand washing, many lives could have been saved.

All new ideas, large or small, meet with some level of resistance, especially if the new idea requires new *behavior.* If we want to change the way people behave, remember that comfortable ideas will not yield easily, even to evidence and authority. In order to change hearts and minds, we need to focus on enhancing how we communicate. We need to be clear, convincing, and accurate.

Do we really believe that minds can be changed with a stream of bullets in a presentation slide deck? If the existing methods of communication aren't working very well, then we need to work out what is missing.

Visual

Over the years we have shared the content of this book with hundreds of people. Al Noel, a principal consultant at Microsoft, had this to say about changing how you approach presentations.

You must free your mind! No more boring lists of bullet points! That stuff does not work. You have to take a much different approach. People absorb stories visually all the time with all our modern communications technology.

Many years ago when I was in the Army, I was assigned to the 101st Airborne Division. At that time, the idea of an Air Assault division that used helicopters extensively was a new idea some people did not always get. One picture in the presentation regarding the division's capability summed it all up. It was a picture of a helicopter flying over difficult terrain.

Any infantry man can just look at that picture and get the message. It is about taking a completely different approach over the obstacle and moving on. No more figuring out better ways to cross the obstacle quicker, faster, and safer; you must take a completely different approach to the problem. You only have to cross something like this once in your life as an infantryman to get the idea and appreciate it. It's the same with the visual approach to creating and telling stories.
—Al Noel

Stories

In their book *Made to Stick,* Chip and Dan Heath talk about an annual class they run at Stanford University. The students are asked to deliver a one-minute persuasive speech to their peers. All the students are provided with the same data. Half of the students must argue for one point of view, the other half for the opposite point of view.

As you might imagine with Stanford students, these are typically good-quality presentations that clearly impart data and arguments. After the presentations, the audience is distracted for a few minutes with a comedy video and then asked to write the key points from each speech they heard, working from memory because they don't have notes to refer to.

The students are surprised at how little they can remember. It's not as though they had a lot to remember, just eight one-minute speeches. These are well-educated people, being presented to by some of the brightest students on the planet. Although only one in ten students will use the presentation to tell a story, leverage emotion, or really focus on a few key messages, the evidence shows that sixty-three percent of the audience can remember facts from the story-telling presentations, compared with only five percent from the rest. This evidence was one of the tipping points for me. The use of stories can make your ideas stick in the minds of your audience.

Should We Blame the Tools?

We make presentations every day. This is especially true in professional settings, where we present ideas, agreements, and updates to peers, superiors, customers, partners, and stakeholders. We even make presentations at home and in our communities. Yet not all presentations are equal. Sometimes, a presentation leads to decisions, actions, commitments, and change. However, far too often, a presentation fails to produce any effect whatsoever. The audience may have learned something, but their actions don't change. So, the question is, was their time well spent?

If, like us, you've sat wearily through boring presentations, maybe you've thought or heard others say, "That's an hour I'll never get back," or "Did we make any progress at all in there?"

But should we blame the tools? After all, Microsoft PowerPoint has become ubiquitous in business and government settings. Speakers at major conferences are expected to use PowerPoint to deliver their presentations. Military commanders use PowerPoint to provide status updates to their superior officers, and teachers at all levels, from grade school through graduate school, use PowerPoint to deliver class lectures. It's clear that PowerPoint has been widely embraced as the de facto mechanism for education, information sharing, and idea sharing.

We don't think the fault lies with the tools. For one thing, PowerPoint and other similar presentation packages are relatively new tools. Poor communication has been happening for a long time. In fact, most of our visual stories have been created by using PowerPoint as a simple design tool.

Finding the Right Tool for the Job

As a tool for convincing people of big ideas, a typical business presentation built from a template of bulleted lists fails in so many ways.

The reasons are plentiful. Different people start with different assumptions, learn in different ways, and need different information to make decisions. Some people are detail-oriented and some like the big picture. Some need a logical argument; others want to understand the impact on people and processes. You cannot provide all possible permutations of the information needed, yet make it easy to navigate and understand with a standard bullet list template. Yet people try, and as a result, members of the audience either become confused or angry about your presentation, or they ignore it. What could be *less* effective than that?

If the standard presentation template approach isn't an effective way to convince people, why do we use it? Einstein said, "Insanity is doing the same thing, over and over again, but expecting different results." And that applies here. Most PowerPoint presentations created to convince people of a new idea are about as effective as using a hammer and chisel to slice bread. It will work, sometimes, but not very often and not very well.

This is a reboot. We are starting over, and questioning the basic idea of the presentation itself.

This book is about how to effectively communicate that a change needs to happen so people will be motivated to take action. The approach we will introduce you to in the following chapters produces a clear communication that we call a **visual story**.

visual story

visual story

Visual story (viz'yoo wel stôr' ĕ) **n.**
1. the telling of an event or series of
events in a form that is, or can be seen
2. a simple and clear visualization of
an idea, presented on a single "sheet
of paper," for the purpose of guiding a
group of people to a specific conclusion.

Sometimes the visual story can be
as simple as a hand-drawn sketch,
sometimes it's a merger of a rich
picture and mindmap, sometimes
a high-production quality
infographic. The key factor is that
it's a story on a single page with the
intent to persuade someone to act
and make a change happen.

To Be Effective, You Have to Affect People

A visual story is a new starting point from which you can then create
presentations, animations, or just stand and speak. It is a proven, simple,
effective technique for communicating an idea in such a compelling way that
your audience will want to act on it.

A visual story does more than communicate an idea. It combines storytelling
techniques with visual design to communicate a message that has been fine-
tuned for your specific audience. A visual story inspires your audience to act.
This matters because an idea that doesn't inspire change or motivate people
to act is impotent and powerless. Even an amazingly good idea, like "wash
your hands before surgery," can go unheeded if not communicated well.

Although literally millions of presentations are made every year, most
fall into three general categories. Presentations are used to CONVINCE,
EDUCATE, or REPORT. Visual stories are useful primarily for situations
where the aim is to convince other people. Presentations designed to educate
the audience or to report on progress can benefit from a lot of what we have
to say, but the process we have developed has a strong focus on reducing
the message down to the minimum necessary to influence the audience to
take an action. A visual story provides a selected set of information, in a
single complete picture, carefully designed to draw your audience from their
starting place to the desired conclusion.

While you may ultimately produce your visual story in many different
formats, we are going to focus on first getting to the one-page view, as we
have found that the focus and effort to get the message to this level enables
a better delivery for a wide range of other formats, from presentations, to
video, to simply standing at a whiteboard and sketching out the ideas. On
the following two pages we illustrate the idea of the visual story, with a visual
story about using the process to rapidly improve an existing presentation. As
this is a common situation we have dedicated Chapter 16 to be a worked
example based on the last two days of this story.

What a difference a day can make

Bob and his team have spent many months developing ideas for a new product. They can describe what it will do, how to build it, and what it will cost.

The team has presented on its product many times, and has standard content that shows the features and lists the advantages.

Sometimes the presentations go well; sometimes the audience seems distracted. The most important audience, with the power to provide the remaining funds, is still to come.

> Hi Bob. On Friday we have a chance to present to the business team on the new product proposal. Would you take the lead please?

> You've been working on this for months. Put some of the content together and do a dry run tomorrow.

> I know we've done a lot of work, but the presentation has over ninety slides and takes forty minutes. We need something shorter.

> It was too complex and too confusing! Too many words and complicated diagrams. I barely listened to you while I was reading all the slides.

> I reworked it last night, really sharpened up the text, removed a lot of diagrams and put in some pictures of people using the new systems.

> I saw your presentation today. Your message is still confusing. At the end, I was wondering what you wanted us to do next. I think you need to take a look at this book.

Monday				Tuesday				Wednesday			
0900	1200	1500	1800	0900	1200	1500	1800	0900	1200	1500	1800

Every day, people make the mistake of presenting what they know, rather than what the audience needs to hear.

A little simplification can go a long way toward improving the audience's experience.

But, if you want to really engage the audience, to get a reaction, it's time to think differently. It's time for a story.

Clarify the goals and the result to be achieved. Map out the content to remove the excess and sharpen the focus.

Translate the content into action. Turn it into a story with characters motivated to achieve the goal.

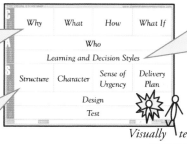

Why	What	How	What If
Who			
Learning and Decision Styles			
Structure	Character	Sense of Urgency	Delivery Plan
Design			
Test			

Assess members of the audience to determine what they need to know.

Visually tell the story.

Define the conflict.

Show the struggle.

Achieve the goal.

Return to ask the audience for support.

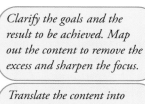

I read this book last night, and I want to see if we can do something different. We have the content; we just don't have a compelling story.

Let's get the team in a room. It's always easier to make progress when we can create and review together.

We'll follow the CAST process to turn our content into a visual story. This will help us put the audience first and tell a story that has real meaning for them.

I don't mind you bringing your work home. The story makes your ideas easy to follow. You know I don't understand most of the technology you use, but with the story and the handout I don't need to.

That was a great way to explain the ideas. I really feel like I know where we're going, and why. You can count on me. One day you'll have to tell me your presentation secrets.

Thursday								Friday			
0800	1000	1200	1400	1600	1800	2000	2200	0900	1200	1500	1800

Most visual stories take longer than a day to create, but if you already have the content, it's possible to make a big difference very quickly.

Chapter 16 shows what Bob and the team did on Thursday and Friday. If you're keen to understand more you can jump ahead, but be warned, we cover a lot of ideas and techniques in the chapters between here and there.

Convincing Evidence

Early in the development of the visual story process, well before it had the name and structure we use in this book, Martin used the technique to help change the relationship between the IT department and the rest of the organization in Her Majesty's Prison Service.

Martin

Every year, the senior executives met to review the strategies for different parts of the organization. Each year, the IT director presented the updated IT strategy to the board. He was usually allocated 15 minutes on the agenda. For many years the IT director had presented a document of approximately eight pages, and each year, the group of executives indicated their approval. There was no real discussion, and the IT department wasn't seen as strategic to the performance of the organization. Each year, real opportunities for change were lost because changes in technology and the Internet were not considered a priority by the senior staff.

A new IT director was appointed at the start of a major period of change. This wasn't a small reorganization. Whole departments were undergoing changes, and at the same time, a major update of the IT infrastructure and line of business systems was planned. I was hired to work on this upgrade and to support the implementation of the IT strategy. It was an ambitious program that would affect every major business function. Over a two-year period, it would replace tens of thousands of computers, upgrade the network and data centers, and replace core business systems.

Failure to convince the executive staff of the need for this strategic, and expensive, change could mean that the people we needed to involve would not be ready, significantly delaying the program and really increasing the costs. There was also a big risk that opportunities for improvements to the business processes would be lost if we didn't secure the engagement needed across the organization. As the date for the annual strategy presentation approached we knew we had a golden opportunity to change the way the prison service worked with its technology team. This opportunity was rare, and because we were both new, we could try something different.

The day of the meeting came, and at the appointed time, we turned the projector off. Instead of showing a PowerPoint deck or an eight-page document, we distributed a large-format, printed copy of a visual story, one page, and held our breath. What they were looking at was a well-known picture of a training prison with a series of small stories around the edges, each relevant to different members of the board, in the context of the overall business of the organization. The stories captured the impact and detail of changes over the next three years.

The original one-page visual story is probably somewhere in the prison service archives, but it would have far more detail than is appropriate to share here. This sketch gives an idea of what the visual story looked like and the topics for the stories.

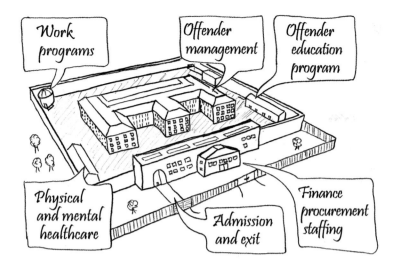

Work programs

Offender management

Offender education program

Physical and mental healthcare

Admission and exit

Finance procurement staffing

The difference was immediate. No one said anything. All eyes were on the visual story. After a few minutes, the IT director began to speak. He talked them through the major technology changes from the perspective of the prison, using different parts of the central image as the starting point for a series of small stories.

After 30 minutes, the questions were piling up. After 45 minutes, the session was called to a halt. We had exceeded our time, but the outcome was very different from prior years. All of the department heads now had an action to establish regular one-on-one briefings with his or her IT representative. It took a little while for the IT strategy to get approval. Many questions now needed answering, but the change in the relationship between IT and the department teams had started.

The Visual Story Process

This book is for visionaries and educators, change agents and revolutionaries, motivators and drivers. If you prefer the status quo, or your business is not changing, you probably don't need this book. But if you want to influence others to make a decision, improve something or agree to a change, read on. We can help you.

We've been experimenting with the production of visual stories for years. We've utilized research from a wide array of fields, conducted some of our own, and looked at the work of many other groups struggling to make effective communications. We have failed as many times as we have succeeded. When we examined why we failed it was clear that we had skipped some part of the analysis, or rushed to create a visualization without first getting clarity on why it mattered to the audience. When we succeeded it was also clear that we had first created a good one-page visual story to clarify the focus of the message before developing other formats to communicate the story.

The visual story looks simple, and in its simplicity, it is powerful. Clear simple messages are easy to consume, use, and follow. *But clarity and simplicity are not easy to produce on demand.*

We have made it as easy as possible to create a visual story, but doing so still requires work — more work than you would normally put into preparing a presentation. Making change is hard. Communicating change is hard. With visual stories you can at least improve your success rate.

What do you have to gain? That's up to you. Where do you want to take the world today?

CAST and the Visual Story Map

2

Over the next few hundred pages we are going to cover a lot of material. Chapter 1 explained why the visual story is important. In this chapter we provide an overview of what we you will learn, and in Chapter 3 we explain how you can get the most from this book. Because we are going to show you how to bring together a wide range of different techniques we thought it would be very important to provide an overview, so you can see how it will all fit together, and also to give an early insight into where all of the techniques we use have come from. Each chapter will provide a lot more detail on the sources for the techniques, and you can find a prioritized list of references in the Appendix.

The Visual Story Map

The diagram below is called a *Visual Story Map*. We developed the Visual Story Map to illustrate the process for creating a visual story, and to show how the steps of the process relate to one another. We named the process *CAST* after the four main steps shown vertically on the far-left side of the Visual Story Map: Content, Audience, Story, and Tell.

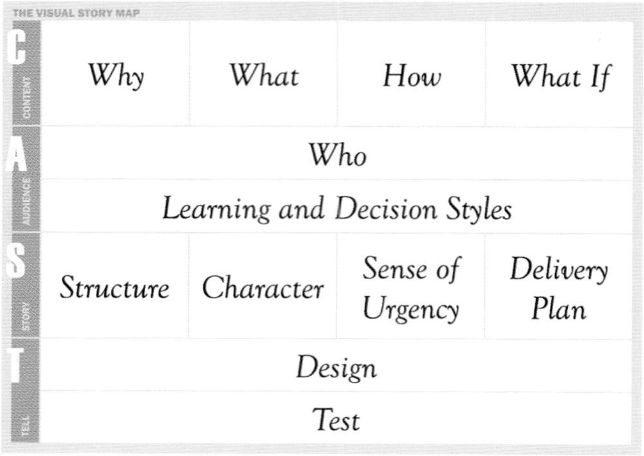

I keep six honest serving-men
(They taught me all I knew);
Their names are What and Where and When
And How and Why and Who.
—*Rudyard Kipling, Nobel Prize-winning*
novelist famous for his short stories.

THE VISUAL STORY MAP

CONTENT	Why	What	How	What If
AUDIENCE	Who			
	Learning and Decision Styles			
STORY	Structure	Character	Sense of Urgency	Delivery Plan
TELL	Design			
	Test			

CONTENT ROW Many presentations have too much content that is not relevant to the decision or change being proposed. If you want your sales team to search for new customers, or your IT group to implement a new content management system, your content must lead the audience to understand why you want them to act, and what they must do.

AUDIENCE ROW You need to understand the people you're telling your story to. What do they need to know? How can you motivate them to respond in the way you intend? Whether you want your design team to develop a new logo, or your CEO to approve a new project, you need to consider the different people in the audience.

STORY ROW When you are clear about the content and your audience, you can focus on the story structure. We draw from centuries of practical experience of how to tell a compelling and interesting story. Using the format of a story, rather than simply presenting information, makes it easy for your audience to identify with your goals, remember your ideas, and agree with your suggestions.

TELL ROW Now you create the words and visuals to focus on the telling of the story. Work out how the story will be conveyed in different formats and test that it has the intended impact. Careful attention to the different ways a visual story can be told can make the difference between a clear story and a muddled message.

Nick

I am responsible for figuring out the simplest way to solve difficult software and technology problems. Often I need to create a solution and then explain it to dozens of different people, each with their own questions and concerns.

Before I understood how to create a visual story I would create a long series of diagrams to explain my ideas, using different pictures for different purposes, or running through a series of diagrams in a presentation. More than once, after throwing picture after picture at my customers, I'd sit back and marvel at my skill and wait, patiently, for my customer to agree. After all, I'd given them all the evidence they needed to see that my design was good, solid, and skillfully produced.

Usually, this approach failed. Sometimes, it failed miserably. I tried for a long time to understand why. Certainly, I understood what I was trying to say. Why didn't they? Was I an eagle working with turkeys? Was I a conceited, self-important geek wrapped up in my own complexity? Was I speaking Hawaiian to a Spaniard?

After Martin shared the techniques for creating visual stories with me, all that changed. He showed me how a well-crafted visual story uses scientific methods, developed through decades of research in psychology, linguistics, design, and education, to motivate audiences to act. After a little practice I was a changed man. Now a single page from me could tell an entire story, not only to help people see what I was trying to say, but also to motivate them to care about the changes I proposed.

My ideas became compelling, and then to my surprise, easy to remember. Some of my visual stories started to "go viral," as I presented a story to one person and he or she used it to present those same ideas to others.

Good CONTENT Makes For Good Stories

Before you create a story, you need to be very clear on what the story will be about. In Chapter 1 we said that the purpose for most visual stories is to motivate your audience to make a decision, take an action, or make a change in their business or life. Chapters 4 through 7 cover the Content row of the Visual Story Map. In these chapters we show you a series of techniques to refine your content to focus on the outcome you want, and to filter ruthlessly to remove anything not directly relevant to the desired action.

Over the decade it took us to become skilled in the CAST techniques, the hardest lesson was accepting the importance of working on the content *first* and then building the story and presentation materials. Every minute you spend understanding the relevance of the content to your audience is returned tenfold when you get the story right.

The Content row includes four elements, Why, What, How, and What If.

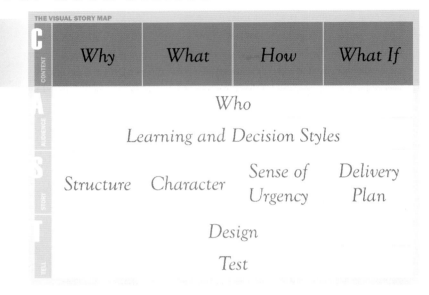

WHY People do not like to change, and where possible most people will avoid making decisions. Your story has to give them a clear reason to act. We find that the best way to be clear, and remain clear, is to make the reasons for change as explicit as possible. This includes identifying any external influences that your audience should react to, as well as the personal goals of your audience that can be tied to your story.

WHAT If the reasons for change are already known to your audience, you can bet that some people have already thought about the "broken" things that need fixing, or the new things that need to be added. However, you must also consider all the "working" things that may need to change, and the things that could be affected but should be left alone. In a business setting the things you might have to think about include processes, buildings, machinery, systems, people, customer experience, and information that will change or be affected by the change.

HOW Wave your hands, say a few words, and everything is different. *This approach only works for Harry Potter.* In most situations decisions take time to implement, and the process of change requires careful planning. Good stories include a lot of action, where something happens, and the content you identify now will form a large part of the visual story. You may be starting something new, stopping something, changing an existing activity, and possibly ensuring that some things remain the same while everything else changes around them. An important step we will cover in the "How" chapter is to show the clear linkage back to "What" has to be changed, and "Why." Linking your plan to the reasons why the story is important to your audience allows you to convince everyone that you understand their concerns.

WHAT IF There are always alternatives, the competing ideas and reasons why your audience might not be as supportive of your idea as you want them to be. You'll need to explain why this change should be supported, even when there are so many other needs and demands. Why should other worthy causes get a lower priority? Why this direction and not another? Through the development of the Content row, we will help you to place your change into the broader context so that you can convince your audience to follow you now, and not wait until a later day that never comes.

The Content row is based on questions or the common interrogatives of "Why," "What," "How," and "What If." While these interrogatives are often used by journalists, they are also used as a structure for the analysis of business problems and for the different ways in which people learn.

During the last decade, many organizations have had great results with a structured approach called the Benefits Dependency Network, developed at the Cranfield University Business School Centre for IS Research. This approach helps organizations understand the benefits of business change programs. We simplified and adapted this approach to create techniques to structure the content for a visual story, and also incorporated ideas from current research on how people learn and make decisions to help focus on what the audience needs to understand.

The "Why," "What," and "How" cells build a logical sequence with strong connectivity that helps underscore the reasoning and motivation in the story. Many stories fail because there are unbelievable leaps for the characters, or actions that seem to have no justification. The work in this row of the Visual Story Map helps your audience understand why they need to change, what to change, and how to change it. When you build this into a visual story you will provide a convincing sequence of activities. The "What If" cell looks at the challenges, consequences, and alternatives. The information gathered here can put a twist in the story that can help make it stick in the minds of the audience

Our understanding of factors that influence the *stickiness* of ideas comes from the book, *Made to Stick,* by Chip and Dan Heath, which is based on work they've been doing over many years. In their book, the Heath brothers describe how to make an idea stick: make it simple, unexpected, concrete, credible, emotional, and tell the idea as a story.

Why did we go to all this effort? Because we believe that applying the most current science will help you to create the most compelling story. We made it easy by taking the research and turning it into a step-by-step process for you to follow.

Motivate Your **AUDIENCE** to Act

Understanding your audience is key to selecting the right story structure, formats, and deciding how to represent your content to lead them effectively to a decision to act. The Audience row, covered in Chapters 8 and 9, consists of two elements, Who, and Learning and Decision Styles.

WHO To convince an audience, you first must figure out who they are. If you know who will be in your audience, you can build an understanding of their interests, their support for your ideas, how much they know about what you want them to do, and how they individually might influence each other. In some cases you may have never met your audience; all you know of them are broad characterizations. For these situations we will look at the use of personas to help develop a focus on the motivations that drive the group.

LEARNING AND DECISION STYLES The way you present your content, from the selection of formats to the order in which you present it to the different members of the audience, should be determined by an understanding of how the audience will react to what you give them. Some people will expect details, others will want to know how your proposal will impact the people in the organization. This section uses research on the different learning and decision styles to help you focus your story in a way that produces the results you need, without missing any cues.

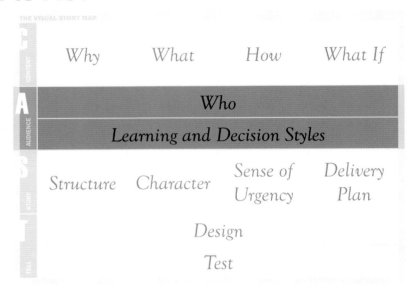

As you will discover in learning the CAST process, we believe that you will need to be ruthless in throwing out extraneous details. Deciding what to keep and what to discard can be tough. The best place to start, we have found, comes from carefully considering the people you want to influence and building the story specifically for them. What motivates them? How do they learn? What kind of information do they require in order to make a decision?

If you want your story to be successful make sure it addresses the important question that is rarely voiced:

"What's in it for me?"

Our methods for audience analysis are built on the best practices from three very different professions: project managers who use stakeholder management techniques, salespeople with their influence maps and methods to convince people to buy into a dream, and professional change managers who understand the process people go through as they adopt change. Martin had a realization, many years ago, that visual stories need to be created with the same insights into the audience that top salespeople use when creating their sales pitches.

When you use a story to make change happen, you're often asking your audience to perform two different and difficult tasks. You are asking them to *learn*, and you are asking them to *decide*. The learning and decision styles that cut across all aspects of the Audience row are drawn from the techniques used by psychologists, sociologists, salespeople, and educators. A technique that has been particularly successful for us is based on research from the 1970s by Bernice McCarthy into how children learn, work that has been developed into techniques now used by educators around the world. It is simple to implement and can be used quickly to act as both a filter and guiding structure to take the content in the top row of the Visual Story Map and ensure that it fits with the range of learning and decision styles of the audience.

Asking a person to learn is different from asking a person to decide.

Martin

I was leading a number of projects to implement new IT solutions into our business. Most of the potential solutions came from some of the biggest companies in the IT industry and we were trying to pick the best combination based on our business needs and the capabilities of the software. We thought we had a good plan, but we had competitors with different plans. Those competitors were not limited to internal people with alternative ideas. They included external salespeople from the big IT companies who were trying to sell us their solutions, regardless of the fit with the other suppliers or our internal capabilities.

The approach of the sales representatives from the big companies was much more influential with our senior managers than our approach was. Each time we met with our senior managers, we found that the external sales teams had already been to see them and set the stage for their next discussions. They had a better story and a better approach for delivering it, and this was based on understanding our executives better than we did! We finally got a solution to fit our needs, but only because we managed to get a vote on the procurement board for the project.

The salespeople were just doing their job, and doing it well. Based on this experience, I concluded that we needed to find out how salespeople sell an idea and then build that approach into the process for creating stories about change.

Give Your Audience a **STORY** to Remember

The Story row of the Visual Story Map guides you through the process of building an effective, interesting, and compelling story. There are four elements in this row, Structure, Character, Sense of Urgency, and Delivery Plan.

STRUCTURE Stories have a beginning, middle, and an end. They take the audience on a journey, and they use idioms, metaphors, rhetoric, and archetypal plotlines to help the audience connect with your ideas. Picking the right format and structure of a story helps to make it memorable and relevant.

CHARACTER Your audience has to care in order to become truly engaged. Characters are critically important for humanizing your message and allowing members of your audience to see themselves, and their success, as being connected with the struggle of the characters in the story. The characters in your story must be meaningful to the audience, but that doesn't mean they all need to be people. In Chapter 11 we look at how to create characters for people, inanimate objects, and concepts — in short, anything that must change.

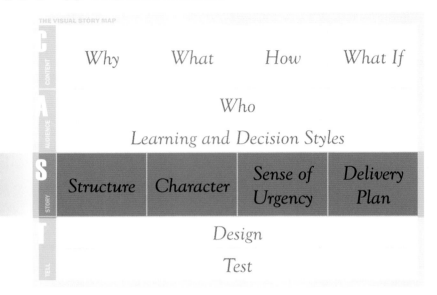

SENSE OF URGENCY There are many types of stories, but they all have one thing in common: the characters are placed in a situation where they must react. The sense of urgency in your story will help you to focus on the story elements that drive your characters, and your audience, toward the conclusion you want them to reach. Is there a conflict to resolve, a puzzle to solve, or an obstacle to overcome? We build on lessons learned from top salespeople to capture urgency, to make your story compelling, and cause your audience to choose to act now.

DELIVERY PLAN We are accustomed to stories being told in many different ways. Sometimes a story belongs at a team meeting, shared with peers, sometimes in a boardroom, and other times in a company cafeteria. Even business stories could be presented as movies or told around a campfire at an offsite retreat. In this part of the CAST process we cover the many different ways you can tell your story, and why having a range of channels can multiply the effectiveness of your message.

In Chapters 10 through 13 we cover the Story row, drawing on multiple sources to provide the structure and scope for the visual story. Our mix of sources starts with Aristotle and spans centuries to include the work of world-famous scriptwriting lecturer, Robert McKee; draws on the seven basic plots of stories identified by Christopher Booker; and the narrative and character structure identified by Vladimir Propp over a century ago. It's a diverse mix intended to provide inspiration and ideas rather than prescriptive rules.

Story, by Robert McKee, is a book for script writers, for the people whose stories we see every day on stage, in films, and on TV. There's a large body of evidence about what makes a great film or a memorable TV show. What McKee points out, quite forcefully in his lectures and training courses, is that no magic formula always wins. We draw on McKee's experience to create the overall story structures and advice about how and when to use them.

From Propp's work and an analysis of common plots, we provide a set of archetypal characters that can help to clarify and define the potential characters in a visual story. In many cases, you know the story will have a hero and a villain and someone who will set the hero on his or her way, but with different plots, the hero can become a villain and vice versa.

Visual stories are not created for entertainment. Visual stories are meant to cause someone to make a decision and to take action. For that to happen, you often need to elicit a sense of urgency. A sense of urgency is often a core concept in sales training, where the salesperson's intent is to entice the consumer to buy today rather than wait until tomorrow to make a decision.

As Martin described in his story about competing with external sales teams, you may have competitors (both external and internal) who are trying to sell their ideas, and the audience is going to make a choice. The key lesson is *not* to ignore their sales tactics, but rather to use them to your advantage. We built the CAST process to leverage the techniques that salespeople use to sell an idea. That way, your presentation can be as compelling as your competition, and thus as successful.

Drive your audience toward the
conclusion you want them to reach.

Visual Stories Are Designed and Tested for Someone to **TELL**

Finally, it's time to pull the parts together to tell the story itself. We cover the Tell row in Chapters 14 and 15, where we look at how to create visual elements for the story, characters, and supporting content, combine those elements in compelling ways, construct a rich one-page picture of the story, and validate that your story can be told and understood in a variety of formats.

Chapter 14 examines *design*, and Chapter 15 shows you how to *test* your story.

Design is a critical component to influence your audience.

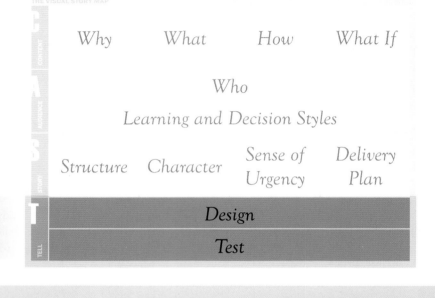

THE VISUAL STORY MAP

Why   What   How   What If

Who

Learning and Decision Styles

Structure   Character   Sense of Urgency   Delivery Plan

Design

Test

DESIGN Whether through the words you say, the words that are written, or the visuals you use, it is the mental image you create that helps to influence your audience. Design is a critical part an effective influencing process. Even a thoughtful, creative, data-rich, and potentially successful story can fall flat on its face if the most convincing visual elements and approaches for your story are not identified and chosen carefully. For example, if you present two different options, one in red text and the other in green text, your visual may be sending a message to some of your audience about what to go ahead with and what to stop, but others who are color-blind may just not get the message.

TEST Did you cover all your bases? Did you include all the information you need in order to make your story compelling? Did you stay away from using too much red? (Just kidding.) Did you practice the "telling" of your story and refine the visual story to both support your telling and the path to a decision? In short, how do you know your visual story is good enough to influence your audience? There are no guarantees, but we know there are common problems that derail stories, and lead to confused audiences. In this last part of the CAST process we bring together a set of six tests that will reduce your risk of failure.

With the CAST process, you now have real clarity on the content and the justification for every element you include. We call this focus *intentional design*. Every part of the visual story is focused on getting to the core message; you don't spend time creating content that you later realize is not relevant, or distracting.

Design is a skill that you continue to develop over a lifetime of practice. However, time after time, we've seen how using just a few of the right techniques can quickly make a fantastic impact on the quality of the result. The surprise to many people is that you get all the way to the fourth row before you start to create the visuals.

When Mark agreed to be a co-author it made a massive difference to our ability to write the book and also to the advice we could provide on design techniques. Mark took the lead writing the design chapter (Chapter 14) to cover techniques for ideation, composition, and content coding to support the development of your story in formats from one-page posters to animations. Truly, seeing is believing. The design section includes guidance drawn from graphics designers and experts in the analysis of visual design, including Edward Tufte, who identifies many of the secrets to effective data visualization in his classic book, *Beautiful Evidence*.

Finally, we looked at the visual stories we have created and a wide range of examples we have seen over the last ten years to identify six tests that, while not a guarantee of success, at least help you to quickly spot the common problems. Testing your visual story includes the necessary steps to ensure you have included, and excluded, all the right things, and also includes examining the potential unintended consequences of your recommendations.

Testing is more than just rehearsal. A communication technique called "Active Listening" encourages the person listening to feed back to the speaker what they are hearing, by paraphrasing or re-wording what they have heard in their own terms. In this way the meaning of the conversation is actively confirmed by both parties. We think of testing as a similar active process, where you will ask your test audience to feed back to you what they heard in the story, how it made them feel, and what they would do as a result of hearing and seeing your visual story.

The CAST acronym for the process, and the current format for the Visual Story Map, happened one day by looking at the grouping of notes on a page. Until this point the process had been represented by the image of a machine taking in the inputs for the story, with levers and controls to select the story and character combinations.

Today we use the Visual Story Map to capture key notes for a visual story, and as a reminder of the key elements that must be considered. We'll look at how you can use the Visual Story Map in the next chapter.

Using CAST to Tell Stories

3

*Tell me and I'll forget;
show me and I may
remember; involve me
and I'll understand.*
—Chinese proverb

*Long after the audience has forgotten your name and the title of
your presentation, they will remember your stories, which is why
Master Presenters are such apt storytellers.*
—*Chip and Dan Heath. Best-selling authors on the subjects of change and how
ideas survive.*

Use the Visual Story Map

The CAST process and the Visual Story Map evolved together. We found there was a need to have a simple visual format to help remember the different activities, and to capture the key information and decisions about how to structure and design the story. The Visual Story Map has evolved into a simple table structure to make it easier to use in printed formats, and to recreate on whiteboards and flipcharts in workshops. You can download a template for the Visual Story Map from our website at www.storiesthatmovemountains.com or from the book's companion website at www.wiley.com/go/storiesthatmovemountains. We use the Visual Story Map in different ways, and we assume that you will as well.

We have found ourselves many times with a deadline looming and a mass of content, ideas, audience information, and partly completed materials. When you've learned the CAST process you will realize it is possible to just grab everything you have and lay it out on a large version of the Visual Story Map, then start to iterate.

On other occasions, we have had groups of people involved in the development of a story, sometimes with key members of the audience taking part. Often, we suggest starting with a brainstorming workshop, and involve everyone interested in the creation of the story. In the brainstorming session, a facilitator draws an empty Visual Story Map on the whiteboard, issues a small pack of sticky notes to each participant, and lets them post anything, anywhere on the board. After fifteen minutes, the facilitator walks along the Visual Story Map, sharing the notes posted. After everyone has the seeds of ideas from their colleagues, a second round of brainstorming and clustering takes place. In just thirty minutes, this process can ensure that everyone's ideas have been heard, and it builds a great data set to start a solid visual story.

Most visual stories are created over a period of weeks, rather than days or hours. The Visual Story Map is useful to keep track of progress and highlight key information as the story develops. Often we see people use an electronic version of the Visual Story Map to share notes across a team, or have a copy posted on the wall in a team room.

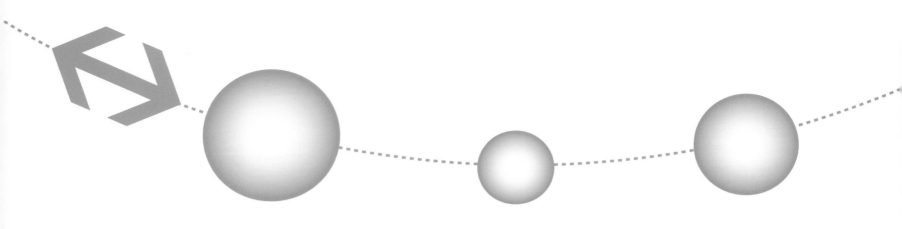

Learn From Our Experience

ITERATE Looking back at the visual stories we have been creating for the last decade, we have never got it right first time. Not once. Not even close. Sometimes it just takes a few days, sometimes months, of working with people, telling the stories, and iterating to get them right. There's a lot of testing to be done, a lot of listening to feedback from others, and iteration of your design.

Each of the sections of the Visual Story Map corresponds to a chapter in this book. At the end of each chapter, you will find a checklist of key things to remember and perform as you go through that part of the CAST process. All of the checklists are laid out the same way to allow you to find them quickly and jump from checklist to checklist to get a simple view of all of the steps. As you iterate over development of your visual story, keep going back to the checklists to help you stay on track.

INTEGRATE We created the CAST process and the Visual Story Map to provide a structure that we know works. One of the strengths is the integration of all the parts to develop a compelling story and visual design that together are focused on exactly what the audience needs to know. If you find yourself skipping a part of the process, or with content in one part of the Visual Story Map that is not integrated with the rest of your content, you should stop and work out what is missing.

In each of the chapters you will see the evolution of two example visual stories. These examples have a consistently colored edge to the pages to allow you to quickly move through the book, following the development of the example content. We have tried to show how the integration works through these examples.

INNOVATE The CAST process brings together a wide range of very powerful techniques, but these are not the only techniques you might use. In some chapters we point to alternative techniques that you could use, and many of you will have experience with other techniques that achieve the same goals as the ones we recommend here. Our recommendation is to first understand what the desired outcome is for each step in the CAST process, and then add your own experience and skills to the techniques we have identified.

Ultimately you should have your own variation of CAST, adapted for the way you work and for the culture of the organization you work in.

Examples of Using CAST

When we decided to write about CAST we looked at many other books to help us decide on a style. Most books use examples to illustrate each point, but we found the examples are either all independent of each other, theoretical, over-simplified, or just show the end result. We decided to be different and create two examples that build up, piece by piece, in each chapter to show what you really have to do to create a good visual story. These examples are built on real situations, with just a few names and details changed to allow us to demonstrate as much as possible from the different techniques. By the end of the book, we will have completed each of the examples, and you will have seen how to use the CAST process.

The first story is about Marina, who wants to start a business to support personal trainers. The challenges and approach in Marina's story could be applied to anyone wanting to influence a small group of people with similar backgrounds or issues. Marina's story also represents a situation where the CAST process is used to help develop the ideas and content used in the story.

The second story is about Tom, the leader of an IT group in a major hospital who wants to gain the support for a significant transformation project. Tom's situation will feel very familiar to many people who have to deal with complex business projects, with many different stakeholders and a range of business objectives. This situation also demonstrates how to build a story into an existing program, and how to plan for the complex delivery process often required in large organizations.

On the following two pages we introduce each of the example visual stories and explain a little about the situations Marina and Tom are facing.

There is a third fictional example in Chapter 16, built by combining factors from a number of visual stories we've created over the years for organizations and interest groups. You have already seen the start of this with the two-page visual story in Chapter 1. In Chapter 16 we develop the last two days of this story into an example of how to use the CAST process in a very short timescale to prepare for important presentations. By contrast, the Personal Trainer and City University Hospital examples each span a number of weeks over which the content is being developed, tested, and delivered.

Build Your Own Example

The worked examples will help you understand the CAST process and many of the individual techniques. We recommend you try creating your own example to test the ideas as you read through each chapter, rather than waiting until you're at the end of the book.

If you work through the sequence with your own example while reading the book, we believe you will have a much clearer idea of where you need to focus when you need to create a visual story in a hurry.

Marina

You can follow the Personal Trainer example by flipping to the pages with yellow borders throughout the book.

Example 1: Personal Trainer

My name is Marina. After spending years as a pharmacy technician and medical administrator, I wanted a new lease on life. I looked around to find something I could be passionate about and decided to go back to college for a two-year degree as a certified personal trainer. As I found out though, the problem with passion is that it might not pay too well. I talked with a number of different gyms but found that working for them was really only a last resort. While the gym would collect $50 for an hour of my time, I would earn only about $15 of that, and then still have to cover my travel costs, other business costs, and pay taxes.

So I decided to look into opening my own small training studio, where customers would come just for personal training. I had a good knowledge of how to run a business, and a husband with great business experience who could help. There is a lot of complexity to opening a studio. Setting up accounts, doing marketing and sales, online and offline advertising, and renewing the billings every month was daunting.

Many times, I wondered aloud if there was just some company that would do some of this grunt work for me. Every day I was spending trying to set up a studio was another day when I couldn't focus on the reason I was doing all this — to be a personal fitness trainer.

So with my husband, I started to consider a radical new idea: Why not create a service that allows personal trainers to set up their own training studio as part of a network? Clients could find the service online and sign up for a nearby training studio, learn about their trainer's philosophy, and share their feedback with other clients in an online social forum.

The service would handle the administration of collecting membership and training fees through electronic subscription payments and then pay the trainers directly via their bank accounts. The service would also handle legal fees, hide banking complexity, provide online marketing, and provide simple step-by-step directions for trainers to set themselves up.

To achieve my goals, I need trainers, especially ones who already own a studio, to become interested in joining the network. We created a name and brand identity for the business, "Optimal Balance," and we have started to create some of the services, along with a website, so we can work with our investors. The visual story has to convince studio owners and personal trainers that this is a viable business. It might take a number of presentations to get enough studio owners signed up, but all I need are ten paying customers to be viable. This story needs to be tuned to the very specific needs of these key people, to excite them to make the decision to be a part of something new.

Tom

You can follow the City University Hospital example by flipping to the pages with blue borders throughout the book.

Example 2: City University Hospital

City University Hospital is one of the top five hospitals in the country. It's a leading research center and training hospital that serves as the major area hospital with more than half a million patients each year. This is a great place to work, where I can be very proud of what we do. My name is Tom. I lead the IT group that provides systems to run everything from patient information to room scheduling.

The hospital trustees recently approved a three-year expansion and transformation plan. This will include a new critical care building at the side of the existing Accident and Emergency unit. Capable of handling 70,000 patient visits per year, this facility will lead the way in adopting new technology and processes to improve patient care.

Unfortunately the IT systems have not had the coordination or investment over the past five years to support this plan. I joined the hospital team when the management board decided to bring IT services back under their control, after a long period of being run by an outside company.

The transformation plan is the first big chance my new team has to make a difference and show how IT really should work. It is great to have this chance, but at the same time, we have to convince a lot of people that we can do this.

Patient data is currently in a mix of systems and on paper. We have islands of information across the hospital and complex processes that have evolved over years to get around the problems this causes. To bring in the IT changes needed to make the new critical-care building a success, we need to get a lot of support from the clinical team, nursing staff and administrators, as well as the financial support from the transformation program's governance board.

Everyone is supportive of the goals for the expansion and transformation plan, but there is a lot of work to do to convince the management and staff of the importance of the IT transformation. They have been working around the existing issues for years and don't realize how much that is compromising their ability to improve in the future. I need a visual story to describe the change we're going to make. This needs to explain the vision we have for the future, how we are going to get there, and how success will depend on widespread participation. I have been through enough big change programs to know this is going to be a team effort across all the departments, and clarity of communication is vital to bring the team together.

"Would you tell me, please, which way I ought to go from here?"
"That depends a good deal on where you want to get to," said the Cat.
"I don't much care where—" said Alice.
"Then it doesn't matter which way you go," said the Cat.
"— so long as I get somewhere," Alice added as an explanation.
"Oh, you're sure to do that," said the Cat, "if you only walk long enough."

—Lewis Carroll, *Alice's Adventures in Wonderland*

Makari. Male Amur Tiger. Taken in 2009 at Wildlife Heritage Foundation, UK.

Tell the Right Story

The most common problem we find, the one that wastes the most time in the process for creating a visual story, is a lack of clarity on the reason for the story.

Many times, we've seen people put in a lot of effort to create a story only to communicate background information or miss the point. If you're not 100 percent sure you have the purpose for the story clearly defined, spend the time required to work through the Content and Audience rows to get clarity.

Organizing is what you do before you do something, so that when you do it, it's not all mixed up.

—Christopher Robin, in A.A. Milne's, Winnie the Pooh

Tell the Story Right

The second most common problem is the creation of a visual story without a clear plan for how it's going to be delivered to the audience that needs to support the change.

We've seen great stories and visuals developed, but never seen by the people who should see them because the authors didn't work out how to get the message to the audience. The Story and Tell rows are designed to ensure that the visual story reaches members of the intended audience, enabling them to act on it.

He who fails to plan is planning to fail.

—Winston Churchill

Imagine how different the Cheshire Cat in Alice's adventures would seem if he had been represented as a tiger. Makari is a beautiful tiger, but he does not have the characteristics we expect for the Cheshire Cat. Think about this as you develop your visual story. Good visual stories balance all the different parts to ensure they fit together. It's worth the effort because doing so can significantly, and positively, affect audience perception and expectation. If you have elements of the visual story that are out of alignment with the rest then the message your audience receives may be that you don't really know where you are going.

C CONTENT	Why	What	How	What If
A AUDIENCE	Who			
	Learning and Decision Styles			
S STORY	Structure	Character	Sense of Urgency	Delivery Plan
T TELL	Design			
	Test			

author: *You*   purpose: *First story*   date: *Now*

© Martin Sykes, Nick Malik, Mark West 2012

Go to www.storiesthatmovemountains.com/ and download the Visual Story Map template now. Use this to create your first visual story as you work through the book.

START ➡

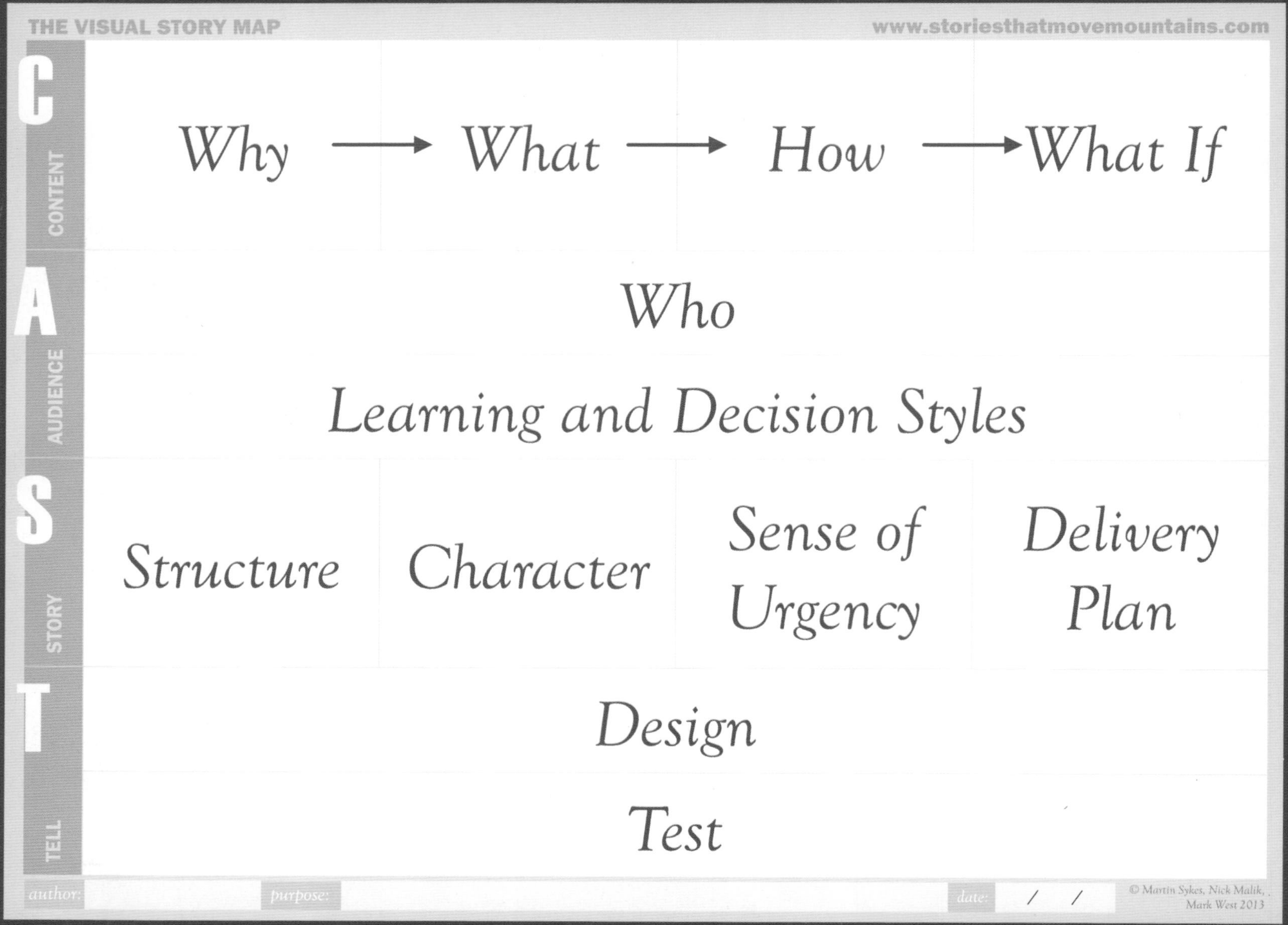

C CONTENT

Why → What → How → What If

A AUDIENCE

Who

Learning and Decision Styles

S STORY

Structure   Character   Sense of   Delivery
                                 Urgency   Plan

T TELL

Design

Test

CONTENT

Why

4

The best way to predict the future is to create it.

—Peter Drucker, management consultant
and 'Father of management theory'

If we have our own why in life, we shall get along with almost any how.

—Friedrich Nietzsche, noted German philosopher
and author of Twilight of the Idols in 1888

The first step in the CAST process is to make clear the reasons why there's a need to change at all. Simon Sinek manages to fill a whole book, *Start with Why*, writing about how the greatest influencers and leaders in the world all start with "Why" before going on to the "How" and "What." The people you want to influence will accept change more readily if they understand why they need to change.

You can use the techniques in this chapter to start filling in your Visual Story Map. The first step is to work out the core reasons for the change you are proposing. Your visual story must successfully communicate those reasons.

In our training sessions, we have found that most people already have a change that they would like to propose, and the visual story becomes a way to describe that change. Assuming that you have a change that you would like to see in your life, your company, or your neighborhood, we would like to start with a simple caution.

It is likely that you have a reason that you want the change to occur... but we are going to ask you to go beyond your personal reasons. This chapter will help you to find the reason that your audience will recognize and identify with. We will help you to find the reason that they will make the change, and to remove yourself from the story.

Associated with your reason for making the change, you may feel that the change is urgent. In a later chapter, we will share techniques for finding the sense of urgency that motivates your audience. The same caution applies in that case as well: you cannot assume that your audience will want to make the change as urgently as you do.

The Three Big Whys

It is not easy to step away from your own motivation entirely. We will give you some tools to examine motivations in a neutral way. In this chapter, our aim is to help you answer the question that matters the most: *Why does your audience need to move this mountain?*

Although each story will have a unique set of factors, we suggest three main reasons why people propose a change:

- **To improve an existing situation.** If this is the type of story you are telling, you need to understand and catalog the pain that the current situation is causing, and show how your solution will diminish it. By pain, we mean any inconvenience, inefficiency, loss of potential gain, or physical, emotional, or financial discomfort. (You will find more about the concept of the *pain chain* and techniques for dealing with the pains later in the chapter.)

- **To bring about something new and useful.** Maybe there's no existing problem to be solved, but your proposal will lead to a new product, event, or process that will increase efficiency, improve revenue, or add excitement. Motivating your audience may be difficult because there's no sense of urgency to draw upon, either from any kind of pain or from a well-understood personal benefit. If this is your story, you have to convince your audience that your proposal will improve their lives, possibly in a way that's never occurred to them. Did anyone ask for the VCR? For the iPad?

- **To fulfill some personal desire or motivation.** This kind of story may be for your own use, or maybe it's meant to appeal to some personal desire shared by many individuals. Personal stories could be about self-improvement, getting a new job, or losing weight.

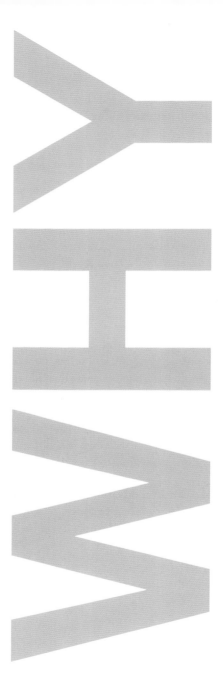

Focusing First on "Why"

We are going to ask you to focus first on answering the question "Why?" However, in our training sessions, most people are tempted to fire up their software and start by creating slides. Sometimes, we hear the justification, "I just wanted to start capturing some thoughts." The trouble is that these thoughts take time and effort to lay out and build into a final presentation. Millions of hours are wasted every year around the world as very busy people start their presentations before they have clearly thought through the message they want to convey. Moreover, most books on improving presentations start with the assumption that you already know the story you want to tell. In this book, we are proposing that you work out your message *first*, in order to understand the problem that you aim to solve.

In this chapter you'll develop a clear understanding of the problem you need to solve, which will drive the rest of the content for the story. Everything that needs to be changed, all activities, need to link to one of the reasons "Why." You'll also use this process to develop a better understanding of your audience. For every reason "Why," you need to identify the individual or group in the audience it relates to.

This process is iterative. Although you start with "Why," you'll quickly start to record notes that you will use when developing the "Who," "What," and "How." Later as you work on these cells, you may identify additional reasons "Why" or need to come back to this part of the map to update details or improve the focus. Don't try to be perfect. The iterative nature of this effort allows you to catch any reasons you missed as you work through the later cells.

All Motivation is Personal

Change is personal. Inanimate objects do not *care* if they're changed. People *care*. People have emotional attachments, desires, and relationships. In order for those emotions to work in your favor, you have to speak to individuals *as people*. If you want members of your audience to care about you, you have to demonstrate that you care about them.

Some changes are driven by altruistic motives, for the welfare of others, but most of the changes you need to communicate have to directly address your audience's question, "What's in it for me?" (We sometimes abbreviate this as WII.FM.) Think of this as the radio station your audience is tuned into, playing in the background while they go about their daily lives. Occasionally, a tune or announcement catches their attention. The reasons "Why" are these announcements and familiar tunes. If you don't trigger the "What's in it for me?" response in the audience, then the story will lose a great deal of its influence.

I don't care

The key to focusing on the right information at this stage of the process is to put yourself into your audience's shoes and think about *what's in it for them*. It may be the achievement of business goals or a personal dream. It could be the desire to be a part of something important that has strong alignment with their personal feeling of self-worth, or the chance to do something interesting for the first time. It could be the desire to be seen as a team player or good employee. In organizations' efforts for change, the reasons for personal participation can be quite different from the higher goals of the organization. You need to understand the grand goals and the personal motivations, and be sure to include both in the story.

When members of the audience understand what they can get from the change, they often have a second question, "What's in it for you?" As the person proposing the change and telling the story, they have a natural desire to understand your motives and reward for the change. This view isn't often built into the story, but it is an important consideration and one you can address right at the start, as you introduce your story to the audience. If your audience does not trust your motives, you cannot expect them to trust the story.

Techniques for Discovering Whys

In the rest of this chapter, we introduce three techniques to help you develop and focus on the "Why." These techniques are called Five Whys, the Pain Chain, and Outcome Mapping. Choose the technique that works best for your situation and try to get to the biggest pain that can realistically be addressed. After all, the solution you propose must be something your audience can credibly deal with.

Five Whys

Understanding why a change is important is often a matter of self-reflection. It's easy to say that a solution "just makes sense" because it makes sense to the author. But if you're going to explain why an idea makes sense to someone else, you need to remove yourself from the picture. For me, this is a kind of analysis game. I use the "Five Whys" method to drill down to the root motivation.

I remember one day when I was taking my children to play at an arcade. My son Andy, who was five years old at the time, decided to play. The interaction went like this:

> Andy: Dad, are we stopping the car?
>
> Me: Yes, we need to stop now.
>
> Andy: Why?
>
> Me: We are pulling into a gas station.
>
> Andy: Why?
>
> Me: We need to put some gas in the car.
>
> Andy: Why?
>
> Me: Because the car needs fuel in order for us to get to the arcade.
>
> Andy: Why?
>
> Me: Because I used up all the gas in the tank already.
>
> Andy: Why?

This game went on for a few more rounds, and ended up in a fit of giggles. Of course, my son was simply having fun, and I knew it . . . so my answers were short on purpose, giving him an opportunity to ask why as many times as he wanted.

As an analysis technique, a game of five whys can be more revealing. For example, in one of my projects, I found myself wanting to convince a group of business leaders that they should work together to create a single eCommerce experience for all of our customers, rather than creating different experiences for each of our products. I started with the premise that I wanted to use a visual story to convey that "we need one experience for our customers." Here are the "Five Why" questions that followed.

WHY do we want a single user experience? Because our customers are currently getting six different eCommerce experiences, and that is not good.

WHY isn't it good? Because each different experience includes different products, sometimes at different prices or with different promotions, and that can be frustrating for the customer.

WHY do they find it frustrating? Because a customer cannot be sure that they're getting the best price unless they try out every possible eCommerce experience, which takes time and builds resentment.

WHY does it take time and cause resentment? It takes time because each experience is different. Going on a "treasure hunt" builds resentment because it looks like we're trying to hide some of our best bargains where no one is likely to find them. This fuels dissatisfaction with the company itself.

WHY do we care about customer satisfaction? Because unsatisfied customers are less like to come back to shop at our site again.

Now the root cause is apparent. After asking "why" five times, the real reason comes out. We want one customer eCommerce experience because anything less will cost us in customer loyalty. Loyalty is something I can measure.

The game of "five whys" demands that you start with your initial thought, and then ask the question "why" five times in a row, going deeper each time. Of course, for some situations, a compelling reason is not five layers away, and in some cases, you may have to go further. However, most people find the answer that they are looking for in "five whys or less."

The example on the following page is the first of our "worked examples" that thread through the book. In this example, Nick and Marina use the Five Why's method to look at the motivation for change in small personal training studios struggling with providing routine business functions for their clients.

So, start with your own belief. When you ask why the first time, you may get down to the *observation* level, where you can point to various observations that are useful. Asking why again requires you to step away from your own observations and perspective and look for underlying trends from someone else's point of view.

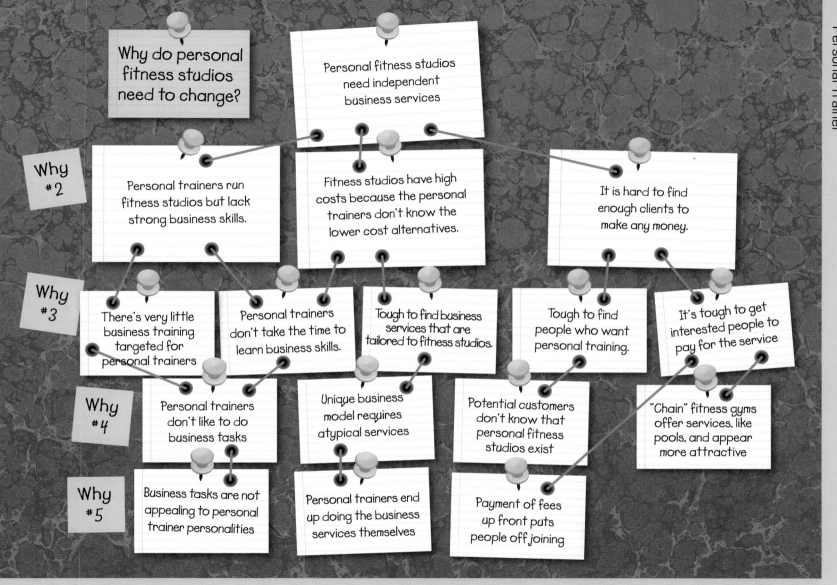

Marina pins index cards to the wall in her study, and uses the Five Whys technique to map out "why" personal trainers would feel the need to use her "Optimal Balance" services for their fitness studios.

Pain Chain

The pain chain concept comes from sales techniques. The idea is that the *pain*, or problem, cascades through an organization but is experienced differently according to each person's level or responsibility. For the visual story, the pain chain technique can help you identify the relevant people or groups in your audience, how the story touches each of them differently, and the variations in the ways in which they're currently responding to the pain.

You can start anywhere in the chain and work in any direction. In the example illustrated by the diagram, the pain starts with a sales director identifying a failure to hit targets. This pain radiates up and down the organization, affecting different people in different ways. Pain occurs at both a personal level, with the sales person losing commission, and at an organizational level by affecting overall business profitability. The root cause of the pain in this example is visible at the bottom of the chain. Economic conditions in the countries where a major customer operates have caused big cash flow problems, resulting in the loss of a future sales opportunity.

Pain chains can work laterally across organizations, and the root cause can start at any point and spread out. The pain chain doesn't help you understand the change over time (which is something the Five Why technique can help with), but it does

help to build a comprehensive picture of the many different people, groups, or organizations involved and their unique perspectives. For the best chance to improve this situation, the story should be developed to address the different pains for everyone in the audience.

Not all of these pain points will be relevant when you build your story, but you will hear one recommendation throughout the book: Make a deliberate decision to include or remove each person on the chain. As you decide, consider the impact on the overall story and the ability of the audience to understand and relate to it. If you remove an influential person from your story's target audience, will members of your audience accept the story? Will they be able to use it and share it?

The pain chain technique often results in wording that sounds negative. This is a part of the mindset about finding "pain." However, when it comes to building the story, the message often needs to be tuned to overcome the pain and realize a more positive message.

Later in this chapter we begin the worked example for City University Hospital. This starts with a mind map of the key problems and then creates a pain chain.

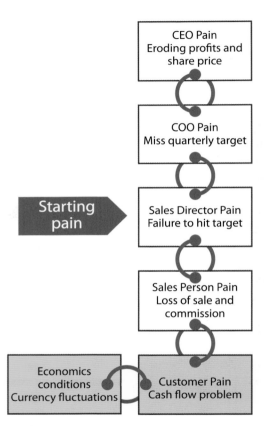

Outcome Mapping

The third technique provides a way to look at how individuals or the organization might respond to events beyond their control. In film and literature, heroes usually find themselves responding to some event that they have no control over. The event may lead them on a journey and to a personal transformation that results in some change in themselves or the world.

Start at the top of the diagram with the stimulus, the event or situation that is driving the change. The stimulus is something out of the immediate control or influence of anyone in the audience for the story. It could be something in the past that has changed attitudes (and therefore is not changeable) or an impending event ranging from a new competitor entering your markets to a potential natural disaster. The important factor is a clear relationship between the stimulus and the ability to achieve a future *goal*. In other words, the existence of pain is not enough by itself. There has to be a relationship between the pain suffered and the failure to reach a valuable goal. In the figure on the right everyone has a goal that they will fail to achieve.

One or more goals can be associated with each stimulus, with some linking or dependency among them. Each goal describes a specific part of the future you want as a result of the change. The outcomes are then a way of measuring or demonstrating that you've reached the goal. Again, there can be multiple outcomes for each goal, and some outcomes relating to multiple goals.

Describe the goals in a rich language that explains what is different in the future. Write how it feels to be there and what the people in your audience will be able to do when the change is complete. Sometimes these future scenarios are best developed by using visualization techniques. Close your eyes and imagine yourself in the future. Look around and experience it. Now, write a paragraph describing the future or draw a quick, rich picture or mind map to capture the key points.

In contrast, be as specific as you can to define measurements to show the detailed change in the outcomes, between today and when the change is complete. For organizational change, the outcomes could be business metrics such as the Order to Cash cycle time; for personal change, the outcome could be the amount of weight lost or time to run a mile. In the best cases, you should be able to define the measure, the current value, the target, and the time it will take to reach that target. The time-basis can be an important element later in the CAST process to help sequence activities for the story.

When you start the CAST process with a lot of existing content, first put your stimuli, your goals, and your outcomes in separate lists. Then take some time to draw connections from each stimulus to one or more goals and from there to one or more outcomes. Once you are done, drop anything that doesn't have a connection to something else. If the connections aren't strong and clear, you need to question whether the content is really relevant to the story.

The worked example in Chapter 16 shows how Outcome Mapping is used to map existing content.

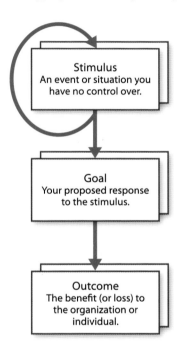

This process is a simplification of a great business analysis technique you can find in the book *"Benefits Management: Delivering Value from IS & IT Investments,"* by John Ward and Elizabeth Daniel.

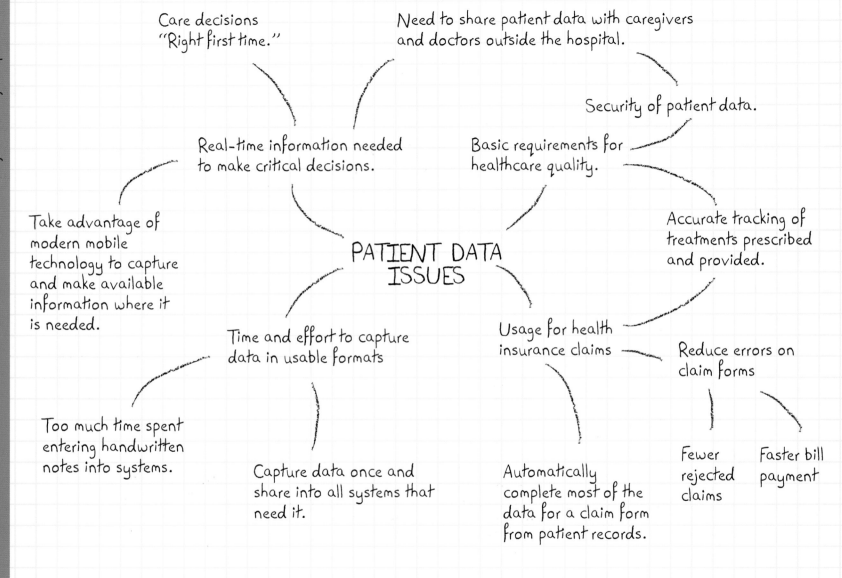

Care decisions "Right first time."

Need to share patient data with caregivers and doctors outside the hospital.

Security of patient data.

Real-time information needed to make critical decisions.

Basic requirements for healthcare quality.

Take advantage of modern mobile technology to capture and make available information where it is needed.

Accurate tracking of treatments prescribed and provided.

PATIENT DATA ISSUES

Time and effort to capture data in usable formats

Usage for health insurance claims

Reduce errors on claim forms

Too much time spent entering handwritten notes into systems.

Capture data once and share into all systems that need it.

Automatically complete most of the data for a claim form from patient records.

Fewer rejected claims

Faster bill payment

The City University Hospital example is used in all the chapters on the CAST process to show how Tom develops his visual story. Most of these pages are taken directly from his notebook to show the work in progress. This page started as a whiteboard from a staff meeting with the COO's leadership team to brainstorm the key patient data issues.

Pain Chain

Claus- CEO
The three-year transformation plan is dependent on tight cost control. Errors in insurance claims cause financial losses equivalent to the total savings we must make in the next three years.

Bernd - COO
IT systems cost money to fix, but the errors from data issues cause financial problems for the hospital and damage its reputation.

Allan – Financial Controller
Difficult to assemble claim forms for health insurance companies from the data in our systems. Many claims are queried or rejected.

Luc – Patient Data Controller
Patient care targets are being missed because of data quality issues. But efforts to improve data quality have met with complaints about the time and effort required.

Nurses
Re-entry of patient data in multiple systems leads to errors which the nurses are held responsible for.

Nurses
Too many different places to record data makes it hard to find information in an emergency.

Insights

1. The pain chain works well when you know the people in the chain.

2. The same problem is felt very differently at different levels in the chain.

3. A lot of people feel the pain, but we need the nurses to make the biggest change.

During the leadership team meeting, Tom had the chance to ask Luc what the patient data issues specifically meant to him. Over the next few days, he had a chance to ask others in the management team and nursing staff the same question, allowing him to build this pain chain from their answers.

It's not about you!

Are your "Whys" for your audience or for you? Perhaps you have a deadline to make the change happen or a sales quota to reach? These reasons may be very strong to you, but mean nothing to your audience. Make sure your objectives remain completely focused on how your audience will change as a result of your story. Why should they think and act differently after they hear your story? **If their attitude is not changed as a result of your story, then why are you wasting everyone's time?**

Positives and Negatives

Look at both the advantages and disadvantages of your proposed change. Think about the future, about reaching the goal of the change and the benefits of getting there. Then think about the barriers and obstacles, the potential downside to the change. It's much better to identify all of these issues and choose whether to address them in your story than to have someone from the audience throw them at you and derail the story. Time after time, we've seen people focus only on the positive when creating their story and be knocked back by a negative view from the audience. Strike first, and acknowledge the negatives; you will gain trust from your audience if they see that you are not hiding part of your agenda.

GAIN > PAIN

The gain from making a change has to outweigh the current pain, plus any temporary discomfort that results from the change itself. For example, learning to use a new data system can be a nuisance, although the system will ultimately save time and make work life easier. Even if you establish that the result is valuable, many people will continue to resist the change if they believe that the change itself will be painful. It will help your story if you can show that the pain will be temporary, but the gain is long term.

Dormant or active pain

Most of the discussion so far has been about active pain. That is, the pain that we can easily identify, that people can describe, and that they're experiencing now. For new products or very new ideas, there may be a dormant pain, something the audience doesn't even know yet as a pain.

In the U.S. pharmaceutical industry, we regularly see new terms being used to describe ailments people have lived with for years. By making such dormant pains visible, giving them a name, and relating them to a current situation, you can generate a desire to have the pain removed.

For example, in order to increase the desire for consumers to buy mouthwash, manufacturers taught us about "gingivitis." Using the medical term for gum inflammation makes the condition sound unpleasant so that it can be addressed. If your change is the introduction of a product that your audience doesn't know that they need, it helps to give the problem a name.

Dormant pain can also relate to problems you've never really considered. Before the recent introduction of the e-book reader, few people would have seen a need to buy one. The convenience of having a library in your pocket wasn't really a concern. Now that there are millions of e-books available, the benefit is clear. However, when the e-book reader was first proposed, the pain was dormant. Is there a dormant pain in your audience just waiting to be identified?

Personal or PROFESSIONAL agenda

Are your reasons "WHY" linked to the personal agendas of your audience or to their professional, social, or work agendas? The difference can be significant for the level of support your story receives. A PERSONAL AGENDA can be a strong influencer for personal commitment. However, without the support of their organization or social group, a personal agenda may be subjugated to the needs of the group, to avoid being seen to be rocking the boat. Linking your "Whys" to a PROFESSIONAL OR WORK AGENDA, on the other hand, many not garner as much enthusiasm, especially if the group doesn't agree on its goals.

Strategic or Tactical Pain

Tactical pain is often the most urgent and personally felt. It can be the pain of job loss, failure to hit targets, or personal credibility. Often this kind of pain is short lived. Although tactical pain can prove very useful for developing a sense of urgency to make a change, it can also disappear quickly once the change is accepted or even through other temporary factors. Strategic pain, on the other hand, is persistent pain that presents a long term obstacle to success; unless the change is accepted and seen all the way through, the strategic pain will remain.

If you have identified strategic pain, make sure it links to some tactical pain, right now, to push your audience into action. If you just have tactical pain, look to see if there is an underlying strategic "why" to be addressed. Use the Five Why method to help with this work.

Be Specific

Detail makes a big difference to credibility and audience attention. Give an example that's important to your audience. Be specific on the relevant numbers. Don't drown the audience in detail, but give them specific information to drive the story.

Can You MEASURE the Improvement?

Can you identify something to measure the pain and that could be used in the future to demonstrate that the change is happening? Is there a measurement to indicate that the change is complete? Describing the end goal in terms of a measurement is a powerful way to demonstrate what a happy ending could look like.

Extreme Focus

Can you define a one-sentence objective? Defining your objective in a short, catchy phrase makes it easy to remember and can help rally your audience around the message. Make is short and directed. No multiple clauses or paragraph-length wording. Not even an elevator pitch. Much shorter. Make it something the audience can experience. Describe your objective as a power phrase that can drive the imagination into the rest of the story. For example:

A COMPUTER ON EVERY DESK AND IN EVERY HOME

Bill Gates

Twice as fast.
Half the price.

Steve Jobs on the iPhone 3G

GOTCHA

Follow these steps to make sure that you are collecting the information needed to explain why the change that you envision is needed.

(!) **Do not judge or over-analyze.** We provided three techniques in this chapter to help you structure your reasons "Why." If you aren't sure you understand the audience's reasons to change, use the pain chain. If your reasons "Why" seem weak, use the Five Why technique to develop more depth of understanding. If you have a lot of information to start with but no structure, build an outcome map. Pick one or use a technique of your own, get the focus, and move on.

(!) **Be ready to iterate.** The aim is to quickly start the CAST process. You will return to this cell to refine and focus on the reasons "Why" as you develop a better understanding of the rest of the top half of the Visual Story Map.

(!) **Beware of building the story for yourself.** When the change involves other people, it's all too easy to put your own desires and values into the story and miss the viewpoint of the audience. Unless the story is for your personal change, remind yourself to describe the "Why" statements from the audience's viewpoint by standing in their shoes and asking, "What's in it for me?" (WII.FM)

- [x] Cover the full range of reasons "Why," and include any "Why nots" as well.

- [x] Check that the reasons for change define the full scope of the pain.

- [x] Define the problem in a way that members of the audience can realistically believe they can address.

- [x] List reasons for change that address the "What's in it for me?" for the different people in the audience.

- [x] Include a one-sentence objective for the core of the story.

- [x] Soften or remove your own self-interests from the list to ensure it reflects the audience's interests.

What

5

> God, give us grace to accept with serenity
> the things that cannot be changed,
> courage to change the things which should
> be changed,
> and the wisdom to distinguish the one from
> the other. "
>
> —Reinhold Niebuhr, American theologian whose writings have influenced American political leaders in the 20th and
> 21st centuries. The quote here is an extract from the Serenity Prayer he wrote in the 1940s.

Most of us make assumptions. We might assume we know the motives behind management decisions, or assume that others understand the situation the same way we do. In many IT departments there was an assumption for many years that computer users had to be managed, that the IT department, or a specialist external company, had to provide all the systems and services required for the business. This is changing rapidly, with employees using Facebook, instant messaging tools, and online access to e-mail. Some companies are even starting to let staff connect their own laptops, home computers and smartphones to the company network. Many organizations are now having problems balancing the responsibilities of the IT organization with the expectations of the employees.

The assumptions about who will manage information and keep it secure must be revisited. Organizations are making new assumptions about the needs of the business and the employee, about the availability of services provided over the Internet, and even which companies that are providing services today will still be around in a few years.

If your audience is already on board with the reasons behind your proposed change, you can bet that some people have already thought about the things that need fixing, or the new things that need to be added to implement the change. That just seems to be human nature. Together, we have helped with hundreds of change initiatives, and it is as rare as finding a talking horse to find a problem where someone has not already assumed what needs to be done to accomplish the goal and how to go about doing it.

Assumptions on the part of your audience can be one of the biggest problems at this stage. As you present your content, your audience will make assumptions about the relative importance of the different things to be changed and about how to change them. In your story, as soon as you begin to tell members of your audience about the problem, they will start to make assumptions about how the change should be implemented.

When you assume you make an ass out of you and me.
——*Oscar Wilde*

Photograph by Steve Fletcher

"But I'm tellin' ya I'm a horse . . . I'm a horse!"

Visual stories are most often short, and are focused on the key elements of the change being proposed or the decision to be made. We find that clearly linking "What" to change with the reasons "Why" makes a big difference in the focus for the story, and reduces the number of assumptions. In this chapter, we introduce you to techniques for figuring out which details to use and which details to leave out, so you can keep your audience focused on the essential points.

In the previous chapters, we may have given the impression that all you need is the Visual Story Map. Sorry. As a single page, the Visual Story Map is a great way to summarize the key elements and structure the content to create a visual story, but for an effective story you are going to need a few more pages to capture and structure your thinking. The results will be worth it.

Elements of Change

In this part of the CAST process, you look at the content you have and identify all elements that will be affected by the change: things, people, and processes or activities.

THINGS can be physical, such as locations, buildings, or machinery. In a more intangible sense this could be a computer program or an information model. We chose the term 'things' quite deliberately, even though it is very vague, to reflect the reality of what can be considered for a change.

PEOPLE may need to behave differently as a result of the change or may need to develop new skills or abilities. There could also be changes to the number of people required for something to happen, or consider changes in organizational behavior and culture. On a personal level, you could change yourself or change your relationship with someone else.

PROCESSES refers to the sequences of activities people do at work or in the context of the change. At the organizational or community level, a process change might include changes in legislation or expectations for working time.

Consider all the impacts that your change will have, not just the ones you're most interested in or those that place your proposal in a flattering light. Research suggests your audience will find you more convincing if you also talk about the parts of the change process that are not going to be popular or easy. When you identify "What" will change, be sure to include all the outcomes, both positive and negative.

Change, by its very definition, means having or doing something differently. However, it's not always about changing something that already exists. Suppose your organization is adding a new division to handle your business in Brazil. A committee may have to be created to recruit and establish the new Brazilian management team, and dissolved when the business is operational. You will need to acquire an office building, hire the rest of the staff, and adapt your business to a new culture. Your original office is still in place after all this, but now with ties to another location; some personnel are not even aware of the new division, others might be moving to Brazil, others may have new colleagues to work with.

In most stories, the central driver of the story is built around a change that the main characters have to deal with. In the Brazilian example this may be the recruitment of the people, and the rest of the changes are necessary but not the main element of your visual story. As you build your visual story, you will need to find this core, but don't assume too quickly that you have the right content. Capture as much as you can using the matrix on the opposite page. Later in this chapter you will map these to the reasons "Why" for the change or decision.

We rarely see all the elements identified at the start of the story continuing through to the end. Some pass from start to finish and are changed, some appear in the middle of the story, and some are lost along the way. There are also some things that don't change but are required to make the story work. These can be elements that the audience might assume to be in scope, as well as elements that don't change but are required to enable the change.

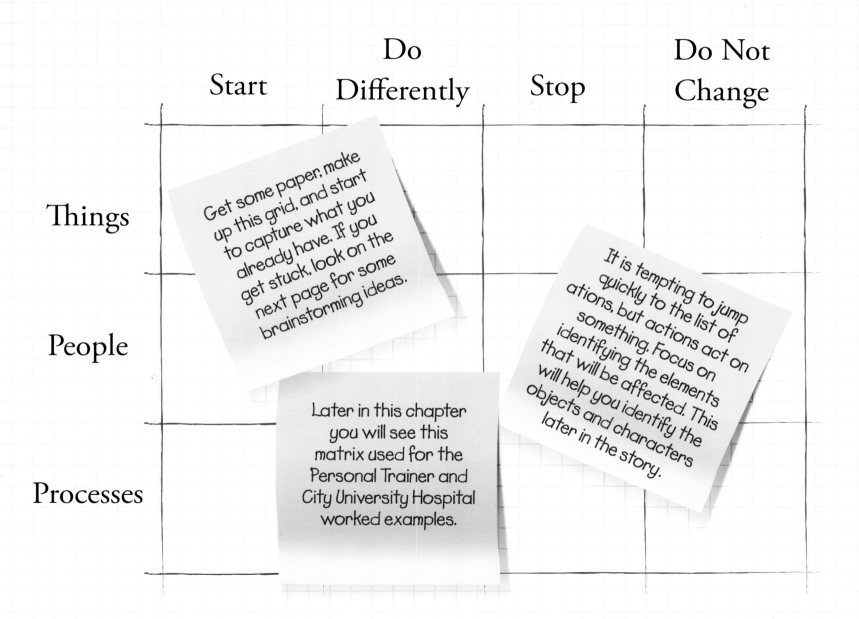

	Start	Do Differently	Stop	Do Not Change
Things	Get some paper, make up this grid, and start to capture what you already have. If you get stuck, look on the next page for some brainstorming ideas.		It is tempting to jump quickly to the list of actions, but actions act on something. Focus on identifying the elements that will be affected. This will help you identify the objects and characters later in the story.	
People				
Processes	Later in this chapter you will see this matrix used for the Personal Trainer and City University Hospital worked examples.			

Brainstorming the Changes

The field of "root cause analysis" took a huge leap forward in 1968 when Kaoru Ishikawa, one of the key influencers of the development of quality-control science in post-war Japan, described a method for discovering the causes for complex system failures. By creating a visual model of "the reasons for failure," he created an easy-to-use tool to help people structure their thinking and explore the commonly repeated reasons for failure. His model, called an *Ishikawa diagram* (or a *fishbone diagram*), has been a core part of quality control ever since.

In effect, Ishikawa's visualization "went viral." He took a simple concept of "brainstorming by category" and put it in a visual diagram that anyone can understand. Although his life and accomplishments are the stuff of quality-control legend, he is best known around the world for this single image and the body of knowledge that led to it.

The method behind the Ishikawa diagram is what is interesting in the context of visual stories. The method, as used today, is a mechanism to encourage creative investigation and, to some extent, brainstorming. We take this method and reuse it specifically for investigating the possible elements that must be changed to address the reasons "Why" that you identified in Chapter 4.

Use this approach if you're having a problem filling in the Elements of Change matrix. If you still find it difficult to work out what to include, that might indicate you still need to do some work to understand the real scope of the change you're proposing.

We have three top-level categories: things; people; and processes. Each of these can be structured into a further set of sub-categories to help identify what needs to change. Here are some examples of what you might include at the next level:

THINGS

- Technology and Tools
- Information Sources
- Facilities and Locations
- Resources
- Finances

PEOPLE

- Culture
- Skills and Experience
- Motivation and Rewards
- Awareness and Interest
- Agreements and Relationships

PROCESSES

- Practices or Procedures
- Success Metrics
- Dependencies
- Business Model
- Operating Model

These sub-categories are mostly relevant to business change activities, but can easily be adjusted to fit personal change stories or broader societal change. Use these as a starting point and adapt them to your situation. We put five sub-categories into each of our top level categories as examples that work well from our experience. You might have more or fewer.

The diagram below gives an idea of how we use the categories with the Elements of Change matrix. This is deliberately a little abstract to allow us to explain the process. If you flip over to the next page you can see how the categories and Elements of Change matrix are used in the Personal Trainer example.

On the left of the large whiteboard in the diagram below are the three top-level categories, and the sub-categories for each of these, drawn as an Ishikawa diagram. You can lay them out like this, or as more of a wheel as we do in the Personal Trainer example. The important aspect is to have a way

to work through the sub-categories and keep asking the same simple question over and over again "What do we need to change in this sub-category?"

Capture each answer on a sticky note. We often use different colors to represent the type of change from the vertical columns on the Elements of Change matrix. This brainstorming exercise may leave you with 15 to 100 stickies, and a lot of ideas. Next, it's time to filter and cluster the ideas together, and place them onto the Elements of Change matrix. The fact that you used colored stickies will help you quickly move the ideas to the appropriate column. As you move the stickies over you can refine the wording and group similar concepts together.

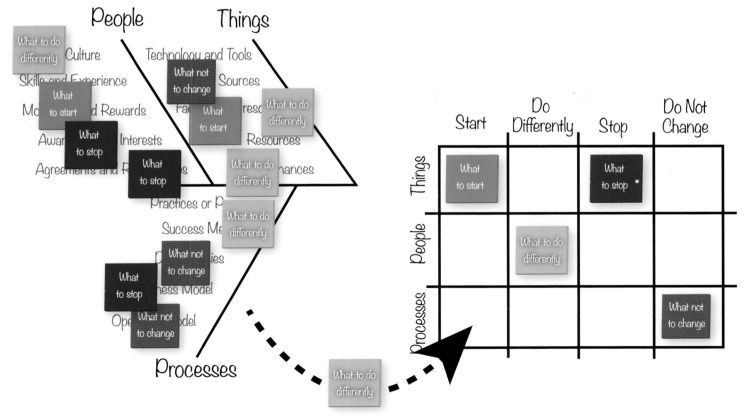

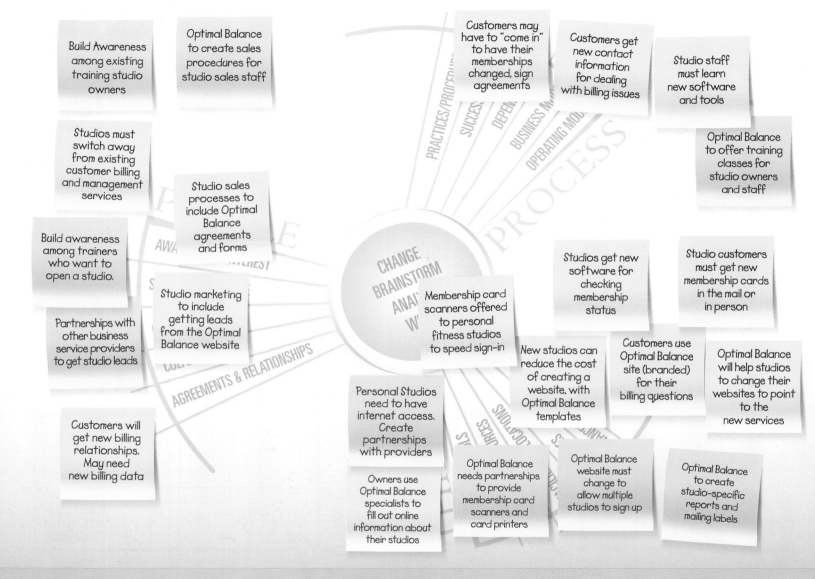

Marina and her husband Nick started with a printout of the brainstorming wheel and attached sticky notes to the areas of the wheel that triggered a thought. The brainstorming process helped her identify many changes necessary for personal fitness studios to use her Optimal Balance service.

	Start	Do Differently	Stop	Do Not Change
Things	Studios get new software for checking membership status; Customers use Optimal Balance website (branded) for their billing questions	Optimal Balance website must change to allow multiple studios to sign up; Optimal Balance to create studio-specific reports and mailing labels; Membership card scanners offered to studios to speed sign-in; Studio customers must get new membership cards in mail or in person	Studios must switch away from existing customer billing and management services; New studios can reduce the cost of creating a website with Optimal Balance templates	Studios can continue to offer their existing services without change; No changes are required in equipment or facilities
People	Optimal Balance to create sales procedures for studio sales staff; Studio staff must learn new software and tools; Build awareness among existing training studio owners; Owners use Optimal Balance specialists to fill out information about their studios	Studio sales processes to include Optimal Balance agreements & forms; Customers will get new billing relationships. May need new billing data; Studio marketing to include getting leads from the Optimal Balance website; Customers may have to "come in" to have their memberships changed, sign agreements		Studios can hire and train their trainers in any way they'd like, without interference
Processes/Activities	Partnerships with other business service providers to get studio leads; Optimal Balance needs partnerships to provide membership card scanners and card printers; Build awareness among trainers who want to open a studio; Studios need to have Internet access. Create partnerships with providers	Optimal Balance will help studios to change their websites to point to the new services; Customers get new contact information for dealing with billing issues; Optimal Balance to offer training classes for studio owners and staff		Studios never forced to sell any products that they don't want to; Studios can present unique offerings, philosophies, and products without interference

It is OK that this column is empty. It means that this particular change does not require us to stop doing many things.

Marina moved the sticky notes over to a grid. She was initially concerned that part of the "Stop" column was empty, but decided that's okay. In reality, her Optimal Balance service is changing things, not stopping them. Marina and Nick used different colored stickies to help them keep track of who had each idea so that later in the day they could add the details for how to make the change happen.

Filter and Focus

You've probably seen a movie where the characters seem to have little motivation, where the relationships among them are contrived, resulting in the story limping along without purpose. The problem in these movies is the same one we see in many presentations: weak or nonexistent relationships among the parts.

To make the connections explicit, it is time to link together all the reasons "Why" from Chapter 4 with "What" to change. Each of the things, people, or processes that will change should link to one or more of the reasons "Why." This helps you to make sure that you aren't considering a change without knowing why. You can skip forward a few pages to the City University Hospital example later in this chapter to see this process with real data, but here we want to use a simpler graphic to explain the process for linking the "Why" and "What" content together.

This process is iterative and may require you to group and break up content to get to a consistent level. We've been asked many times what the right level is, but there is no right answer. It all depends on the level of detail needed for the story.

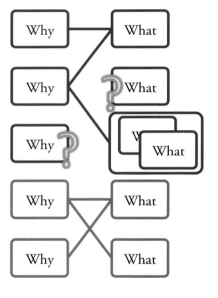

This is the first time you will link items of content together. It will not be the last. So get started and use the time to develop a good understanding of the relationships. You just need to follow these four rules:

- If almost every "Why" is connected to almost every "What," you haven't spent enough time cleanly separating the items. Perhaps you need to cluster and go up a level.

- If one "Why" is connected to many "Whats," perhaps the "Whats" should be clustered together into a higher level group.

- If a "Why" isn't connected to a "What," either something is missing in the "Whats" or the "Why" should be removed.

- If a "What" isn't connected to a "Why," either something is missing in the "Whys" or the "What" should be removed.

This process can get messy, but as with a Sudoku puzzle, just keep going around, and the pieces will slowly work out. Don't worry too much about how things are clustering together; if they're connected, you may need to treat them as a group in the story in order for it to make sense.

If you have to update the "Whys" to make the connectivity work, turn back to Chapter 4, and quickly run through the checklist at the end of that chapter again.

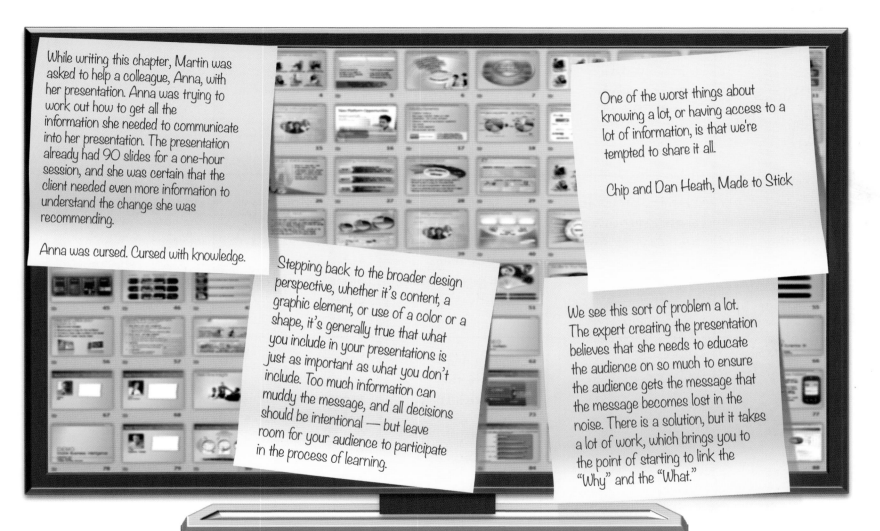

While writing this chapter, Martin was asked to help a colleague, Anna, with her presentation. Anna was trying to work out how to get all the information she needed to communicate into her presentation. The presentation already had 90 slides for a one-hour session, and she was certain that the client needed even more information to understand the change she was recommending.

Anna was cursed. Cursed with knowledge.

One of the worst things about knowing a lot, or having access to a lot of information, is that we're tempted to share it all.

Chip and Dan Heath, Made to Stick

Stepping back to the broader design perspective, whether it's content, a graphic element, or use of a color or a shape, it's generally true that what you include in your presentations is just as important as what you don't include. Too much information can muddy the message, and all decisions should be intentional — but leave room for your audience to participate in the process of learning.

We see this sort of problem a lot. The expert creating the presentation believes that she needs to educate the audience on so much to ensure the audience gets the message that the message becomes lost in the noise. There is a solution, but it takes a lot of work, which brings you to the point of starting to link the "Why" and the "What."

	Start	Do Differently	Stop	Do Not Change
Things	Review patient notes files to create examples for training.	Create a direct link between the prescription system and patient notes files to automatically link prescriptions to the care provided profile.		
People	Learning circles to share experience and new ideas to simplify and improve data capture.	Training on hospital systems to focus on effective data capture for nurses, using common terms instead of narratives.	Stop doctors and specialists writing their own patient notes, or handwriting on patient notes printouts.	Responsibility for the correctness of information remains with the person recording the information.
Processes		Simplify and automate the insurance billing process.	Stop the daily end-of-shift process that copies handwritten notes into the patient files. This should be made redundant.	Pharmacists will continue to cross check between patient notes and the prescribing system when dispensing prescriptions, to ensure patient safety.

Tom continued to analyze his notes from the staff meeting and ad hoc interviews, to create a first pass at understanding what should change. It's a good start, but putting them into this framework made him realize that there may still be quite a few assumptions in the project, and a few gaps, to revisit.

WHY

INSURANCE CLAIMS

- ☐ Reduce the number of rejections.

- ☐ Reduce time spent responding to queries.

- ☐ Reduce time and effort to submit a claim.

DATA QUALITY

- ☐ Capture data once.

- ☐ ALL data captured in electronic patient notes files.

- ☐ Reduce data coding errors.

WHAT

Data Standards

Data Capture
- ☐ Stop the daily end-of-shift process that copies handwritten notes into the patient files.
- ☐ Everyone must capture patient data into the electronic patient notes system.

Data Validation

Data Integration
- ☐ Create a direct link between the prescription system and patient notes files to automatically link prescriptions to the care provided profile.

Patient Reports

Insurance Claims
- ☐ Simplify and automate the insurance billing process.

Training and Development
- ☐ Create examples from the patient notes files.
- ☐ Use learning circles to share experience and new ideas to simplify and improve data capture.
- ☐ Focus training on effective data capture for nurses, using common terms instead of narratives.

Insights

First mapping of the WHY and WHAT has left more questions than answers!

Mapping the cleaned up list of WHYs to the changes, grouped into the list of business processes we have been using on the project so far, shows we haven't thought enough about data validation or patient reports with the leadership team.

Perhaps data standards and patient reports should be filtered out of the story? They did not get highlighted in the leadership meeting or the WHY-WHAT mapping.

Tom's IT team has been working on the patient data problem for some time and has been using a set of business process names for all the major activities. To bring his notes together with these, Tom uses the business process names to group the changes. He also takes a little time divide the reasons for the change into two groups around insurance claims and data quality.

G✋TCHA

- - - *Follow these steps to make sure that you are collecting the information needed to explain WHAT has to change.*

(!) **Consider all the elements that will be affected.** Make sure you're including the downsides of the changes as well as the positives. Go back to the reasons for the change in the "Why" cell to record these reasons.

(!) **Remove the interesting, but irrelevant.** There may be many interesting facts and problems associated with the change or decision you are focused on. But if they are not linked directly to a reason for the change you should consider removing them, no matter how interesting they are.

(!) **Are you creating new content?** If you start to fill in gaps with new ideas, rather than structure and filter what you already have, you're using the model to identify stuff that's missing in your thinking. Make sure you have this clear before you move on to developing the story.

- ☑ Map your existing content to the Elements of Change matrix.

- ☑ Use the Brainstorming Categories to iterate through the "Whats" to group, expand, and refine them.

- ☑ Filter and focus to link the "What" and "Why" together.

- ☑ If there's a "What" or "Why" with no relationship, something must be added or removed!

- ☑ Is your ego tied to the story? Probably! That's okay; it will add to the passion when you deliver the story. Just make sure the content is focused on the audience's problem.

How

6

A journey of a thousand miles begins with a single step.

Lao-tzu, Chinese philosopher and author of the Tao Te Ching (604 BC - 531 BC)

> *Vision without action is a daydream.*
> *Action without vision is a* nightmare
>
> — Japanese Proverb

When an organization plans a new project, someone, typically a project manager, must list all the tasks that will be required, break these activities down to a level of detail suitable for determining the resources necessary, and then track and manage these activities as the change is implemented. We are going to do something similar in this chapter for the content of your visual story. The information that you capture in this chapter is the basis for the sequence of activities that the characters in the story will follow, literally or metaphorically.

As you consider "How" a change must take place, think about the sequence of events that your characters will follow. The sequence has to be realistic for the audience to believe in it, and they should be able to identify with the progress of the characters. Your story may have unexpected turns, sub-plots to deal with specific issues, and climaxes where everything is put at risk. The story cannot be an unordered jumble of scenes that make no sense to the audience. Flashbacks and convoluted intertwined storylines of unrelated participants are best left to Hollywood directors with eight figure production budgets. But we are jumping ahead a little. We will develop the structure of the story in Chapter 10. For now all the steps need to be identified, and at the right level of detail.

If you just show people what the change needs to be, they'll take the path to get to it, right? This is an erroneous assumption that leads to smart people producing no results.

The reason that the CAST process starts with the "Why" and the "What" should be clear by now. In a visual story, you need to understand "Why" the audience should want to change, and "What" will have to change to reach the destination. Without the anchor of "Why" and "What," there's no hope of selecting the right activities to include in the story.

This chapter provides you with some techniques to define "the way forward" part of your visual story. These tools help you to build the "How" from the "What", and then structure the "How" into a sequence that can be told in a story.

If you build it, they will come.

Traceability

Traceability and Milestones

Traceability in the context of a visual story means that you can draw a line from "Why" something needs to be done to "What" to change and then forward to "How" you intend to accomplish it.

The value of traceability comes when filtering out the activities at this step. If you cannot show that your plan for a company Facebook page will address the need to be more proactive at resolving customer complaints, then perhaps you do not need the Facebook page. For most people, this example will seem fairly obvious; however, in many change programs, there are activities that seem obvious to the person proposing them that, on inspection, aren't actually required to make the change happen. Many times, activities are missing from the implementation plan that should be performed, but no one spotted them.

Inevitably, some activities will be difficult to do. Often, these get passed around because no one wants to be responsible for them. Worse, these activities could be left to the end of the project in the hope some magic will happen. Difficult challenges make better stories than easy activities. Your audience wants to hear how the characters will address the challenges, so ensure these difficult yet important activities are a core part of your story.

For project planners, all activities are scheduled and sequenced according to dependencies and resources. Sequencing is important. Just as a home builder erects walls only after the foundation is in place, a project planner looks for these sequences and dependencies. At natural points along the way toward your change, there are milestones where a set of activities are completed and some major part of the change can be seen. These milestones are key elements for your story. They become the points where your characters will pull together to reach a goal before moving on to the next part of the change.

Q. What is the difference between a typical project plan and the model created for the visual story?

A. A typical project plan includes *all* activities, not just the most important ones. The filtering and focus you're about to do make the difference. For the visual story, you need to focus on the steps that have the greatest meaning to the audience, on the steps that directly lead to the resolution of the issues they have, and on the milestones where the change makes significant progress.

To describe a journey across Las Vegas you can simply sketch out the major junctions and any special turning instructions. There is no need to go into detail about all the buildings and side streets you will pass.

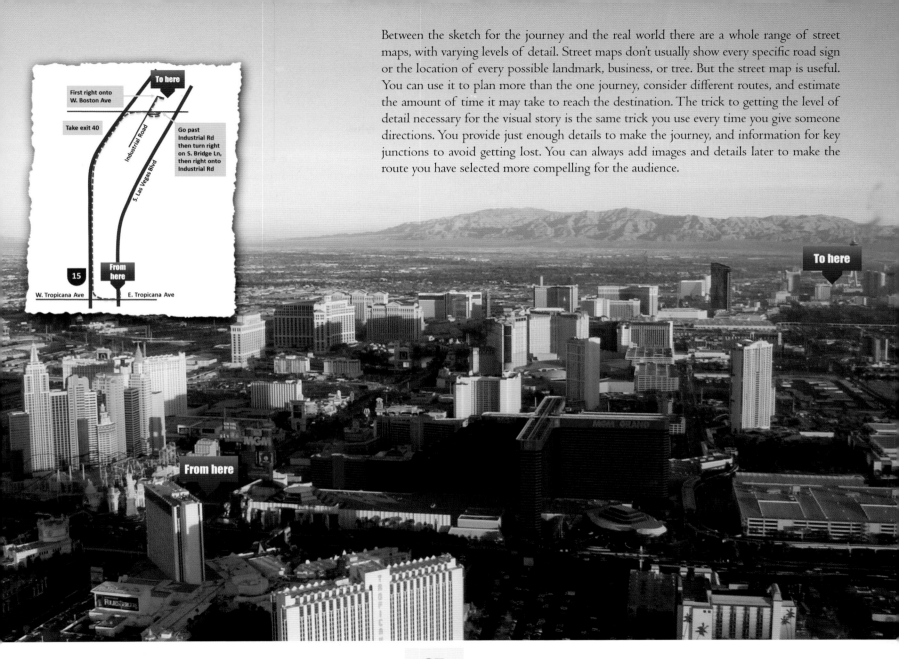

To here

First right onto
W. Boston Ave

Take exit 40

Industrial Road

S. Las Vegas Blvd

Go past
Industrial Rd
then turn right
on S. Bridge Ln,
then right onto
Industrial Rd

15

From
here

W. Tropicana Ave   E. Tropicana Ave

From here

To here

Between the sketch for the journey and the real world there are a whole range of street maps, with varying levels of detail. Street maps don't usually show every specific road sign or the location of every possible landmark, business, or tree. But the street map is useful. You can use it to plan more than the one journey, consider different routes, and estimate the amount of time it may take to reach the destination. The trick to getting the level of detail necessary for the visual story is the same trick you use every time you give someone directions. You provide just enough details to make the journey, and information for key junctions to avoid getting lost. You can always add images and details later to make the route you have selected more compelling for the audience.

Finding the "How"

You know "Why" you want to make the change, and you know "What" to change, now, you need to focus on *"How"* that change will come about, and answer the question, "What steps will we take in order to close the gap between where we are and where we should be?" This answer may require some detailed analysis.

You may already have your answer. Take a moment now to bring together all the content you have that describes how your change will happen. This content can include strategies, project plans, sets of activities, and to-do lists. You cannot share all of the details in most visual stories, but you will need some details to start with and a good reason to believe that you know, at a minimum, how all the changes will be made.

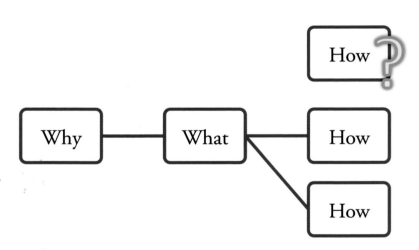

Every activity you identify in this chapter should link to a "What" you identified in the last chapter. If you can't find a "What" for an activity, but you do have a "Why" you want to link it to, go back a step and work out the "What" that should be there! Often this happens because the "What" does not exist yet, and your activity may be creating it for the first time.

Many people with a story to tell are intelligent, thoughtful, and ineffective. One of the most difficult, but important, parts of a visual story is the focus on key elements that need to change. This focus can turn an ineffective story into one with real impact. At the start of the CAST process you identified "Why" the audience should care about the outcome of the story. You have to ruthlessly focus on the important things, the things most essential to your audience, so they will pay attention.

Start with the Elements of Change matrix created in Chapter 5 (or if you have already done some grouping of the "What" as Tom has done in the City University Hospital example, start with the groups you already have) and find a set of the people, processes, and things that will typically have to be changed together. There are no right answers, but you have to start somewhere, so just do that — start somewhere! This might bring together the things people use and the processes they work with.

Next, take the first cluster of "Whats" and write down how they will be changed. You don't need to do it for each "What" individually as the reason they are in the cluster is because they are related to each other, but every cluster must have some activity associated with it, even if that activity is "Leave as is" for the "Do not change" items. If you have something in your project plan or to-do list that doesn't map across to an idea of "What" to change, you have a choice — either remove it from your planning or go back and add a new "What."

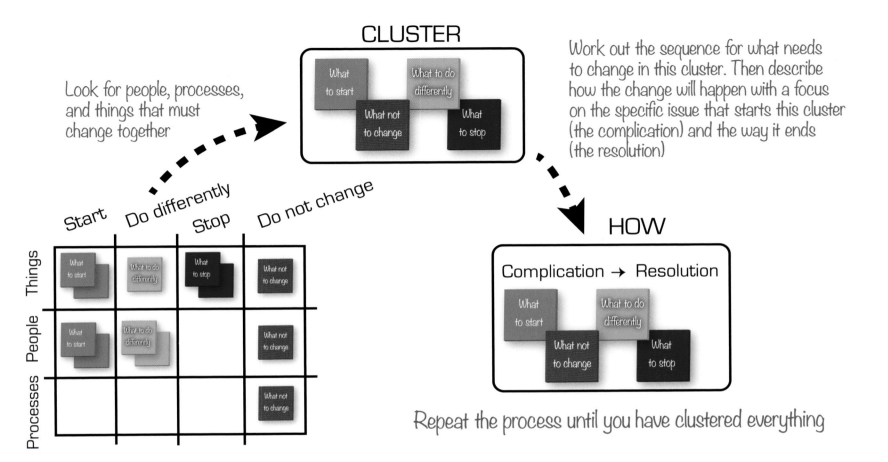

CLUSTER

Look for people, processes, and things that must change together

What to start

What to do differently

What not to change

What to stop

Work out the sequence for what needs to change in this cluster. Then describe how the change will happen with a focus on the specific issue that starts this cluster (the complication) and the way it ends (the resolution)

Start   Do differently   Stop   Do not change

Things
People
Processes

	Start	Do differently	Stop	Do not change
Things	What to start	What to do differently	What to stop	What not to change
People	What to start	What to do differently		What not to change
Processes				What not to change

HOW

Complication → Resolution

What to start

What to do differently

What not to change

What to stop

Repeat the process until you have clustered everything

If you find that you need to put the same steps with different clusters, perhaps the clusters need a reshuffle or the level of detail you're considering for a "What" and a "How" are actually at very different levels. Iterate through this process until you're comfortable that it makes sense, and keep making the clusters until you have taken everything from the Elements of Change matrix. Look back at the Hospital example in Chapter 5, where Tom generated a list of "Whats," and then look at the continuation of the example later in this chapter where each of those clusters are now associated with specific steps for "How" they will be addressed.`

A quick way to test if your clusters are at the right level for the visual story is to define the specific complication or issue that exists at the start of the activity described in the cluster, and then check that the activity in the cluster comes to a resolution. This complication-resolution check will prove very useful when building the story structure in Chapter 10.

Understanding the Dependencies

Mapping the dependencies can take minutes or hours. It really depends on how well structured your content already is. The goal is *not* to create a final and comprehensive plan, but to understand the steps necessary and name them. (Project managers understand this activity well, but you aren't planning a project; you're creating a story with well-designed visuals.) Many visual stories are created in organizations with project teams that will already have a project plan, but now need to work out *how to communicate the change the plan describes.* If this is your situation, it's likely you'll have brought the activities from your plan directly into this chapter.

For many people new to creating visual stories, it can seem like a lot of effort. In some cases, they are right, and in a few minutes, you might be able to get your information down on a page and be totally happy with it.

To test your content, try constructing a sentence like this:

We are going to do HOW to change WHAT because WHY.

Make these sentences for all the relevant combinations in your content to be sure you have enough detail to make sense of the relationships. In the Personal Trainer story you might read one of the combinations as:

"We are going to *run a staff training program* for *staff to learn new sign in procedures* as a part of *providing professional problem resolution.*"

On the opposite page you can see how Marina has developed her thinking for the Personal Trainer story. She has been refining her content and really focused her thinking down to just four activities, shown in the "How" column. Behind each of these is a lot of detail that may be brought out in the story later. For planning and structuring the content, this is an ideal level to work at. Marina has also color-coded the "What" and "How" to show the relationship between them.

Marina has gone a long way to identify the "Hows" in her story, and to link them to the "Whats" and "Whys," but there is another significant step, and that is to work out the sequence for the "Hows." Everything is unlikely to happen at the same time, and even if it could, your story has to have a sequence for you to be able to tell it. It is now time to clarify the sequence of events and key milestones.

WHY	WHAT	HOW
Happy customers = loyal customers		
Reduce billing mistakes	Train staff to collect data for Optimal Balance	
Professional problem resolution	Train staff to call Optimal Balance for help	
	Transition away from existing billing services	Staff Training Program
Reduced costs = higher profit		
Lower operating costs	Train staff to call potential new customers	
	Staff learn new sign-in procedures	
Greater demand = higher rates = higher profit		
Automatically tracked list of potenrial new customers	Change registration form packet	Paperwork Refresh Process
	Inform customers to call Optimal Balance for help	
	Update sales materials to show benefits	
Effectively turn "prospects" into "customers"	Clients issued new membership cards	New sign-in scanner and membership cards
	Studio websites updated to include advanced capabilities	Website Integration Project

Marina fired up her PC and created a simple slide for the information she had collected. She clustered the work to identify four big projects she would need to make the business a success. Now Marina can see what needs to happen and how it relates to "Why."

Cum hoc ergo propter hoc

The phrase *"Cum hoc ergo propter hoc" is* Latin for "with this, therefore because of this." This phrase is sometimes described to as "CORRELATION IMPLIES CAUSATION," assuming that when two events occur together there is often a claimed cause and effect relationship. But simply being adjacent in time is not sufficient to prove causality. On the other hand, using the idea of traceability to relate the "Why," "What," and "How" ensures that you will have a causation clearly defined for correlation and be able to show this evidence if required.

Start with a whiteboard or large sheet of paper and put the "Whys" and "Whats" on the left side, with lines for the relationships you identified in Chapter 5. Leave plenty of space on the right for the "How" information, because you're going to lay this out on a timeline. Because the pieces usually move around a lot as you work out the sequence, we recommend using sticky notes or something similar for the "How" information. Create a sticky note for each of the activities identified in the last exercise. Place each one on the whiteboard to the right of the "What" that it relates to. Space the "How" out as you do this along a horizontal timeline, with the start of the story on the left, working right to the conclusion. As you build the timeline, add in connections to show dependencies where one set of activities cannot start until a preceding set has completed.

As you put each sticky note on the whiteboard, try to group them into combinations that have high interdependency. Within each group, some steps will be either very difficult or very meaningful to the story (in terms of the impact on the "What" or "Why"). These steps are the ones to highlight for use in the visual story, because they will provide climaxes and turning points.

Stories build through these turning points until they reach a climax where the audience cannot see any way back. In the best of stories, the hero reaches a point where he or she has no choice but to commit everything to overcome the final challenge. We will explain this in much more detail in Chapter 10 when you build the story from the content you have here. For now you need to ensure that the most important challenges are identified and brought to the highest level. Also, be certain to highlight your milestones, especially where the resolution of an activity is a major step toward achieving one of the reasons "Why" for the visual story.

There are plenty of drawing applications that can help you quickly lay out the boxes and lines and keep them all linked together as you move them around (even PowerPoint). Just remember that the aim is to structure the information, not waste time on layouts.

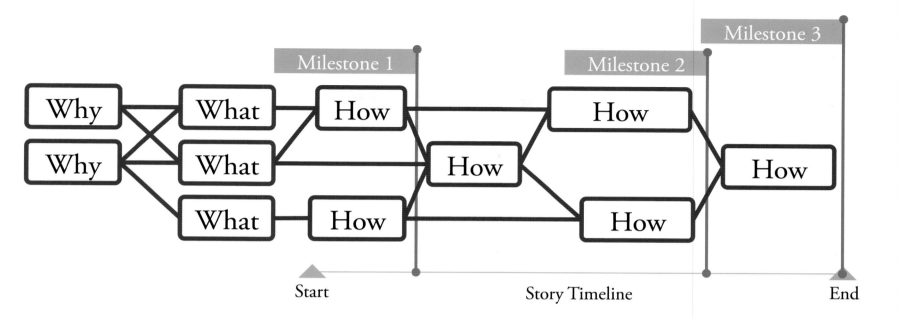

You are aiming to build something that looks like the diagram above, although your diagram will have a lot more content in each of the "Why," "What," and "How" boxes. Sometimes it helps to break the "How" boxes down into the next level of detail to be sure you have the right flow; it really depends on how detailed you left your content in the last exercise.

The challenge here is to ensure that each "How" logically follows the ones that go before it. On the following page you can see how Tom structured his content for the City University Hospital example. As he did the analysis he found there were some parts of his project that were not well defined, and some that were not necessary for the visual story. Tom's milestones came from his project plan. Because of the dependencies between activities Tom needs everything to be completed for a milestone before the activities for the next milestone can begin.

Chapter 16 shows another worked example with traceability from the "Why" through to the "How," with a more complex set of dependencies. All three worked examples show a different level of detail and mapping of the content. There is no single right answer for the number of top-level challenges and milestones. It depends on both the complexity of your story and the format you'll choose later to tell your story. Do a first pass now to create your first structure, aiming for three to five milestones, and see how this works.

WHAT

Data Standards

Data Capture

Data Validation

Data Integration

Patient Reports

Insurance Claims

Training and
Development

HOW

Milestone: Clinical systems operational
Milestone: New IT systems ready
Milestone: New interface ready for tests

- ☐ Implement new standard data definitions
- ☐ Map existing data to new definitions
- ☐ Implement new, simpler data entry screens, focused on clinical tasks
- ☐ Deploy mobile devices for data capture and to display patient notes
- ☐ Change input processes to capture all information related to a diagnosis
- ☐ Create business rules to support data validation and integration between systems
- ☐ Implement machine readable tags on patient bracelets for data entry and retrieval of notes.
- ☐ Automated daily reports to spot potential gaps in patient care records for immediate attention
- ☐ Automatic generation of insurance claims at regular intervals and on patient discharge
- ☐ Training program
  - ☐ The importance of patient data capture
  - ☐ How to use the new interfaces and devices

Tom uses the project plan that his IT team has already started to identify the key project activities that fit with the themes emerging for the visual story. He doesn't need to worry about the resources and details of timings, but this does provide a sequence for major activities and insight into three key milestones that might relate to the story.

Insights

1. We have two stories here, one about the change to patient data capture and usage in the hospital, and one about the billing for care to insurance companies. There is a lot in common, but perhaps we need two different versions.

2. The data standards work is a key enabler, but it is mainly of interest to the IT team. No wonder the last presentation to the project steering committee felt like it hadn't gone well. The mapping indicates that none of our key people care about the data standards; it's just a prerequisite to the work that adds real value.

   Action: Drop Data Standards from the visual story. These are vital for the project, but we don't need to include them in the story to get support for the major changes.

3. Patient reports are an important part of the project but did not get highlighted in the WHY-WHAT analysis. Our focus with the teams so far has been on the hard work of the data capture changes and not on the improved patient report outputs, which should make big differences to the availability of information to nurses and doctors.

   Action: Doing this mapping has highlighted that no one understands the value from the improved patient reports. Go back to the WHY-WHAT mapping and create a link from "ALL data captured in electronic patient notes files" to Patient Reports. Include details that the Patient Reports are built on the new patient notes data.

Tom reviewed all the project activities with Ralf. The work so far has identified a number of areas to focus on and some differences between what his team has thought important and what others in the hospital think are important.

GOTCHA

Follow these steps to make sure that you're collecting the information needed to explain "How" the change that you envision will happen.

(!) **Project plans rarely focus on the activities for a good story.** A project plan is structured around resources and aggregating smaller tasks into larger ones for manageability. A story is based on conflict and interaction, where the important tasks are those with the greatest meaning to the characters and the audience. Milestones in project plans are typically at the completion of major steps in the change process. Milestones for the visual story are where the greatest challenges are overcome.

(!) **Keep a record of the different versions as you filter and cluster the content.** You may find later you need to get back to a greater level of detail or a structure you had at an earlier point. A camera can be a quick and easy way to do this. Most phones today come with a camera that can capture great images of whiteboards or pages of notes. Just get used to snapping as you go along. If you don't need the images, you can easily delete them.

(!) **Avoid analysis paralysis by working with someone else.** Sometimes, it seems like there are so many combinations you don't know where to start. Don't worry about getting everything right the first time. Just set yourself a time limit. Do a first pass, being as ruthless as you can; then present your plan to a friend or colleague. We often find this analysis a lot easier with a second person to help, just listening to the ideas and giving feedback.

?

☑ First cluster the "Whats," and then for each cluster identify "How" the change will happen, noting the complication, resolution, and any examples.

☑ Use your existing plans and to-do lists as the starting point, but ensure that every "How" can be clearly linked to a "What" and through to a "Why."

☑ Every "What" must have at least one "How" defined for it.

☑ Create a dependency analysis for the "Why," "What," and "How," and then identify the milestones for the visual story.

What If

7

At first, I see pictures of a story in my mind. Then creating the story comes from asking questions of myself. I guess you might call it the 'what if - what then' approach to writing and illustration.

—*Chris Van Allsburg, Caldecott medalist, author and illustrator of children's books*

*What if you slept? And **what if**, in your sleep, you dreamed? And **what if**, in your dream, you went to heaven and there plucked a strange and beautiful flower? And **what if**, when you awoke, you had the flower in your hand? Ah, what then?*

—*Samuel Taylor Coleridge, English poet, philosopher, and co-founder of the Romantic Movement in England*

The preceding three chapters focus on what you want to happen. Life is rarely so straightforward that there's just one path to follow. Members of your audience may have different ideas, options, or alternative outcomes in mind. After they hear your story, they may also start to speculate on future possibilities, on what they could do if the change you're proposing happens, and on the alternative ways to get there. How can you take the lead and avoid having the audience redirect the story?

DON'T LET THEM STEAL YOUR THUNDER
Why wait for someone else to point out the risks, challenges, or potential downside in the story. Do it yourself, steal the argument, and deal with the issues. After you've raised the issues, putting them in context and explaining how they can be resolved, gives you a better chance of convincing the audience of your story.

EVERYTHING IS RELATIVE
You can make your options look better by comparing them to less attractive alternatives. If doing nothing or other realistic alternatives would cost more than what you are proposing, or result in a worse position for the audience, you want to understand these differences and consider using them in the story to set a frame of reference that supports your case. If the audience thinks things are bad now, you can show how they could be worse. The moral is that a risk taken today may be easier to handle than the problem waiting around the corner — but only if you're willing to take the lead and look around the corner.

In this chapter, we introduce two techniques that can help you to identify the "What If" options to consider: walking backward through the story, and contemplating alternative scenarios. Use these, or any of your own, to develop the ideas; then go back to the "Why-What-How" timeline model you created in Chapter 6 and annotate it with these ideas.

WHAT IF another company gets to market first with the same idea you have?

WHAT IF we run out of water this summer?

WHAT IF the economy doesn't recover this year?

WHAT IF we could win more deals using stories?

WHAT IF we can reduce costs by 20 percent?

WHAT IF this were such a good place to work we'd have the best people wanting to join us?

WHAT IF the key factors change?

Exercise

Pick some of your favorite movies or stories and examine them to identify key sequences or locations. How would the story change if these were different? How different would the story of The Godfather have been if it had taken place in Mexico City or New Delhi instead of New York City?

Walking Backward Through the Story

Sometimes the best way to work through all the "What Ifs" is to execute the change and see what happens! Not really, but virtually, through the power of imagination. The technique we suggest here is to walk backward through the timeline of the story.

Why go backward? Going through the steps in reverse order breaks the normal thought processes and helps to undercover assumptions and different perspectives.

Martin

This technique is one my personal favorites and one I've used many times to explore a story under development.

I learned how to do it 12 years ago, and in the preceding text, where it says "walk backward," I mean this literally. There is something about physically moving yourself along a timeline that helps to step through the story. I often start with my back to the wall, which represents today, and stepping forward for as many steps as there are milestones in the story. As I walk forward, I imagine myself moving forward in time until I reach the end of the story. Then I close my eyes, imagine the future, and start talking about it.

I start by putting myself in the position of someone in the audience at the end of the story. The first step is to visualize the world of this person when the change is completed, using the full range of emotions and senses in the description. I think about what the person can do. How colleagues, friends, and everyone else in the story will interact with them. When I've fully described the end of the story, I take a step back to the last milestone in the "Why-What-How" timeline.

I repeat the process of describing what it feels like to be at this point in the story, what the challenges ahead are like, and how the person passed through the last set of challenges. I tend to keep my eyes closed throughout the whole process to help me focus on the visualization and use a partner to walk me through a script similar to the one on the next page. The partner can then remind me of the key messages for the milestone after each step.

In this way, step-by-step, I go back to the start of the story. At which point, I open my eyes and review the notes. This is a process that can really benefit from having a partner who can listen to you and capture notes. If you don't have a partner, simply speak out loud and record your voice (most smartphones now have this capability).

Sometimes, I go through this process for a number of different people in the story to get different perspectives. This process helps to identify a broader range of risks and issues from the perspective of different people.

You are now back to today.

Talk about what it feels like to consider taking on this change. *Open your eyes and review the notes.*

Step back.

Go back to the previous milestone in the "Why-What-How" timeline. Talk about what it feels like to be there, to have completed the last steps, and how you are feeling about the next steps. Think about what you can do at this point in the future that you cannot do today.

Start here.

Stand with plenty of space behind you. Close your eyes. Put yourself in the future, when the change has happened. Talk about what it *feels* like to be here. The change has been made. What can you do after the change that you cannot do today?

Alternative Scenarios

We cannot predict the future, but we can plan for it. In *The Art of the Long View*, Peter Schwartz describes a technique called *Scenario Planning* to look at the "What Ifs." The technique goes well beyond simply forecasting the future and starts to identify how to prepare for it and spot when the circumstances are right for certain scenarios to happen. If you find yourself in a situation where the alternative outcomes are a big part of your story, it could be worth your time to develop detailed descriptions of the alternative scenarios and really understand the critical factors that will lead to one or the other.

Here we provide a much simplified version of the Scenario Planning concept that you can use on your own or in small groups to help consider the "What Ifs" for your story. Start by going back to the "Whys" and look at the Outcome Mapping approach. Behind the goals for the story are situations and forces that are driving the change. Look at these drivers and consider "what if" those drivers change.

Here's an example to illustrate our point. In western India, a drought has been getting progressively worse. The government policy in the area has been to provide water for industrial-scale sugar cane operations first, and local food production last. Crops are failing, and thousands of poor people are moving to the cities of Mumbai and Pune. This mass migration is driving the need for change. A non-profit agency, hoping to influence government officials to change their policies and support agriculture aims to use Scenario Planning to describe the alternative scenarios that could arise.

The first driver is a series of recent droughts that indicate the environment is changing. A second driver is the support for industrial sugar cane, which consumes large quantities of water.

Continuing with the Indian drought example, the two driving forces of water availability and the relocation of the population are plotted as two dimensions on the diagram opposite. If you were working through the full Scenario Planning process, you would now spend a lot of time developing the story for each of the different combinations. For your a visual story, it's often enough to have a good idea about the differences between the four variations and then work out where your story fits.

In your situation, you might have many driving forces at play. To keep the scenario process manageable and within a reasonable timeframe, try to limit yourself to the two primary driving forces. For each driving force, identify the extremes of possible outcomes and check whether you can rule out immediately any impossible combinations.

In this example, the story assumes droughts will continue and people will continue to migrate to the city as the rural areas dry out and earning a living becomes harder. What if the rains return next year? What if the migration to cities slows down, because it mainly consisted of young people who have now moved? What if reducing the water allocated for sugar cane doesn't make the water available to poor farmers? In this scenario, you might consider developing a dialogue among your characters to raise the key points and address when it's realistic to decide whether the driving forces behind the story have changed.

The whole situation of a story can change dramatically on certain key factors or events. Understanding what these are will help you strengthen the story and consider the alternatives your audience may want to discuss. As we continue with the worked examples on the following pages, Tom and Marina first consider what might not go as planned, then each look to the future to describe how an ideal outcome might feel.

More information on the West Indian drought used for this example can be found on the AlertNet website at http://www.trust.org/alertnet/news/west-india-drought-fuels-migration-to-cities.

Rainfall returns to the long-term normal.

Urbanization continues with water consumption increasing as water resources are not considered a problem.

Rural communities have the water supplies to support the population.

Urbanization

Water supply

People move to the cities.

People stay in the rural towns.

Urbanization crisis is caused by water shortage. Focus of the story.

Rural communities have insufficient water, leading to emergency requirement for social and health support.

Droughts get worse.

Risks

1. When we change over to the new interfaces for data capture, the nurses and doctors will have to put in extra time for the training, and then it will take longer initially for them to work through the new interfaces. The risk is that they slip back to using paper notes, and the benefits of the new systems to capture data at point of measurement are lost.

2. We cannot get the new mobile devices deployed until after the software is updated. For a while, the nurses will need to keep going back to the fixed PCs to enter data. The risk again is that they use paper notes throughout the day and just enter at the end of day. This would mean that the nurses might not have the information to answer the extra questions the new business rules ask for, and no ability to quickly capture it.

Alternatives

1. Wait for another hospital to implement these changes, and then copy them. This could be a delay of a number of years, during which we would continue to lose revenue.

2. Make no changes until the mobile devices and patient tags are ready. Much more of a big-bang change in processes and work practices; that could cause bigger issues on the first few days.

3. Hire specific people to focus on the insurance claims process, to improve quality and reduce the rejection rate. This fixes the symptom, not the problem, and we would always require these people.

When Tom did the review with Ralf, he also spent time talking about the risks and potential alternative approaches. They covered a lot of ideas, but agreed these were the major ones that the stories would need to consider.

What will the future feel like after the changes?

Emergency situations on the ward can be handled by any nurse, with confidence that they can see the latest information.

Always able to pick up a mobile device, scan a patient tag, and get the latest patient report.

Everyone working on the ward knows how to enter data into the system.

Feels like everyone is pulling together. A strong team around the patient.

You can trust the patient data to be correct and up-to-date.

Insurance-based revenue is compensating for public funding cuts. The feeling that cuts are coming, which we have lived with for years, does not seem as strong.

This feels like a leading edge hospital. A place where we have invested in things that make a difference to patient care.

My concerns over patient care issues from poor data are gone!

Nurses and doctors are sharing more information about the care plans for patients. Nurses are feeling a lot more involved, and doctors are seeing the positive benefits in patients getting the right care.

Management teams are happy with the insurance billing levels.

City University Hospital

To understand how the patient data changes will impact the hospital, Tom decides to ask Luc for a little help. Luc has been involved in a lot of the thinking for the changes. Tom asks Luc to close his eyes and imagine himself on a ward in two years time, with everything working well. "What does it **feel** like?" he asks. The notes above capture Luc's response.

What if not enough studios sign up?

What if gyms offer better pay to trainers?

What if demand for personal training declines?

What if a studio gets too many customers?

The value proposition of the Optimal Balance system is threefold: reduce the costs to run a small studio; help new studios to start by simplifying the complex financial concerns; and offer the ability for clients to transition from one studio to another.

Until there are many studios in the system, the third value proposition won't matter. While important, the ability to move between studios is not necessary to make the business case compelling.

There are two reasons that a personal trainer would open his or her own studio: more control, and better pay. If commercial gyms improve their pay, trainers may not want to run their own gyms.

Running a studio is easier and more profitable with the Optimal Balance system, so we should focus on the control aspects and highlight the income advantage to the trainer, who will also be the owner, as this scenario is pretty unlikely anyway.

Demographic and economic changes may impact the local market for personal training.

Since the Optimal Balance system reduces cost and hassle, and potentially provides some new customers, it allows studios to cope better with economic hardships than they would on their own.

The Optimal Balance system cannot prevent a studio from going out of business. Optimal Balance will continue to recruit new studios to overcome the turnover in existing partners.

This is a nice problem to have, but still a problem. Most studios have a limited capacity for personal training time.

The nice thing about the Optimal Balance system is that a client can visit a nearby studio while your studio hires staff or buys equipment to increase capacity.

In other words, you don't have to say "No" because you are full. You can say "Yes, but I'll need you to use our partner a few miles away for a week or two."

Marina thought about the underlying factors that could change. She built a slide with a response for each factor, to be prepared for questions when pitching the idea to personal trainers and fitness studios.

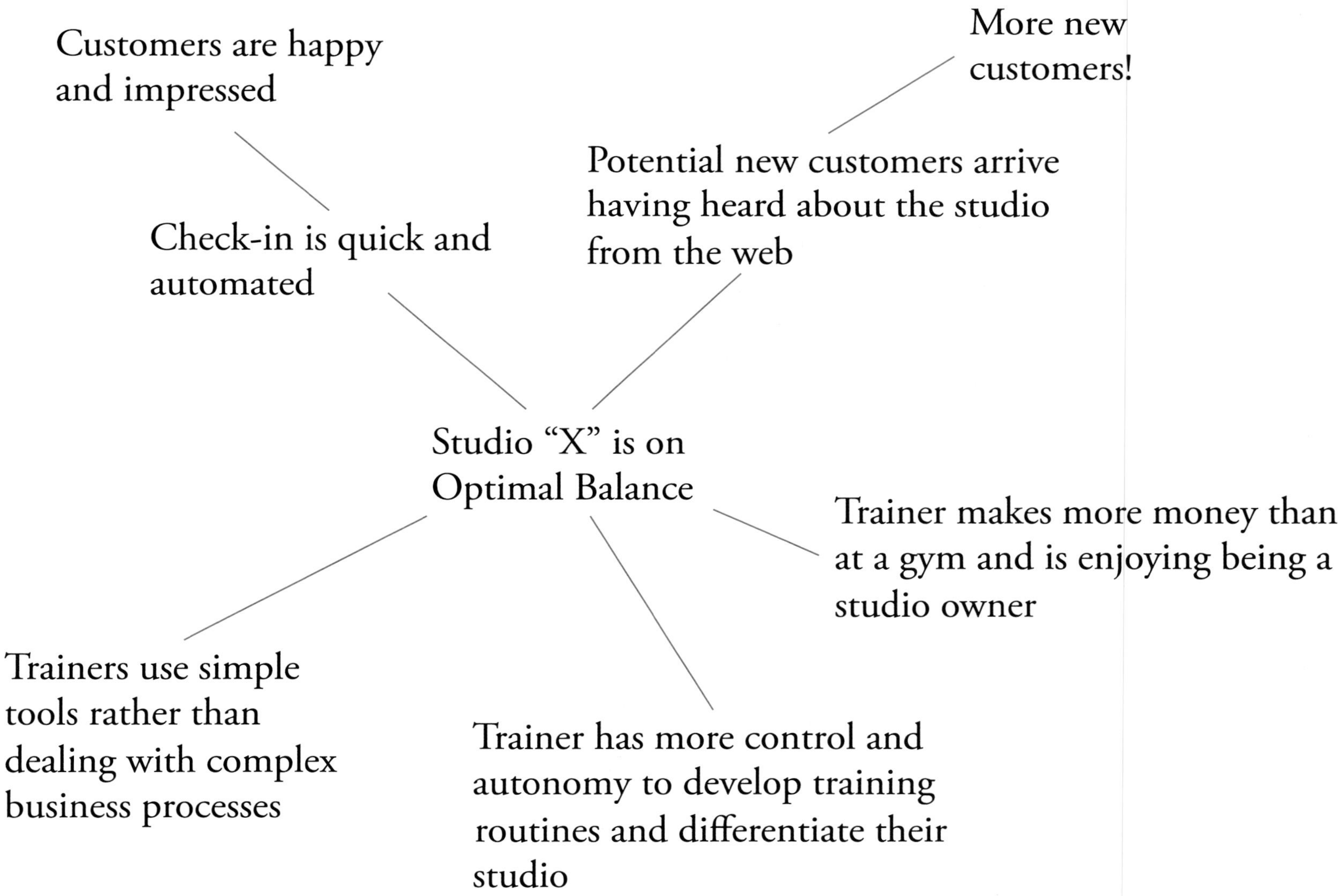

Customers are happy
and impressed

More new
customers!

Potential new customers arrive
having heard about the studio
from the web

Check-in is quick and
automated

Studio "X" is on
Optimal Balance

Trainer makes more money than
at a gym and is enjoying being a
studio owner

Trainers use simple
tools rather than
dealing with complex
business processes

Trainer has more control and
autonomy to develop training
routines and differentiate their
studio

Marina thought about what the future would look like for a studio that joined the program. She added this information to her slides and then took a printout to her friends who own studios to check her ideas.

G✋TCHA

Follow these steps to make sure that you are collecting the information needed to understand the options, alternatives, and potentially different outcomes.

Stop at the end. The act of visualizing the future and considering what else is possible when you get there can result in a desire to take the story further and build a next step into the story. Although doing so can increase the benefits and give you a positive outcome to describe, it can also increase the scope of your change to the point the audience considers it unrealistic and decides not to even start. In most cases, it's better to define the earliest possible ending, where the major challenge has been overcome and where there's a new starting position from which a new story can begin.

Make the preferred alternative clear. The "What Ifs" you consider for risks and alternatives will help you better define the journey you want members of the audience to take. If the alternate journeys are too similar to the journey you're proposing, there's a chance the audience will get confused about which route to take. Demonstrate how your recommended approach is clearly different from the alternatives.

Avoid the multiple-choice ending. There should be no doubt about the ending. When telling the story, you might let the audience make the last leap, but the ending should be so obvious that there's no chance the audience can follow your story and pick an alternative ending. The scenario approach can help you, the creator of the visual story, determine the alternatives and the key factors that you must emphasize in order to ensure that the audience ends up where you intended them to.

☑ Be very focused in order to strengthen the story and call out the risks before anyone else does.

☑ Identify the future consequences, the possibilities the audience can consider that come from acting on the story.

☑ Understand the alternative stories (scenarios) the audience might consider and the comparison you need to make to ensure that they choose your story.

☑ Annotate the "Why-What-How" timeline with the "What-Ifs."

It is not the daily increase
but the daily decrease. Hack
away at the unessential.

—*Bruce Lee, possibly the most influential martial artist*
of the 20th century

A successful book is not made of
what is in it, but what is left out of it.

—*Mark Twain, American author and humorist*

Art is the elimination of
the unnecessary.

—*Pablo Picasso, Spanish painter, sculptor, and co-founder of*
the cubist movement

Ever heard the story about the
violin maker who was asked how
he made a violin? He answered that
he started with a piece of wood, and
removed everything that wasn't a
violin. Well, that's just what you've
been doing in the last four chapters.

The 80/20 Rule: Eighty percent of your
impact will come from twenty percent of the
content you first try to put in the story!

Final Thoughts on the Story CONTENT

CONTENT

Focus

The first row of the Visual Story Map culminates here with a reminder to focus. Your content is now structured and the relationships defined to link all the activities to clear motivations. You can now fill in the top row of a Visual Story Map with a few key words and messages for each of the "Why," "What," "How," and "What If," cells and understand clearly how they fit together. Don't throw away the details; you will need them later, but you now have the core for the story.

As you go through the rest of the CAST process, to structure the story and visual design, you will develop a number of versions of the visual story. These will vary in their level of detail, from the full presentation down to the elevator pitch, and possibly even a single sentence. The foundation you've developed in the last four chapters will allow these versions to be consistent and to build on one another.

What if, after all this filtering and focusing, you realize there's not enough content to really fill a one-hour presentation? Then don't do a one-hour presentation! Rescope your communication to something that better fits the time it takes to deliver the message. This could be a five-minute presentation, a podcast, a well-structured e-mail or a poster on the wall for all to see.

That's been one of my mantras — focus and simplicity. Simple can be harder than complex: You have to work hard to get your thinking clean to make it simple. But it's worth it in the end because once you get there, you can move mountains.

—Steve Jobs, 1998

Be Specific. Be Interesting

Specific content engages the audience. It's simply more interesting than generalizations. The number one mistake in presentations has nothing to do with bullet points or reading from the slides, and everything to do with the message being too abstract. The presentation may be strong on concept and recommendation but not provide any evidence or content that the audience can personally relate to.

A compelling visual story is all about taking the concepts and recommendations and turning them into concrete and specific examples that grab the audience's attention and make its members want to hear all of it.

It's time now to take the focus you have on your content and see it through the eyes of your audience.

You can go from doing something quite silly to something dead serious in the blink of an eye, and if you're making those connections with your audience then they're going to go right along with it.

—Bruce Springsteen, as interviewed by Nick Hornby in the Observer Music Monthly, 17 July 2005

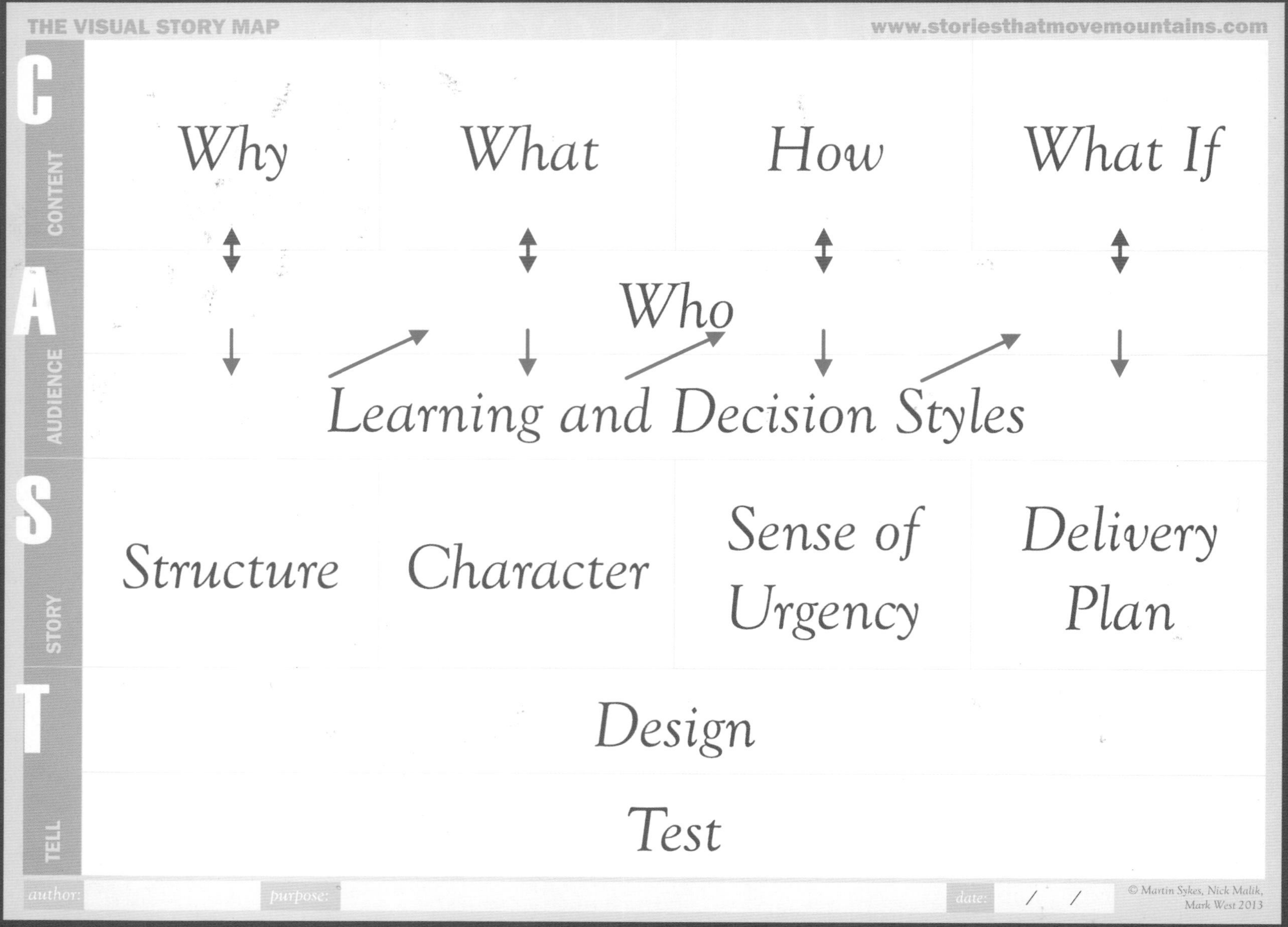

THE VISUAL STORY MAP
www.storiesthatmovemountains.com
C
CONTENT
Why
What
How
What If
A
AUDIENCE
Who
Learning and Decision Styles
S
STORY
Structure
Character
Sense of Urgency
Delivery Plan
T
TELL
Design
Test
author:
purpose:
date: / /
© Martin Sykes, Nick Malik, Mark West 2013

AUDIENCE

Who

8

I don't know what the key to success is, but the key to failure is trying to please everyone.

—Seth Godin, American serial entrepreneur and author

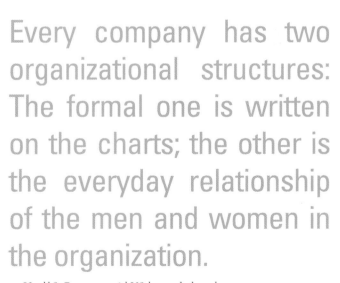

Every company has two organizational structures: The formal one is written on the charts; the other is the everyday relationship of the men and women in the organization.

—Harold S. Geneen, successful U.S. business leader and CEO of ITT from 1959 to 1977

Convincing everyone of an idea is nearly impossible, even if the idea is amazingly compelling. So don't try to convince everyone. Every time you dilute your message to accommodate an additional person, you risk reducing its effectiveness. In this chapter, we ask you to focus on the specific people you need to convince. You must first figure out who they are.

The CAST process focuses on using stories to influence decisions, or to make change happen. Whether you are out to change the world or yourself, you need clarity of purpose and a message to make audiences commit. CAST has been designed to help you plan the delivery approach for different sizes of audience, with a process to map your content to a story structure based on an audience analysis. The first step in understanding your audience is to be clear on the size of the audience.

As more people started to use CAST and the Visual Story Map, it became apparent that these visual stories have real impact on people's lives. One lady created a visual story to help her get a promotion. Posted on her kitchen door and pasted into the front of her work notebook, this one-page visual story reminded her every day why she needed to change, what she had to do, and how she would do it with the help of her friends and colleagues.

Interest groups often represent a shared purpose or ideal. The purpose and activities seem obvious for everyone in the group. You may be lobbying for legislative changes, or championing a cultural change, but for those on the outside the purpose is often less clear, and the reasoning that holds the group together can seem one-sided. The visual story must communicate the reason to care so that the audience moves to support the goal of the interest group.

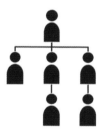

In organizations, the visual story is often used to gain support for large projects. These projects often come with major organizational change, and that usually means getting many people to agree to put time, effort, and budgets into doing something differently. Logic and financial models are important, but to get commitment, you also need a way to capture emotional needs and clearly define the path to a better future.

Changing the world doesn't need a budget of millions or a cast of thousands, although no doubt they can help. Social media sites from YouTube to Facebook have dramatically changed the reach and impact organizations can have. For audiences on this scale, the visual story needs to be developed with greater awareness of cultural diversity and the full range of learning and decision styles.

There is a good reason for how the Visual Story Map is structured, especially the way the first and second rows fit together. In every one of the "Why," "What," "How," and "What If" cells, you have been identifying content for the story *and also* defining who the audience is. Look back a few pages to the Visual Story Map shown at the start of the Audience section and you will see arrows indicating a bidirectional flow from each of the first four cells into "Who" and then from "Who" down to the next cell for Learning and Decision Styles. This is just a little reminder that CAST is not a linear process. As you are refining your content you will identify the audience, and as you develop the details about your audience you will identify content you need to include.

The task of the visual storyteller is to match the motivations of the key people in the audience with the reasons "Why" identified in Chapter 4. Motivations include the degree of personal benefit, alignment with beliefs, and contribution to the change activities. These are not mutually exclusive motivations, just different perspectives. When listening to the story, each person in the audience will respond to a different mix of messages that appeal to his specific motivations. Each person will weigh the issues behind the story differently and judge the story based on his or her experience and context. You can never control other people's decisions. But you can link your story to their problems and differentiate your story from other options they may be considering.

Storytellers need feedback to help them understand whether the story is having the desired effect. Most importantly, a storyteller needs to get that feedback in time to be able to adapt the story. Storytellers must listen and observe, as well as they present. Understanding the personal details for the audience is the first step in collecting and understanding feedback.

Companies and organizations don't make decisions. They don't make change happen. People do. When it comes to making decisions in organizations, not all votes are equal. In this chapter, we look at how to find common ground with your audience, and use a technique called *power mapping*. Power maps help you identify the audience, understand who has the power to influence or make a decision, and work out whom to listen to, and observe.

Don't try to convince everyone

Too often, the designer of a presentation or other communication assumes that the background and goals of the audience are similar to his or her own. In the worst cases, the presenter also assumes that the audience is made up of nearly identical individuals who will all respond the same way to the presentation.

The next time you find yourself thinking about an audience, remember the Terracotta Army. These figures were created for the Chinese Emperor Qin Shi Huang in 210-209 BC. At first glance they look like row upon row of identical statues, but in reality each of the more than 8000 soldiers is different.

We are not suggesting you have to work out the details for each member of your audience, but accepting that they are individuals leads to the next step. When you build a visual story, you have to identify what it is that they have in common. Whatever they have in common gives you a starting point, or foundation, on which you can build a story that will interest your audience. This context for each member of the audience can include experiences, beliefs about the future, and knowledge of the subject matter you bring in your story.

Finding the Common Ground

If there is a more important key to communication than finding common ground, I certainly can't think of it. Common ground is the place where people can discuss differences, share ideas, find solutions, and start creating something together. Too often people see communication as the process of transmitting massive amounts of information to other people. But that's the wrong picture. Communication is a journey. The more that people have in common, the better the chance that they can take that journey together.

—John C. Maxwell, *authority on leadership. He has written more than 60 books, with over 19 million copies sold.*

Every individual in your audience has some existing knowledge or context relevant to your story. Imagine this context as a map in the mind of each individual. The areas of the mental map can be described in different levels of detail, some with real experience and some with a theoretical knowledge. This map may be tiny, inaccurate, or the result of years of experience. It is their mental map. It is constantly being updated, and every map is unique. For your story to have meaning, it must have sufficient overlap with the mental maps of your audience. It is the overlap, or common ground, that allows members of your audience to understand the story and incorporate it with their existing knowledge.

We all have a set of filters that we use to judge information we receive, to compare it with our own mental maps, and to decide what information gets updated. In Chapter 1, we talk about the experience of Stanford students and the improvement of recall through the use of stories. The story is helping to get the information past the filters and into the mental map.

Existing Mental Map + Your Story = New Mental Map

This doesn't mean that all individuals will end up with the same mental map, but your story should start in a shared context, and through the actions in the story you will change their maps, to help them reach the decision you want.

Take a moment to look at the "Why-What-How" relationship model you defined in Chapter 6. Every item on the model maps to a person in the audience who has a pain, owns the thing to be changed, or has a role in making the change happen. Before you go any further, start by making a list of all these people. You will filter this down to focus on the critical people, but until you have worked out what common ground there is, and the power relationships among your audience members, don't make any assumptions.

Assume that the area of this page represents everything that could ever be known, experienced, or believed about your story's subject matter. To keep the idea simple, also assume that the context for each individual in your audience could be contained within a circle on this page. You are represented by the blue circle.

The green circles represent the context for three of the key decision makers.

Everyone has a different context. The overlap (in gray) among these circles is a good place to start for many stories, building on a shared context, or common ground. In the overlap, you will need to look for common experiences on which to base a story that will have a strong personal impact. When researching your story, take some time to listen to your audience so that you can find that shared context.

As the story extends outside this shared context, you may need to educate members of the audience, to extend their knowledge with the content of the story. In some cases, you may also find you have some audience members with a very different context than the story, or than most of the rest of the audience (shown in red). The story may become the only shared context for the whole audience. Sometimes when we spot this situation, it's a clue to include a general metaphor or analogy in the story that all the different personal contexts can relate to, in order to bring the entire audience into the story.

For example, Martin and Nick have both worked as enterprise architects. This role in corporate IT organizations is often hard to describe, and an enterprise architect's context has little overlap with the context of many of the people they work with. In telling a story to help people understand what an enterprise architect is, both Martin and Nick have used the analogy of city planners, relating the planning of IT systems to the planning required to lay out services for a city.

Now take the list of people you created and start to write down what you know they have in common. You probably cannot create this as a series of circles; life is really not that simple. But, you can write out what you believe each of your audience members knows about the story, and use some simple clustering to find out what they have in common.

Creating a Power Map

Power follows the golden rule: The person with the gold makes the rules.

At the start of this chapter, we talked about focusing on the right people in the audience. This focus starts with the people who have the power to make the decision or the change happen. Although not always true, the person with the funds to make the change happen often has the final decision. But money isn't the only source of power. In families, interest groups, corporations, and government, very few changes are really made by a democratic process where everyone has an equal say.

The real power is often invisible, with little relation to the title on the office door, the position on the organizational chart, or the elder on the family tree. The real power also changes regularly, and may differ depending on the decision to be made. You need to understand who has power, and what kind of power it is. This understanding will help you structure the story to fit the influence styles required for different types of power, and it will also be very important when planning the delivery of the story (which you find out about in Chapter 13).

As you gather information, you can build a *power map* to identify who has power to make a decision, to influence the decision, to enable the change to happen, to lead others, or to block the decision. You should also identify any potential members of the audience who you do *not* want to support your position, because if they are supporters, others will automatically be against you.

Sources of Power

POSITION OF AUTHORITY In a recognized hierarchy, the person in this position possesses the ability to deploy and use the power of anyone under them.

MONEY Whether through direct budget, donation, or the ability to purchase any other form of power, money is one of the most significant power bases.

TRACK RECORD A demonstrated ability to be successful that makes people consider your requests more favorably.

ACCESS The ability to control access to other people or to information is a significant source of power in modern organizations.

COMMON INTERESTS These may be shared goals or a common enemy. The power of a common interest can influence people to share a common decision.

THOUGHT LEADER The person to whom others turn when an idea is required or an innovation must be reviewed.

SOCIAL INFLUENCE People are more apt to buy from people they like. Social networks and relationships can bring the right people together and influence them.

EXPERTISE Direct and demonstrable experience of the subject matter of the story is a strong influencing power.

USEFULNESS The ability to deliver the outcome proposed in the story is a strong influencer for decision makers.

PERSONALITY Charisma, presence, or simply the right personality type can make a huge difference in the ability to influence.

The best salespeople build power maps from their first visit to a customer. They ask questions about the organizational structure and the people in the various roles, and, at the same time, they're listening for the *characteristics* of power.

The diagram opposite is Tom's power map from the City University Hospital example. It shows the relationships among the members of the audience, and notes which members have specific sources of power. The people in green represent the primary audience, who report to Bernd, the chief nurse and operating officer. Bernd is keen to see the improvements, but also new in the role and is being careful not to make early mistakes. Just last month, he was in the position Franco now occupies, with Ralf as a trusted direct-report who demonstrated again and again the ability to generate good ideas.

Allan, the financial controller, can influence Bernd's decision by providing specific funding to support the change. Allan has always had a good relationship with Franco who has been a loyal supporter of Allan's initiatives over the past eight years.

Claus, the chief executive, will not take a direct role in the decision, because it's Bernd's responsibility, but Claus can tacitly approve the decision, which will give Bernd greater confidence in the suitability of the change. Karen joined Bernd's team after two years as a special assistant to Claus, building the business case for the new investment, and she has the ability to gain direct access to Claus.

Luc is responsible for patient data and would be instrumental in implementing the changes. He has a strong relationship with the nurses, having moved last year from a role as a senior nurse, and has already implemented some key improvements in the hospital's nursing teams. Luc and Karen have a common interest in business-process improvement with a focus on the measureable impact.

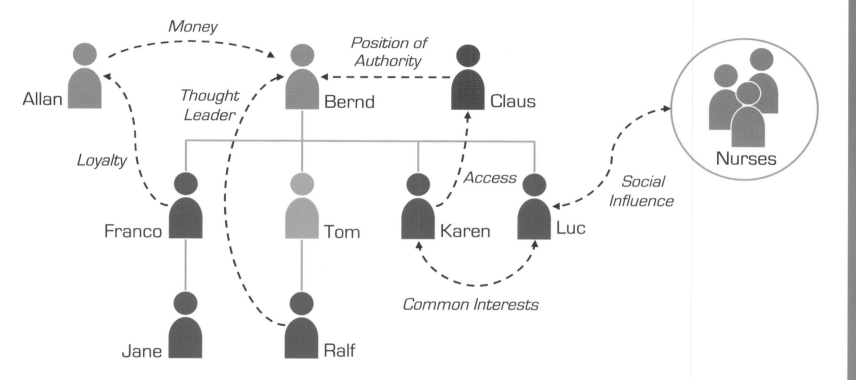

Tom's power map for the City University Hospital audience.

What if I have a really big audience or don't know enough about their context?

In the examples discussed throughout the book, there are situations where it's not possible to define the context for someone in the audience. There are far too many nurses in the hospital to address individually, and too many different personal trainers in Marina's Optimal Balance story to focus on just one. So what should you do?

In situations like these, we create *personas* to represent one or more of the groups in the audience. A persona is a hypothetical person, based on real data. It embodies the key experiences, attitudes, and knowledge of the target audience group. A persona is not one person from the target audience group, or the last person you talked with. It is created by integrating data that may come from interviews, observation, and marketing data, and it represents a specific segment of the audience. If your story will influence the persona to change, it should have the greatest positive impact on the audience segment it represents.

Personas can include a great deal of useful information about the fictional "everyman" that they represent. A persona can include age, location, ethnic group, education level, income, common experiences, attitudes, in fact anything that helps to provide enough detail in the description to properly represent the audience segment. It will also include this segment's specific pain or issue relevant to the story. Later in this chapter you will see the persona for Sharon, a Senior Nurse in the City University Hospital.

The power map diagram is an easy way to think about your audience and consider whom to focus on. For large power maps or situations where there's a complex mapping from people to the "Why," "What," and "How," creating a full mapping table like the one shown opposite from the City University Hospital can be a good idea. This table records the direct relationships to the content for the visual story. If this is a little too much for your story, then take a look at the example on the following page from the Personal Trainer story, which focuses on mapping the audience to their motivations, taken from the analysis of the "Why."

In addition to understanding the power relationships, you need to consider the different roles the audience members will play with respect to the story and the decision. We split these into three categories:

KEY DECISION MAKERS The people who have the power to say *Yes*. In the power map diagram on the previous page, these people are shown in blue.

PRIMARY AUDIENCE People whom you intend to communicate with directly. In the power map on the previous page, these people are shown in green and blue.

SECONDARY AUDIENCE People who may hear the story from someone in the primary audience, or through indirect communication such as posters, video, or e-mail. These people can be powerful supporters for the story, but ultimately have less power to influence the key decision makers. In the example from the previous page, these people are shown in gray.

You might also consider identifying already-known attitudes that may need to be changed or that could be supportive. Spend time now getting this analysis right. In Chapters 9 through 13, you'll use this information to keep your story focused on the audience.

Audience Member	Role & Power	Why	What	How	Attitude	Notes	Desired action
Allan (Financial Controller)	Decision maker Money	Must balance costs with the need for change.			Neutral	Low	Agree to release funds to make the change happen
Bernd (Chief Nurse and Operating Officer)	Decision maker Money; Position of authority	Grow the reputation of the hospital.	Critical Care unit	Implement expansion and transformation plans.	Negative	New in role. Being very careful not to make mistakes as Claus (CEO) is watching closely.	Agree to implement the changes
Luc (Patient Data Controller)	Primary audience Common interest with Karen; Social influence with Nurses	Achieve goals for data quality and error rates.	Patient data	Implement new patient data management systems.	Positive		Support the decision
Ralf (Operations Manager)	Gatekeeper Thought leadership				Neutral	Bernd will not listen to the story unless Ralf recommends	Be a positive supporter and recommend to Bernd.
Nurses	Primary and secondary audience: Social influence	Reduce time spent entering data and improve quality.	Manage patient information.	Change the data entry process.	Positive		Influence Luc to support the decision.

A selection of Tom's detailed notes for the City University Hospital audience.

Audience Member	Description	Motivational Hook	Importance
Studio owners who are trainers	These trainers have built a business and may or may not need help	Want to reduce the complexity of managing the financials and customer service	The most common target customer
Studio owners who are not trainers	These business people have hired trainers to work in their studios	Want to reduce costs and offer additional benefits to attract new customers	Fairly uncommon
Trainers wanting to own a studio	These trainers are either students, or are working in a gym and desire to break out	Simple and quick way to get from "dream" to "reality" of running your own training studio	Common, but often don't have the resources to get started. Need to find the good candidates and spend time to "develop them" into an Optimal Balance customer
Advisors to existing studio owners	These business people and friends influence the decisions of studio owners	They want their friends to do well, and may need to see that Optimal Balance has worked for others	Not normally a target group, but worth considering
Trainers at large gyms	These trainers may view a local studio as "the competition"	Emphasize message that trainers who join Optimal Balance were once "like them" to reduce resistance	Possibly unfriendly audience; may say negative things about smaller studios. Potential future customer.

(left margin: Personal Trainer)

Marina identifies each of the different kinds of trainers and studio owners that she will be presenting the Optimal Balance idea to, and notes some of their motivations.

Persona of a Senior Nurse: Sharon

Sharon usually manages a day shift on the ward. She is very supportive of the need for improvements in the way information is shared between everyone who works with the patients.

"Doctors and nurses need to be able to get complete and up-to-date patient information whenever they need it."

She doesn't like to be called a manager as that implies to her a non-clinical role, but a large part of her work is orchestrating and coordinating the work of everyone else on the ward during the shift.

One of the work practices that annoys her is when specialists visit a patient on the ward, agree on a course of action, and don't alert the nurses. Sharon has previously worked in a hospital that had very good paper-based patient notes and knows how useful they can be, but also how important it is for everyone (including specialists) to know how to complete them consistently.

"Electronic patient notes from all disciplines would transform the way we work."

She is a regular user of the patient data systems, but finds them frustrating with a poor design that takes a lot of time to enter standard patient information. Sharon has big concerns that her nursing team doesn't know enough about how to use the IT systems, and that doctors will be the focus for training.

"You often need to find patient information quickly, when a doctor asks a question, or when there is a concern over medication."

Sharon keeps her own handwritten daily notes with critical information on the current patients. She would be glad to stop doing this, but doesn't see how the hospital would provide enough computers.

The hospital example was used in detail earlier in this chapter, so we will avoid repeating Tom's notes on it. However, Tom also creates a persona for a nurse, to represent the nurses group in the visual story. This person brings together many different aspects of the nurses at the hospital and identifies a number of the key issues he has heard from them.

Follow these steps to make sure you are focusing on the audience with the power to make the change you want.

(!) **Don't overanalyze other people's motives.** It would be a mistake to spend too long deliberating on the motives of your audience. Doing so can distort your own thinking and overcomplicate the story. Very few people are capable of (or interested in) Machiavellian plotting. Most have a fairly simple set of motives.

(!) **Let someone else be the hero.** Just remember that there's a big difference between leading the way and being the hero in the story. You rarely want to be seen as the hero. This is a role you want members of the audience to be able to identify with.

(!) **Know the role of the audience members in the decision-making process.** Often, very few people can say *Yes,* and many can contribute to *No.* To make a positive change, you don't need everyone to say *Yes,* just the key decision makers, so long as the others do not say *No.*

(!) **Iteration is core to the CAST process.** As you read this chapter, don't be surprised if you realize you need to go back and revisit your earlier work. After you've created a few visual stories with the CAST process, you'll naturally begin to treat the cells on the Content row as a group, starting your work from any cell and moving around as you gather and structure your ideas. In your first attempts we suggest you keep to the sequence, to give yourself a little structure.

☑ For each of the "Why," "What," "How," and "What If" elements, identify all the people who should be considered for the audience and for a role in the story.

☑ Name the decision-making individuals or groups involved in the change who have the power to say Yes, and the source of their power.

☑ Understand the background for each audience segment and key individuals to align the context of their experience with the basis for the visual story.

☑ Create a power map for the audience members with their current attitude toward the change you're proposing.

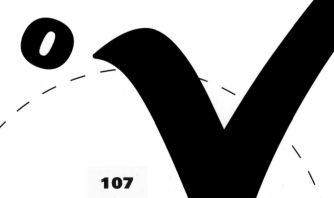

Learning and Decision Styles

9

Nothing is more difficult, and therefore more precious, than to be able to decide.

——Napoleon Bonaparte, French 19th Century military and political leader

> I am always ready to learn although I do not always like being taught.
> —Winston Churchill, British 20th Century Prime Minister and awarded Nobel prize for literature

Categorizing Your Audience

There are many different ways to categorize people. Psychologists, sociologists, and management gurus use different schemes, depending on the problem they want to solve. Categorization models look at everything from personality styles to how a person might deal with innovation. We're going to look at two different ways to categorize people that are useful for storytelling: one model for learning styles and one model for decision styles.

Before diving into the categorization models we use in CAST, let's set some realistic expectations for what we need to support the creation of visual stories. Hundreds of academic papers and dozens of books have been written on a subject we cover here in just a few pages. We can't claim that the models we've chosen are the best or the most suitable for every situation, but we know from personal experience that the models we use in this chapter work well to support the creation of visual stories. We simplify the analysis process behind the models significantly, and we do not explain the theory or evidence behind them. If you want to learn more about these techniques, check out the recommendations in the Appendix at the end of the book.

Preferences, Not Prescriptions

The important activity in this chapter is to identify the core styles appropriate for the key decision makers and influencers in your audience. With this information, you can achieve the right balance between explanation and proposition in your story, and you can phrase it in a way that best educates and influences the audience.

Before going further, we'd like to throw in a word of caution: People defy categorization. You may find that a person learns differently depending on whether the content is a personal passion, or a necessity for work. You may also find that a person uses a different way of making decisions depending on his or her abilities and experience, or if it's been a rough day. Please treat the categorizations as a good guideline, not a perfect science, on the way that your audience learns and decides so that you can tailor your message accordingly.

You don't have to be a mind reader to get through this part of the CAST process. We will ask you to consider the learning and decision styles for your audience, and then take your best shot. Think about how well-aligned members of the audience are with the content of the story. Think about what they need to know in order to make a decision.

A second caution: You have your own learning and decision style preferences as well. Be careful not to create the story for yourself. It is all too common for people to present their stories in a way that relates best to their own preferred styles. Put your audience first. If you don't know your audience, ask. If no one else can tell you about them, then you must consider how to address the full range of learning and decision styles, and not just your own preferred styles.

Learning Styles

In just a few minutes on the Internet, you can find a range of different approaches to learning styles. While doing research for this book, we came across one paper that identified 71 different approaches, some with very little basis in evidence or measurable impact.*

The learning styles approach we will use comes from the work of Bernice McCarthy. In the 1970s, McCarthy looked at how children were being taught and noticed a lot of focus on one approach, teaching facts, and very little on explaining the reasons why or how things worked. The model she created is very similar to ones developed by other people, and in particular can be mapped to Carl Jung's psychological types. You may have come across these same basic ideas if you've ever taken a Myers-Briggs Type Indicator.

Many of the approaches identify a small number of dimensions and then create a set of categories by combining either end of each dimension. McCarthy used two dimensions to describe the learner's approach to information in her learning styles:

* Coffield, F., Moseley, D., Hall, E. and Ecclestone, K. (2004) Learning styles and pedagogy in post-16 learning: a systematic and critical review. London: Learning and Skills Research Centre.

PERCEPTION OF INFORMATION, FROM ABSTRACT TO EXPERIENCE

At the abstract end of this dimension, learners are considering patterns, ideas, and concepts, whereas at the experience end, they are doing, recalling, or imagining an activity or experience.

PROCESSING INFORMATION, FROM ACTION TO REFLECTION

At the action end of this dimension, learners are taking an active role, gathering, interacting, or doing what is being learned, whereas in reflection, learners are reviewing what they have learned and restructuring their mental models.

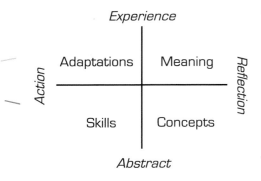

People don't sit at one end or the other of these dimensions, but have a preference for a particular approach and a *sweet spot* somewhere on each dimension. You can see in the diagram how these two dimensions can be brought together to create four learning styles. There's still a lot of variety for the individual in each style. You need to consider the learning styles to target for the audience of your visual story, and how you will ensure a balance of content between content to support learning, and content to drive toward a decision.

Meaning
EXPERIENCE — REFLECTION
WHY?

Meaning-type learners have a strong desire to make connections and understand the reasons *why*. If they don't understand why something is important they will lose interest.

APPROACH: *Make sure that the motives for the characters and the message of the story are clearly stated early in the story to ensure your audience keeps listening to the conclusion.*

Concepts
ABSTRACT — REFLECTION
WHAT?

Concepts learners have a preference for analytical learning, working from the overview down to the detail. They seek out the facts and research additional materials and expert opinion.

APPROACH: *Build key facts into the story, and have the ability to drill down further as required to support the credibility of the content.*

Skills
ABSTRACT — ACTION
HOW?

Skills-type learners want to know *how* the change will be accomplished. They are practical and are focused on building, creating, and understanding what it will take to make the change happen.

APPROACH: *Don't just list the changes to be made; explain the steps to go through, the specific skills and behaviors needed to be successful.*

Adaptations
EXPERIENCE — ACTION
WHAT IF?

Adaptations learners might consider themselves pathfinders or innovators. They're interested in the new opportunities and potential problems and will often be the first to adopt the change, learning by trial and error.

APPROACH: *Be clear on the challenges, the opportunities that can be created, and the unknowns that need to be explored and resolved.*

The names of the four learning styles may seem a little academic, but come from McCarthy's original work. We could have changed them to catchier names, but at least this way the names will match with the many supporting resources you can find online. Find out more about the learning styles at www.aboutlearning.com. Consider your own learning style and how it affects the way you're absorbing the information in this book.

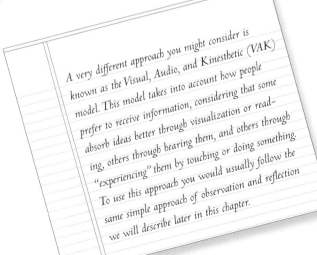

A very different approach you might consider is known as the Visual, Audio, and Kinesthetic (VAK) model. This model takes into account how people prefer to receive information, considering that some absorb ideas better through visualization or read-ing, others through hearing them, and others through "experiencing" them by touching or doing something. To use this approach you would usually follow the same simple approach of observation and reflection we will describe later in this chapter.

Decision Styles

While doing the background research for this chapter, it became apparent there are as many, if not more, variations for decision styles as there are for learning styles. It's a significant topic for management books. But we won't assume that there is one right answer. If such a thing were to exist, we wouldn't see such a variety of ideas.

What we can say is that people have a preference for making decisions in a particular way. The pressure of time or of finding themselves in a situation where they have no knowledge or experience may force them to change styles, but may also cause them to defer making a decision until they are comfortable with it.

In the late 1980s, three researchers, Alan Rowe, James Boulgarides, and Richard Mason, wrote a series of books and papers based on a decision styles categorization scheme they created, which used two dimensions, in a similar way to McCarthy's learning styles:

COGNITIVE COMPLEXITY

At one end of the scale are people who must have consistency and well-structured information, whereas at the other end are people who can handle high levels of ambiguity and complex intermixed ideas.

VALUE ORIENTATION

At one end of this dimension, people are task-focused on the specific activities and details; at the other end, there is a social focus, with concerns more toward the impact on other people, organizations, and social groups.

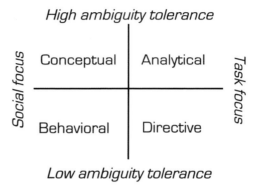

For many people, a decision style is an unconscious preference. A broad range of factors drives this choice, including cultural background, age, social class, education, peer pressure, and organization style. As a result, it's difficult to provide generalizations about the mix of decision styles that will be meaningful for specific situations. When you assess your audience, you may occasionally find that key decision makers seem to be a little mixed up. An individual may have an inherent decision style, but may deviate from it based on circumstances such as organization culture or time pressure. When circumstances change they may fall back on their inherent style.

Some psychologists argue that we use different reasoning processes for appeals to logic than for more emotional questions, and that this greatly impacts the way in which decisions are made. A decision maker who typically relies on an analytical approach may change his or her decision style if the topic of a visual story has strong emotional content.

Consider the decision styles of your audience and determine how you will ensure that you build up to the decision with content that will facilitate an easy decision-making process. As with learning, the two decision-making dimensions result in four decision-making styles that inform your visual story.

Directive
**LOW AMBIGUITY TOLERANCE
— TASK FOCUS**

Conceptual
**HIGH AMBIGUITY TOLERANCE
— SOCIAL FOCUS**

Analytical
**HIGH AMBIGUITY TOLERANCE
— TASK FOCUS**

Behavioral
**LOW AMBIGUITY TOLERANCE
— SOCIAL FOCUS**

Directive-style decision makers are often focused on financial results and are objective-oriented. They trust facts and structured information with an impersonal approach.

APPROACH: *Deliver the important points as quickly as possible, and give supporting details only when requested. Explain how the change will happen, the key milestones, and when it will be possible to see the results.*

Conceptual-style decision makers love the big picture. They're typically creative people who consider numerous options and look for patterns. They're comfortable considering the long-term and with risk management.

APPROACH: *Provide one or more high-level scenarios and develop them in the story. The focus is on concept rather than action. Ask these people to contribute ideas, but avoid asking them to review the details.*

Analytical decision makers prefer details and enjoy analysis. Being able to drill into the details and to show traceability and the logical flow can be critical to their acceptance of a story. These people may need more time to process the detailed information than other styles of decision makers.

APPROACH: *Be prepared to answer questions. Everything does not need to be presented but should be available if required. Include these people in reviews only when you have enough details.*

Behavioral decision makers focus on the impact on others and the organization. The low tolerance for ambiguity means they want clarity on how the change will affect individuals and the organization, focusing on the welfare of others and how they will feel about the change.

APPROACH: *Include descriptions of how the change will affect the characters in the story. The response of these people to the visual story may be intuitive and emotional. They often tend to avoid conflict and prefer open conversations to reach consensus decisions.*

For both the learning and the decision styles, you can find much more information online. But the most common question is about how to use them when you cannot really ask your audience to take an assessment. For the purposes of creating a visual story you simply need to have an idea of the mix of styles in your audience, and any strong preferences for key audience members, such as your key decision makers.

The first step in choosing which learning and decision styles you should address is a simple review from your experience with the key audience members, using the descriptions on the previous pages. In the hospital example on the following pages you can see how Tom did this for his key decision makers. When we have trained people in the CAST process we get questions at this stage, asking for checklists or specific questions to ask. In our experience, we have found the best way is simply to talk with your colleagues about their experience with the audience members and you will spot the characteristics we have described.

If you have the opportunity to meet with members of the audience you can ask them some quite direct questions. For example, you could ask a key decision maker something like, "During the presentation would you like us to drill into the details, or talk more about the process?" A question like this can often lead into a short conversation where you gain a lot of insight into their learning and decision styles, and might also provide you with an opportunity to provide a little background to the story.

In the diagram below, the blue icons represent the key decision makers and the yellow icons represent the primary audience. Across the center of the diagram the two Learning and Decision triangles are used to consider the balance for the story between educating the audience and setting the scene for a decision to be made. Some visual stories may require a great deal of detailed information before a decision can be made; for others, the facts may be known, and it's the argument for the decision that is important.

With an understanding of the learning and decision styles, you can start to consider how to focus the content more clearly on the audience's needs. In the personal story on the opposite page you can see how you might start to think about the content specifically for the full mix of styles in the audience. In the following chapters you will see many more opportunities to use the learning and decision styles to help focus the message of the story for the audience.

Map your audience and decision makers.

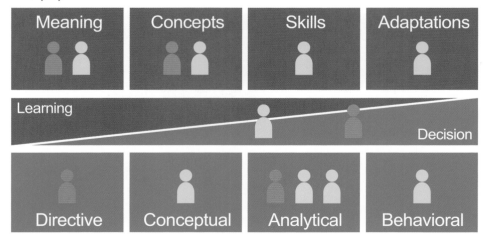

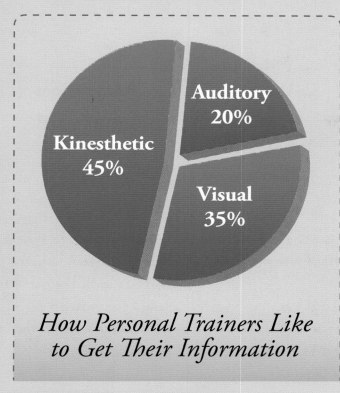

How Personal Trainers Like to Get Their Information

COVERING THE LEARNING STYLES

MEANING
To allow you to focus on your customers instead of business trivia.

CONCEPTS
Focus on business services (what are they) and how a training studio needs special business services.

SKILLS
Walk the audience through a scenario that shows how their life will change with Optimal Balance.

ADAPTATIONS
Emphasize different types of studio operations that can use Optimal Balance services.

DECISION STYLES

DIRECTIVE	CONCEPTUAL	ANALYTICAL	BEHAVIORAL
Cite statistics that show that personal training studios are a risky business.	Imagine a world where the trainer has time for his clients instead of paperwork.	Have a full package of information available to review, including forms and procedures.	Focus on how the clients will feel with new, efficient, modern procedures in place.

Marina considers the trainers and business owners she knows. She has some data from a study she participated in that used the VAK method, but since the presentation has to be given to people she doesn't know, she decides to include information designed to address each of the different styles.

Learning Styles

Meaning	Concepts	Skills	Adaptations
Allan	Ralf	Bernd	Luc
Claus	Jane	Karen	
	Franco		

Allan and Claus both regularly ask about the reasons why in project review meetings, but spend little time on the implementation details.

Ralf is well known in the hospital for his analytical skills and the ability to describe the concepts for new ideas.

Jane and Franco often pull in expert opinions and request further research.

Bernd is always keen to understand the process.

Karen built her reputation in the hospital by creating change programs.

Luc's approach to change has been seen a number of times with the nursing teams to involve a series of small changes with regular checks.

The nurses are a very broad mix and will probably represent all the different styles for learning and decisions.

Gut feel – the visual story is a so/so split between learning about the options and driving a group commitment to make the changes happen.

Tom allocates people to the learning and decision styles based on his observation of their behaviors. This is not a rigorous approach, but it is enough to get a feel for the distribution of styles.

Decision Styles

Directive	Conceptual	Analytical	Behavioral
Claus	Bernd Ralf	Allan Karen Jane	Franco Luc

Directive — Claus is results-oriented and drives the hospital through performance measures. His favorite saying is, "Be bright, be brief, be gone!"

Conceptual — Bernd and Ralf both have a similar style for decisions. They walk up to the whiteboard and sketch out the scope of the problem, working on the big picture to be sure they understand it before making a decision.

Analytical — All of these people regularly sit in our meetings, checking the numbers and the traceability through the analysis in proposals. If anything does not fit, they will not make a decision without sending someone away to check the analysis.

Behavioral — Both Franco and Luc regularly ask about the impact of changes on their people before pushing forward with decisions.

Insights

Personal style – learn by doing (adaptations) and conceptual decision maker. ≫ The audience covers the full range of styles, with only a small overlap to my personal style. Will need to work hard to cover all the styles in the visual story. At least the key decision maker is the same decision style!

Understanding the styles for the audience will help Tom to customize individual deliveries, and also help him to consider how his personal style differs from that of the audience. Unless he deliberately adapts to present his content in the styles necessary for the audience, there is a big chance they will not be ready to fully support the IT changes.

GOTCHA

Follow these steps to make sure you have identified the learning and decision-making factors relevant to the delivery of the story.

(!) **When you just don't know.** If there is no way to determine the optimal approach for an audience, you can use neutral words and let the audience interpret according to their own representational style. Your natural style will be easier for you . . . but beware. To have the strongest rapport with your audience, aim to work across all of the learning and decision styles.

(!) **Many senior managers use a directive decision style.** You have to decide if that is their preferred style or one they've adopted to cope with time pressure. If you believe it is an adopted style, consider using what you believe to be their preferred decision style as well as the directive style to increase your chance of getting a favorable decision.

(!) **Decisions are influenced by personal risk.** Psychologists have identified that people are basically risk-averse when considering how they will benefit and are more inclined to take risks when they are faced with a loss.* This is true even when the core decision is essentially the same. If you need people to take a risk, it may be better to discuss loss rather than reward.

* Brafman, O., Brafman, R., Sway. (2009) The Irresistible Pull of Irrational Behavior.

☑ Identify the learning styles for the audience and specifically for key decision makers.

☑ Identify the decision styles for the audience and specifically for key decision makers.

☑ Look back at the power map for the audience and annotate with the learning and decision styles. Are there audience groups that have the same styles? If so, you might want to pull them together to hear a specific version of the story focused on their styles.

☑ Decide how much of your efforts should go into educating your audience compared with the efforts to influence their decision.

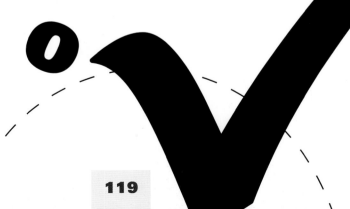

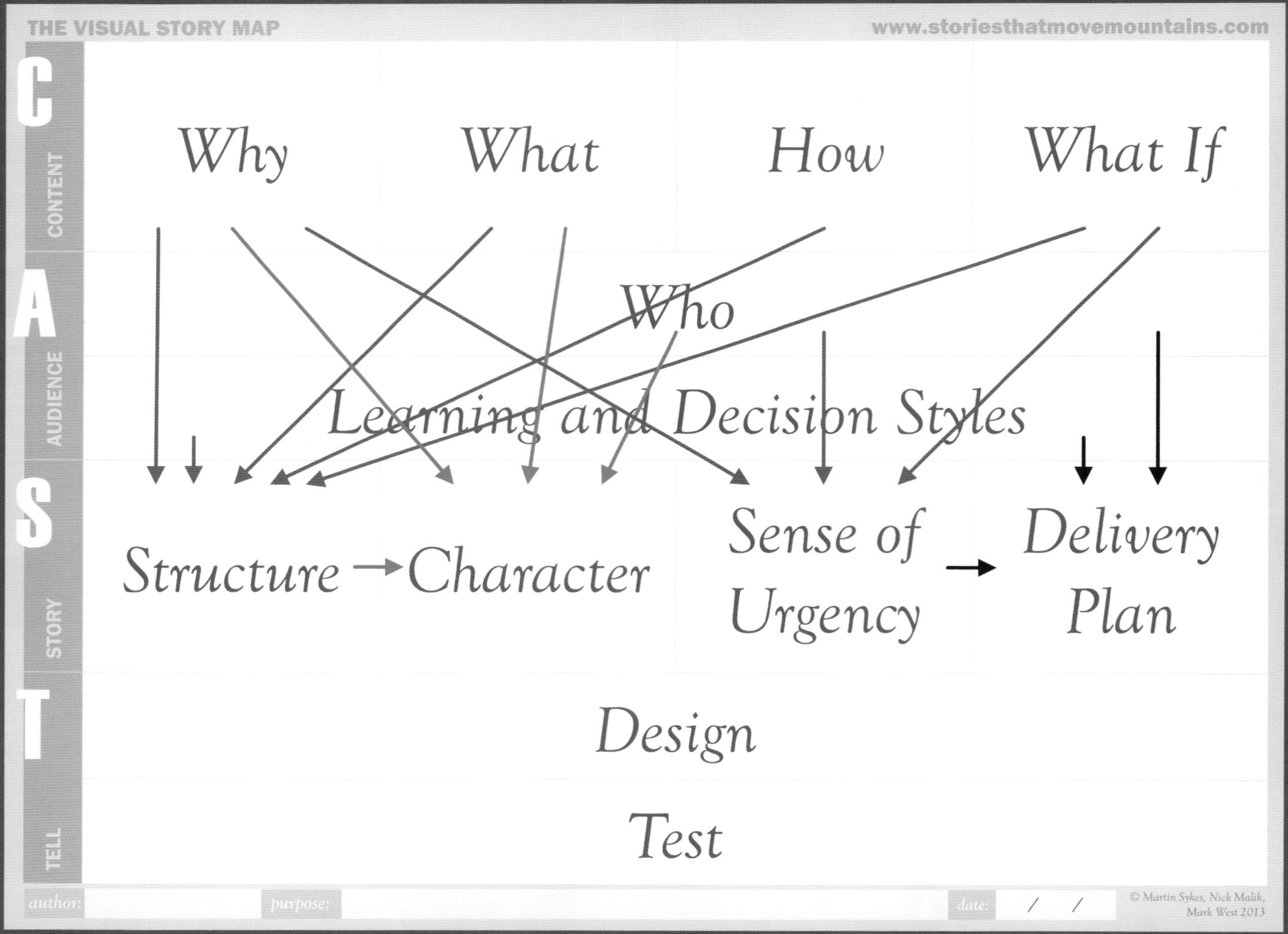

THE VISUAL STORY MAP
www.storiesthatmovemountains.com
C
CONTENT
A
AUDIENCE
S
STORY
T
TELL
Why
What
How
What If
Who
Learning and Decision Styles
Structure
Character
Sense of Urgency
Delivery Plan
Design
Test
author:
purpose:
date: / /
© Martin Sykes, Nick Malik, Mark West 2013

STORY

Structure

10

Story is about principles, not rules.

Robert McKee, screenwriting lecturer and author of the screenwriters' bible: Story: Substance, Structure, Style and the Principles of Screenwriting

I find that most people know what a story is until they sit down to write one.

Flannery O'Conner, twentieth century American Writer

People have forgotten how to tell a story. Stories don't have a middle or an end anymore. They usually have a beginning that never stops beginning.

Steven Spielberg, American film director, screenwriter and producer

In this chapter, you will look at how to create the structure for the story. Fortunately, there has been a lot of research into how to structure a story, starting with Aristotle.

> **Aristotle (384–322 BCE) wrote about the golden rules of successful storytelling. More than 2300 years later, they are still completely relevant. Which just goes to show how important storytelling is to people. Aristotle prioritized the essential elements of a story as:**
>
> 1. **Plot**
> 2. **Character**
> 3. **Theme or idea**
> 4. **Diction (dialogue)**
> 5. **Spectacle and décor (visuals)**
> 6. **Chorus (music)**

The visual story contains the specific interactions of the characters, as a series of events, actions, and reactions. Stories are not just a series of facts and conclusion, which is what we see in many corporate presentations or other attempts to influence people. The narrative in a real story has a beginning, middle, and end, with the potential for diversions along the way.

The first rule of successful storytelling is to have a good plot. A plot is the simplified structure of the story that identifies the key events, turning points, actions and reactions. Many people have claimed that, across all stories, there are a small number of generic plots. Any story is really just a variation on these plots. Depending on their perspective, or how abstractly they want to define a plot, different authors have suggested the number of basic plots varies between 3, 7, 20, or even 36. Later in this chapter, we will explore the seven plots identified in 35 years of research by Christopher Booker, and also explain how these can be represented in visual stories.

Characters serve your plot, and will push your story along. Aristotle said that characters should have qualities we wish to emulate, to see in ourselves, or should show qualities we want to avoid. Your choice of characters impacts the selection of plot, as much as the selection of plot identifies the characters you need.

Aristotle's third rule of storytelling is to have a clear theme. The theme is the underlying meaning you want the audience to leave with. It is the material we discussed in our chapter on "Why." The theme becomes their interpretation of what they have seen and heard and their understanding of why it is important to them. Sometimes this theme is explicit but it can also be implicit and open to the audience to extract the meaning. For your visual stories, you are attempting to influence decisions and change, so you may want the theme to be explicit. For stories with these kinds of goals, understanding the theme, or "Why," of a story is a critical element. That is why we focus on it first in the CAST process.

We cover each of the elements of Aristotle's analysis of story, but not in the same order. Character is covered in the next chapter. After that we cover the sense of urgency that drives the theme. The dialogue and visuals are considered in the design chapter (we don't usually find a high demand for music in visual stories). Plot, character, and theme are so inter-related that in reality you cannot develop one without the other. You may find it best to read through the next two chapters before returning here to start developing your own plot ideas.

Plot Structure

As well as the golden rules for storytelling, Aristotle also described the basic three-act structure of dramatic storytelling. The three acts are *Setup* (of the location and characters), *Confrontation* (with an obstacle, issue, or major disruption), and *Resolution* (with a climax and resolution of the issue).

Over the past 100 years, the explosion in film, theater, and television has created a massive industry around the generation of screenplays, resulting in an evolution of the Aristotelian model. In this discussion, we draw on concepts developed by many great scriptwriters. This modern format is ideal for visual stories because it has been truly tested to have an impact on audiences and to be deliverable in many different formats. It's not a magic formula to follow slavishly, but more of a guideline. If you're new to this process, this format is a very basic way to build your story. Let's take a look at the structure.

ACT I: The Setup

We start with the "normal world" of the hero, before he or she is presented with the challenge in the story. This is shown in the diagram as the Equilibrium phase of Act I. In the middle of Act I is the Inciting Incident, one of the most important parts of the story, signaling the beginning of the Disruption stage. This is the first major turning point for the hero, and for it to make sense you have to first set up an understanding of the world of the hero. You want this incident to touch the audience at an emotional level, to draw on their sense of urgency, and to set the theme for the story (more on this later in this chapter).

We use the term *hero* in this chapter for the principle character in the story. In the next chapter, we develop a better idea of the characteristics of the hero and identify the other characters you will need.

For example, any story about the impact on people and business around the Gulf of Mexico resulting from the Deepwater Horizon oil spill of 2010 would have the inciting incident as the explosion on the drilling rig on April 20 of that year. No explosion, no story.

At the end of Act I, you pass through the Point of No Return. This is when your audience should have a clear understanding of what the story is about and why the hero (and the audience) should care about it. For the hero, it is the point where there is no going back to the normality described at the start of the story.

On our diagram of the basic plot, we show a red line for the tension building throughout the story. The tension begins to build from the Inciting Incident and rises at the Point of No Return. If there is no tension, the audience will find it impossible to believe the motivation for the hero to act.

Act II: The Confrontation

As you can see in the diagram, we split Act II into two parts: first, the Reaction phase, where the hero is reacting to the situation; second, the Struggle, where the hero has found the situation isn't as easy to resolve as he or she thought and refocuses, takes control, and builds a plan to handle the situation. The midpoint separating these two phases, which we label as False Hope, is an important step in the plot where it is clear the hero cannot just continue to react but must take control. This turning point indicates the start of a struggle that may have one major activity where the tension increases or, more likely, a series of activities as the hero takes two steps forward but then gets knocked back by something not considered or anticipated.

Act II contains the bulk of evidence and activities in the story. It should show the audience the path they will need to take, and you should work out how to remind them a number of times of the central reason for the story, tied to the actions of the hero.

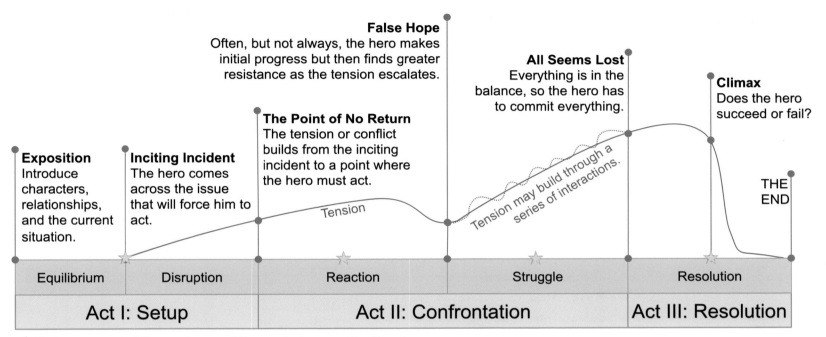

False Hope
Often, but not always, the hero makes initial progress but then finds greater resistance as the tension escalates.

All Seems Lost
Everything is in the balance, so the hero has to commit everything.

Climax
Does the hero succeed or fail?

The Point of No Return
The tension or conflict builds from the inciting incident to a point where the hero must act.

Exposition
Introduce characters, relationships, and the current situation.

Inciting Incident
The hero comes across the issue that will force him to act.

Tension

Tension may build through a series of interactions.

THE END

| Equilibrium | Disruption | Reaction | Struggle | Resolution |

| Act I: Setup | Act II: Confrontation | Act III: Resolution |

⭐ *Set up or remind the audience of the central reason for the story.*

Act III: The Resolution

As Act III starts, the hero may nearly fail. This is the point where the biggest issue surfaces and the hero has to recommit everything. Often, this is also the point where another character comes to the aid of the hero with the resources he or she needs. Now the hero is ready for the climax, and may succeed or fail. Your aim here is to have the audience supporting the hero and the action he or she must take. This will help to gain their commitment for the call to action at the end of the story. If you have a twist in your story, now is the time to play it, to make the ending more memorable.

The story does not end with the climax. In most cases, you will take a little time to describe the future world, the new normal that the hero has fought for. This helps to provide a feeling of closure for the audience and a desire for them to participate in the same change.

If you want to learn more about the art of scriptwriting and the sources used for this model, take a look at the book *Story: Substance, Structure, Style and the Principles of Screenwriting,* by Robert McKee, which covers all aspects of scriptwriting. Other sources we used while developing our approach came from *Screenplay,* by scriptwriting legend Syd Field; *Storycraft,* by Jack Hart; and *The Anatomy of Story,* by John Truby.

PLOT BUILDING: THE SEVEN BASIC PLOTS

In the 1970s, Christopher Booker, an English journalist and author, started to consider the possibility that there were only a small number of archetypal plots behind all the stories we tell, and he spent 30 years researching thousands of works to identify seven basic plots.

In the following pages, we have created a datasheet for each plot with a simple description, examples of use from common stories, and the main stages. At the bottom of each datasheet is a suggestion for a one-page visual layout. One of the most common outcomes of the CAST process is a one-page visual story. There are no standard patterns to use for each basic plot, but we have tried to create at least one idea for each plot from visual stories that we have seen work well in the past. Use this suggestion in the design chapter to get started with your layouts. You can see how Marina selected a plot for her personal trainer business plan in the worked example pages following the datasheets.

TIP

A basic plot can be used with a wide range of characters in many different settings. These are very generic templates which you overlay on the plot structure from the previous page. Many stories have a core basic plot and a number of subplots using other basic plots. The combination of these plots helps to drive the action sequence for individual characters, and build tension into the story, by showing how different characters are experiencing the events in the story in different ways. A story about a major knowledge management project could be an adventure into the unknown for most of the characters (and the audience), but for another character, who is a knowledge management specialist consultant, could reflect the normal shape of events, and their subplot may be about renewing their career.

DESIGN TEAM

MARTIN SYKES
NICK MALIK
MARK D. WEST

Information contained in the description of the seven basic plots is derived from Christopher Booker, The Seven Basic Plots, Continuum Publishing Group, a Bloomsbury Company (2005), and from Andrew Abela, Advanced Presentations by Design, John Wiley & Sons, Inc. (2008). This material is reproduced with the kind permission of the publishers.
We have used just seven basic plots, which are enough in most cases to start the story development process, but if you need a few more examples the book '20 Master Plots and how to build them,' by Ronald Tobias, provides additional combinations and variations.

BASIC PLOT: OVERCOMING THE MONSTER

The hero must overcome a dark, all-powerful creature/person/entity that has exerted a destructive force over other people or a place.

STORY EXAMPLES: Star Wars, Jaws, The Silence of the Lambs

BUSINESS EXAMPLE: Facing a major threat to our business

MAIN STAGES	EXAMPLE
1. The Call	Identify the threat to the business.
2. Initial Success	Make a first response to quickly but superficially address the threat.
3. Confrontation	The threat is seen to be much more significant than first thought.
4. Final Ordeal	Every effort now needs to be made to deal with the threat.
5. Miraculous Escape	Identify a critical weakness that can be attacked, or a clever change in situation to defeat the threat.

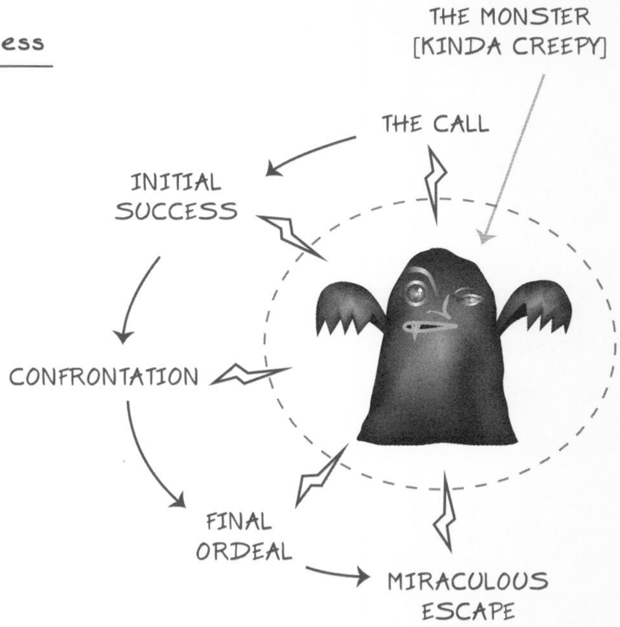

THE MONSTER
[KINDA CREEPY]

THE CALL

INITIAL
SUCCESS

CONFRONTATION

FINAL
ORDEAL

MIRACULOUS
ESCAPE

VISUAL DESIGN IDEAS

Place the core of the story, the monster, in the center of the page and flow the key stages of the story around it.

Use arrows or symbols to ensure that the audience follows the flow correctly.

BASIC PLOT: THE QUEST

The hero cannot rest until he arrives at or attains an all-important, and often distant, goal. Throughout the journey, the hero will find allies and resources, and will meet obstacles and forces trying to stop him from achieving his goal.

STORY EXAMPLES: The Lord of the Rings, Raiders of the Lost Ark

BUSINESS EXAMPLE: Embarking on a major new product initiative

MAIN STAGES	EXAMPLE
1. The Call	An objective is identified that at first may fail to get priority but is eventually recognized as worth the effort.
2. The Journey	Key resources are identified and brought together to achieve the objective.
3. Arrival and Frustration	What was first defined to be the objective is arrived at, but it is clear the objective is incomplete.
4. The Final Ordeals	A final effort is required to overcome a significant challenge.
5. The Goal	The objective of the quest is achieved and the results applied to create a new future.

VISUAL DESIGN IDEAS

Use the visual metaphor of a journey, starting on the left with the call and following a climb into the hills for the journey. Arrive at a plateau to find a broken bridge. The goal is a perfect view once the bridge can be crossed. The same idea can use streets, mountains, or any terrain over which the journey can take place. The story often has geospatial change as it progresses, which allows for images that follow a changing landscape.

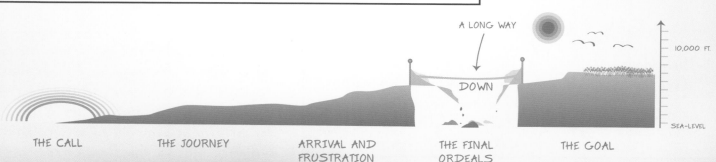

A LONG WAY

DOWN

10,000 FT.

SEA-LEVEL

THE CALL   THE JOURNEY   ARRIVAL AND FRUSTRATION   THE FINAL ORDEALS   THE GOAL

BASIC PLOT: VOYAGE AND RETURN

Like the Quest, this plot is based on a journey. Most often, the hero was not planning the journey and is transported to a very different world, and then back again. On this journey, the hero gains a deeper personal understanding of the world around him.

STORY EXAMPLES: Wizard of Oz, Alice in Wonderland, Back to the Future

BUSINESS EXAMPLE: Sharing an important experience; Investigating a new way of working

MAIN STAGES   EXAMPLE

MAIN STAGES	EXAMPLE
1. Fall into Another World	A new technology is identified that fundamentally changes the way people work.
2. Initial Fascination	Everyone jumps on board and explores the possibilities.
3. Frustration	No one knows what will work and what will not. Time and investment is misplaced.
4. Nightmare	A competitor using the technology rises. There is a chance that everything might be lost.
5. Thrilling Escape and Return	Work out how to take the best from the new technology and apply to the old business.

FALL INTO ANOTHER WORLD

INITIAL FASCINATION

FRUSTRATION

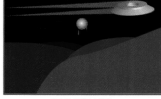
NIGHTMARE

THRILLING ESCAPE AND RETURN

VISUAL DESIGN IDEAS

A comic strip with five cells can be a great approach to represent the alternative world. In each of the first four cells you would use a similar background to represent key features of the alternative world. As the story progresses through each stage the foreground would highlight first the aspects that are fascinating, then focus on frustration and nightmare. The last cell shows the return to normality with the lessons, ideas, or technologies that the hero is bringing back to their normal world.

BASIC PLOT: COMEDY

Comedy has today come to mean anything that is funny. Booker uses the term as it was first defined by Aristotle, where characters suffer from misdirection and misunderstanding. The confusion and bewilderment can be resolved only when the misunderstandings have each been cleared up.

STORY EXAMPLES:

All's Well That Ends Well, When Harry Met Sally

BUSINESS EXAMPLE:

Resolving misunderstanding among different working groups

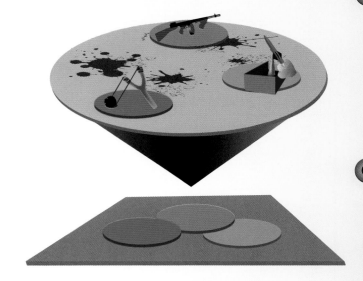

MAIN STAGES	EXAMPLE
1. Confusion	Multiple groups are working toward similar goals but at cross purposes, with competing and conflicting activities.
2. Nightmare	The confusion over direction results in increasing tensions and rivalry, with groups trying to outwit and shut others down.
3. New Information Transforms the Situation	An external agent shows them the errors they have made, gives a common cause, and brings the groups together.

VISUAL DESIGN IDEAS

Spread the different groups around the page with clear borders for each.

Place the nightmare activities in the spaces between the groups to show the interactions between them.

Show the new situation clearly separated by a visual device that makes it clear a transformation has happened.

BASIC PLOT: TRAGEDY

In a tragedy, the central character sets in motion a series of actions that bring about his or her own downfall. The downfall will often instill feelings of fear or pity in the audience, even though the obsession of the hero is often something that would be outside the normal rules of society.

STORY EXAMPLES:

Hamlet, Macbeth

BUSINESS EXAMPLE:

Business about to go bankrupt because of mismanagement

MAIN STAGES	EXAMPLE
1. Anticipation	Preparation and plans made for the business to grow quickly.
2. Dream	Early success leads to dreams of greater things.
3. Frustration	The plan starts to unravel and unforeseen obstacles arise, each worse than the last, but each overcome with effort.
4. Nightmare	The last issue is so large there is nothing left to overcome it. The business has gambled too far.
5. Destruction	New products are failing, market share is dropping, and revenue is plummeting.

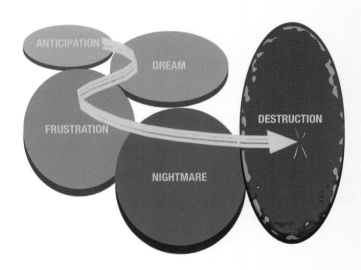

VISUAL DESIGN IDEAS

Emphasize the horror of the ending with the space allocated to each stage getting bigger as the story progresses.

Use images or charts from each stage to illustrate the initial plan, and then the failure of it.

BASIC PLOT: REBIRTH

In rebirth stories the hero appears to be under a dark spell. Although the spell can come from an outside agent, it often is one of the hero's own making. The hero can break free from the dark spell only through the actions of good forces, often from another character. In fiction, love is often the good power, which then implies two intertwined heroic characters. For visual stories in business or organizations, the power is often an external agent that brings new hope or partnership. Ultimately, the good power provides the resources to break free, but the critical action is still something the hero needs to provide.

STORY EXAMPLES: Sleeping Beauty, A Christmas Carol, Beauty and the Beast

BUSINESS EXAMPLE: Recovery after long period

MAIN STAGES	EXAMPLE
1. Hero Falls Under a Dark Power	A well-run business develops technologies to track customers to better understand their purchasing habits.
2. All Seems Well for a While	Business grows well with the new customer information.
3. Living Death	Customers and regulators reject the intrusion, leaving the business putting all efforts into recovering its reputation.
4. Apparent Triumph of Dark Power	Customers are turning away from the company and regulation is limiting operations.
5. Miraculous Redemption	A new leader sets a return to the original principles of the business and brings a new product to win back the customers.

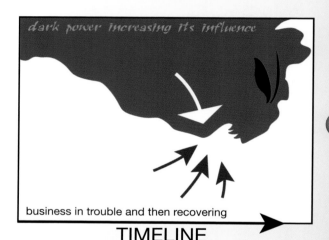

dark power increasing its influence

business in trouble and then recovering

TIMELINE

VISUAL DESIGN IDEAS

Think of the page as a timeline flowing from left to right. Now split the vertical into two parts: the upper part represents the growing dark power and the lower the success of the business. Create this as a background against which you then add the details of the story as events along the way.

BASIC PLOT: RAGS TO RICHES

In plots based on Rags to Riches, the hero seems to rise from nothing to great riches or status. Just as the hero begins to enjoy the new world, the success is swiftly removed. Now the hero must struggle against some villain or opposition to be able to return to the successful state.

STORY EXAMPLES: Cinderella, Aladdin, Great Expectations

BUSINESS EXAMPLE: Sudden success

MAIN STAGES	EXAMPLE
1. Initial Wretchedness	A small company has tried and failed to grow, but continues to limp along.
2. Initial Success	A new product is created that is very different from the original purpose of the business; it draws a lot of attention, especially from potential major partners.
3. Central Crisis	The business has to decide whether to stay with the tried-and-tested safe business or to put all effort into the new product.
4. Independence and Final Ordeal	The business decides to split and bring in the tresources for the new product.
5. Final Union	The major partner forms a strong long-term relationship.

Text describes the initial wretchedness

First view of the source of riches

Incorporating the source of riches in the final union

Cut away to show intial success

cut away to show central crises

cut away to show final ordeal

Use a cutaway to show the internals of the organization

VISUAL DESIGN IDEAS

The external agency that is providing the riches plays a big role in the story. It could be another person or company, an invention, or the discovery of new natural resources. It is going to be important in Stages 2 and 5. The rest of the story is focused on the struggle of the hero. In this image, we show the heroic company with a view of its building, split into three stages, with cutaways to show the activity internally as the story progresses and additional bubbles to bring in the activity with the external source of success.

Rebirth

Works well for studios that have had a hard time being sustainable. The dark spell can be the "weight" of routine business issues.

The Quest

Could be compelling for new trainers starting out, who have a big goal of owning their own studio.

Overcoming the Monster

There is not a good "enemy" with a weakness that can be overcome in this situation.

Comedy

The business problem is not driven by misunderstandings that can be easily cleared up.

Voyage and Return

There is no "event" to start the journey for a studio. The best it could be is an example of a personal trainer working at another studio.

Tragedy

Not appropriate. We want a positive outcome that encourages personal trainers to join Optimal Balance.

Rags to Riches

Only really suitable for studios that are already in crises and want to use Optimal Balance as a part of their recovery.

Marina tested the different options for the plot of the story, writing them on cards and posting them on her office wall where she could shuffle them as she considered the alternatives. Over a few days of review, two plots rose to the top. She tentatively chose "Rebirth" but "The Quest" could work as well.

Rebirth Story Structure

Dark Power → **Temporary Success** → **Living Death** → **Apparent Triumph** → **Miraculous Redemption**

Whether it is naive, optimistic, or arrogant, the personal trainer thinks that he can successfully run his own business with no actual business skills or previous experience.	After a while, the stream of clients starts to run in the opposite direction. More people are leaving than joining. Customer service problems, contract problems, and billing mistakes impact client perception and take their toll on the personal trainer's time.	The owner buys Optimal Balance services and soon has time to dedicate to training clients and getting people excited about their own health. There are still business tasks to do, but they are not so "oppressive" now. New and existing customers get a much better experience.	Existing clients from other jobs, and some friends and family join the new studio. As clients they are very forgiving of early missteps. The business seems to be a success.	The owner dedicates more and more time to the business side, and gets many of the problems worked out, but the fire goes out of him. There just doesn't seem to be a way out. This isn't the job he wanted to end up with.

Drawing out the story structure, Marina chooses to stick with "rebirth" as the plot for the visual story.

VISUALIZING THE STORY

The visual component of a visual story can be developed to closely follow the storyline, as we showed in the basic plot design ideas earlier, or can be structured around one consistent organizing pattern. These organizing patterns are useful when you might use the visual component with a number of different story variations, or when your visual needs to provide the detailed evidence behind the assertions in the story. You can assemble the visual so that it supports the story, even if it doesn't directly illustrate it.

Here's an example to illustrate the problem. Our audience needs to decide on major capital investments for an airline. The story revolves around the way the airline has grown in the past and the predictions for the future, with key characters that include a typical business passenger, pilots, flight attendants, and operations staff. You now need to choose a pattern for the visual to support the story, rather than to tell the story. The sticky notes show a range of the most common patterns.

Chronological

With this pattern, you describe events in the order in which they take place (or should). This is a very common pattern, and particularly appropriate when it's important to present a neutral review of the history of a situation. It's usually impossible to include everything in the timeline, so the hard part is deciding what to exclude, without appearing to lead the audience, or leaving out relevant details. In our air travel example, this might show the key changes in the market for the airline since it started.

Logical Argument

The logical argument pattern involves visualizing the research for the story, building up an evidential case to argue for the specific outcome you recommend. Use this pattern when there is a strong logical consequence that can be developed, and visualize this as a chain or flow of logical steps to the conclusion.

Sequential

This pattern is useful when the story has to explain a step-by-step process. You might use this pattern if the reason for following the sequence is a vital part of the story, and you want the audience to pay attention to the sequence in their decision making process. In the air travel example, this might be a visual of the complex process that is followed to select, order, and commission new aircraft.

Geospatial

This pattern may use a map, a real image of a location, or a set of directions as a background to represent key elements of the story. The air travel example could use a world map to show the locations where the airline operates, how it has changed over time, and the potential new routes that could be operated in the future with different choices of new aircraft.

Cause and Effect

This pattern shows how one thing leads to another. You can work forward starting with the cause or backward starting with the effect. The Five Whys approach we introduced in Chapter 4 is an example of this in action. When looking back in time at events that have already happened, the cause and effect may not follow logically (people are not always logical), but they should be consistent with the real events. When looking into the future, you need to be careful to clearly describe the motivations and reasons for cause and effect sequences. One poor assumption can destroy the whole sequence for the audience.

Problem-Solution (Options)

When you have a very clear problem and one or more solutions, the visual pattern can be as simple as showing these as two sides of the same page. On the problem side, you might fully describe the background, impact, and long-term consequences. On the solution side, you might include the effort, resources, timescale, and final outcome. A variation of this is where there are a number of potential solutions on the page with the same attributes described for each to allow for comparison of the options. In our example, the problem may be how to grow the business, with a range of solutions that consider investments in aircraft, alliances, and purchasing routes.

Compare and Contrast

This pattern is useful for focusing on similarities and/or differences between topics, concepts, or ideas. Show the audience a point-by-point comparison of the items. With our story about air travel, we might compare and contrast, plane by plane, the costs of operations, capacity, and facilities for travelers.

Topic/Classification

You might use this pattern when your story presents a group of ideas or objects. Identify each of the ideas or objects and then sequence them logically according to an attribute they all possess. For our story about the next generation of air travel, we might provide a series of planes, each increasing in terms of range, with a different challenge involved in the use of each one.

Give it a twist.

Sometimes the ending of one of the basic plots might be 'inverted' to give a shock to the audience. In film, this might be when the monster returns or the happy couple fails to get together. In visual stories, this approach can be used with a chronological approach, where your story as a review of past events. The audience thought the problem was resolved, and now you need to wake them up to the return of a competitor, or that a second effort is required to complete a change across the whole organization.

Surprise!

You can put surprises anywhere in your story, from data that no one expects, to the sudden shift of villain to hero, to surprise endings. Surprises make the story easier to remember. They provide a memorable hook for the brain to recall the rest of the story associated with the surprise.

WHERE DO WE GO FROM HERE?

If you don't have a conclusion to your story where your hero wins, just stop the story at the climax and ask your audience "What now?" For this to work, you need to ensure that they are totally committed to the journey the hero has taken up to this point. If you can engage your audience in the discussion of how they would complete the story, you can bring about their commitment to the story. Get your audience to experience the story.

REMEMBER WHEN . . . ?

In Chapter 8, we talk about identifying the shared context between your audience and the story. You can do this at the level of the whole story, and for specific points you want to make. These specific points can pull the audience into your story by drawing on their experiences to drive action in the story.

No two people have had the same experiences, so how do you find common ground to start from? One approach is to look for the universal experiences that most people in your audience will have had. Here are a few ideas for universal experiences:

- Starting at a new school
- Feeling of being alone in a crowd
- Going on a journey
- Regretting having done something
- Having an argument
- An unbelievable coincidence

You can start this part of your story with "Remember a time when you . . ." and then move to the same experience for the characters in your story.

You have probably seen a movie with a large number of flashbacks and convoluted timelines that required you to really engage to follow what was happening and piece it all together. The Quentin Tarantino movie *Pulp Fiction* is a great example of this. Avoid trying to create these until you have really mastered the art of storytelling. There are two key reasons for this: keeping the audience focused on the outcome you want, and keeping the tension building to the climax. You want the audience to understand the message clearly and make a decision, not wonder about the complexity of the message. It's entirely possible to start in the middle of the story, at a point you might consider to be today and then, before looking to the future, look back in time to understand how we got here. In most cases, this is about as complex as you want to make it.

Sure, a story should have a beginning, a middle and an ending, but not necessarily in that order!

Jean-Luc Goddard

Nesting and Embedding
(or How to Tell Many Stories at the Same Time)

Sometimes you know that no matter how hard you filter and focus, there is a lot to communicate and a very real danger that your audience's attention will start to drift. This situation often involves a lot of background that needs to be communicated to the audience before they can make sense of the bigger story.

If your content has many individual parts that you need to communicate, you could spend time on each part and then bring it all together at the end. The problem is that each part is a unique story, and every time one of them is brought to a close, the audience will wonder if you're reaching a conclusion. This is no way to build tension. An alternative approach is to have a main story with nested mini-stories so that you can keep bringing the audience back to the main story. You can nest a number of stories inside the main story to provide a sense of continuity and direction to the end of the main story. In some cases, you can also weave a number of stories together to explain different perspectives; then you can bring them together at the end.

You are aiming for the audience to have a sense of completion at the point where you are bringing the story to a climax (and a lack of it until then). When you leave one story to dive into another, you leave a trail with the audience that they know you will come back to. This is a clear indication that there's more to come. Just be sure that, in your planning, each subplot serves a purpose to bring the audience to the decision you will recommend. A subplot may be there to act as an influencer, to provide a learning point, or to break a complex idea in the story into a number of threads that can be dealt with separately and then combined in the main body.

This is a common technique for the master storyteller but can take practice, so on your first attempts, play it carefully and stick to simple embedded stories to make a key point. The diagram illustrates the use of four subplots sequentially within a main story, to set the scene and drive the action between the main stages of the storyline.

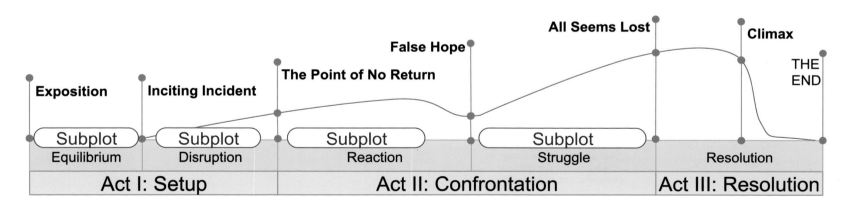

Using Reality and Fiction

We are often asked by people using the CAST process for the first time how to balance content based on real events with fictional content. Sometimes you may want to use a real story to illustrate the situation but then need to move to a hypothetical situation for the future.

Let's pick two different aspects of the story that could each be real or fictional. The *setting* for the story—the place, and the people, a business, organization, or even a family—could be real or fictional. The *situation*—the relationships, incidents, actions, and outcomes—could also be based on reality or be fictional. These setting and the situation are completely independent and lead to four different combinations, as illustrated in the diagram below.

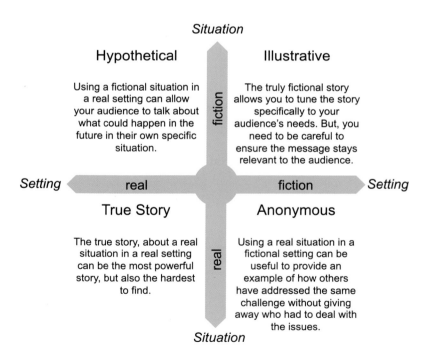

To provide consistency for the audience, the core plot of your visual story should typically follow only one of these four combinations. However, a common variation is to tell a true story for Act I, including the inciting incident, but then to move to a hypothetical, anonymous, or illustrative approach for the remainder, which is setting a view of the future. You are, in essence, telling the audience that they are today at the end of Act I and must commit to change. A similar effect can be had by telling the story as a true story up to the False Hope position, midway through Act II, implying that the audience has been reactive so far and now they need to come together with a plan and commit to action.

Around any core plot, you might include small anecdotes, examples, or subplots to illustrate specific points. These might typically be short true stories that exemplify an attribute of a character in the story or anonymous stories to explain how others have responded to the same situation (for many stories, the reason they're anonymous is because you legally, commercially, or morally cannot provide real details).

Hope's Story

While writing the book we ran across the story of Hope, which has been reproduced in full here. Robyn, the author, had e-mailed this story to a large business executive audience. When we talked with Robyn we found it had received a lot of positive feedback. It draws on a universal experience of owning and caring for a pet, but manages to bring from that experience key lessons for the business leaders. This is a great example of the short true story that can add impact to a broader story about developing people. You could, of course, create a fictional story to drive home the same points.

A few months after losing my beloved dog, Moca, of 12 years, I began looking for another companion. A friend who worked with a shelter in Puerto Rico sent me some pictures, and I was immediately drawn to Hope, a year-old mixed breed recovering from an injury it was believed she incurred during her time spent abandoned on the streets.

When we met her, she took a few steps toward me and fell, and then never seemed to fully regain her footing. We thought it was due to her long trip, nervousness, and new surroundings, but she didn't improve when we got her home.

Watching her struggle to walk was heartbreaking, as she could take only a couple of steps and fall over. She couldn't even get herself upright from the hardwood floors, dragging herself around the house instead.

While Hope did show signs of injury as the shelter in Puerto Rico suspected, our vet's diagnosis was more dire: She had a neurological condition that caused permanent disability. She would not get better.

If Hope's potential was limited, then we had to give her the tools to make the best use of the skills she had.

A small sock with a non-skid surface helped her walk on the hardwood floors, and a dog boot stabilized her for outdoors. After a couple of tumbles down the stairs, we got on hands and knees and manipulated her legs up and down so she could better understand the movements. The right motivation came when the cat ran downstairs for refuge during a game of chase!

Unexpected mentoring came from Sunny, our dog sitter's own mixed-breed dog with hip dysplasia. The two canines spent a week together, and Hope learned all of Sunny's tricks on how to overcome a physical limitation.

Hope has been with us just five months, and the progress has been amazing. There is still evidence of her neurological condition, but she has figured out ways to compensate and gained confidence in her unconventional methods.

Hope is now a regular at the dog park, running and playing with the pack, albeit for limited lengths of time. She chases the ball in the yard and the cat up and down the stairs. She can even jump onto the bed and couch, and into the back of the car on her own.

While we may have taught her how to live a dog's life, there's a lot more that I learned from her. Whether it's developing pets or people, there are some basic principles:

- Pay attention to what your people need and work to get them the appropriate resources.

- The right environment can make a big difference. Hope would have never gotten better among 150 dogs in a shelter, but she thrived with one-on-one support.

- Find incentives to get the required outcomes.

  Peer mentors can sometimes achieve what supervisors can't.

- Confidence begets confidence. If your team feels like they let you down, it will become a self-fulfilling prophesy.

Putting All the Parts Together

At the start of this chapter, we talked about plot structure. On the basic three-act structure, we showed the red line of increasing tension to the climax. As you shape your visual story, ask yourself, "How can I build tension by making things harder for my hero?" Look for ways to bring out the key challenges and activities you identified when you looked at the "How" and "What If" to drive the story deeper into situations where commitment to act is required. To keep the attention of your audience, the story needs to build towards more and more conflict, effort, or struggle.

Unless you are a master storyteller, the use of flashbacks and a mixed up timeline will break the sequence of events and fail to raise the tension. When your audience has to guess why something has happened (or has not happened), even for just a moment, they will start to disengage. Confidence that the outcome of your visual story is believable is increased with a strong sequence of cause and effect in the story.

> ## Repeat the *reason to act*, not the action.

Repetition is the enemy of escalating tension. In Chapter 6 we talked about the use of complication and resolution to set the start and end for the activities you identified as you developed each of the "Hows" for the story. If the resolution for each complication always involves the hero personally taking charge and working late to solve the problem, then you are repeating an idea. This repetition decreases in impact each time it is used.

Instead of repetition, you need to have different ways for your hero and the associated characters to take on each complication, to build tension. If the activities you identified for your "Hows" in Chapter 6 are all different, you can simply present the struggle needed to overcome each challenge. On the other hand, if those activities are similar, but necessary, you may need to work hard to find ways to identify significant differences between the challenges. If you fail to make the hero's sequence of actions clear and distinct, the tension will not build, and the audience will lose interest in wanting to know how the story will finish.

Note that repeating an activity is very different than repeating the reason why the hero has to act. You should repeat the reasons to act many times through the story, usually with the sense of urgency, which you will develop in Chapter 12, and sometimes with other factors derived from the work you did developing the "Whys."

If you find that one part of your visual story is having to explain what just happened, you need to reverse it to set up the situation in such a way that the resulting action is an obvious consequence. For example, you don't say the factory needs to close and then explain that it costs three times as much to produce there than in another location. You introduce the other location and its costs; then say you cannot compete, and the factory needs to close.

We have shown a number of different ways to turn your content into a story, and on the following pages you will see how in the City University Hospital example Tom selects two different basic plots to create two stories for his audience. This example will build to show how one visual can be used with two slightly different stories to provide a consistent message to an audience that has two groups with different reasons for each group to act.

In a Hurry?

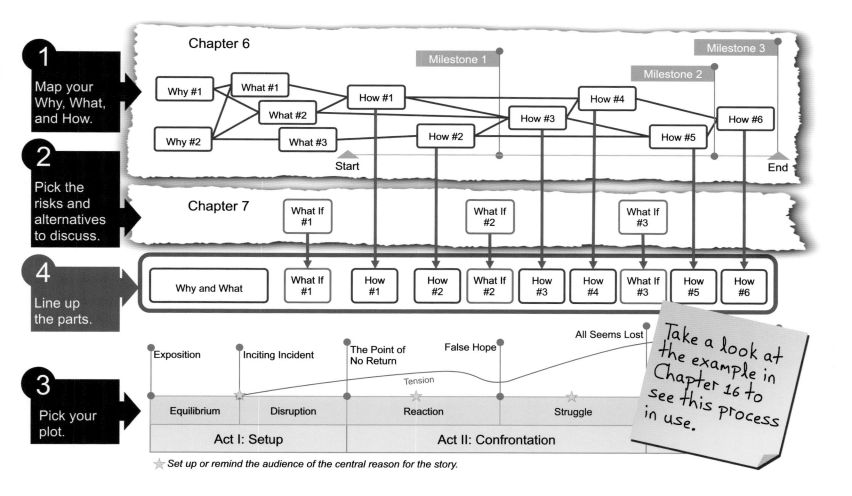

1 Map your Why, What, and How.

2 Pick the risks and alternatives to discuss.

4 Line up the parts.

3 Pick your plot.

Chapter 6

Why #1	What #1
Why #2	What #2
	What #3

How #1 — How #2 — How #3 — How #4 — How #5 — How #6

Milestone 1   Milestone 2   Milestone 3

Start   End

Chapter 7

What If #1   What If #2   What If #3

Why and What | What If #1 | How #1 | How #2 | What If #2 | How #3 | How #4 | What If #3 | How #5 | How #6

Exposition   Inciting Incident   The Point of No Return   False Hope   All Seems Lost

Tension

Equilibrium   Disruption   Reaction   Struggle

Act I: Setup   Act II: Confrontation

☆ *Set up or remind the audience of the central reason for the story.*

Take a look at the example in Chapter 16 to see this process in use.

	Electronic Patient Data	Securing Insurance Revenue
Overcoming the Monster	Patient data issues can be seen as a monster that puts patients at risk, with the nurses and doctors as heroes.	The same patient data issues are preventing us from capturing the full revenue.
The Quest	The goal could be having one source of the "truth" about patient data, available anywhere it is needed.	The goal could be defined as a big increase in revenue from claims, or at least heavily cutting the rejection rate.
Voyage and Return	The "other world" in the voyage could be another hospital that has already been through this kind of change.	Perhaps use another hospital or even the changes in insurance industry claims automation as an example.

Comedy	Comedy requires some kind of misunderstanding that can be resolved. It would be a big stretch to describe the situation as a misunderstanding.
Tragedy	Not feeling like a good plot for either story. We don't want to imply a failure from our decisions!
Rebirth	We could try to describe the current issues as some kind of dark spell, but that feels quite contrived.
Rags to Riches	We already have high revenue from insurance claims, and it's not likely to crash, so there is little to build a rags to riches cycle with.

Tom brought together a few people from his team and had a short workshop to test each of the seven basic plots with the ideas for the visual stories. A first step was to accept that there were two interconnected stories, but with quite different goals. Tom has made notes on three of the plots that seemed to have a good fit and to record why four were quickly discussed and rejected.

Implement new, simpler data entry screens, focused on clinical tasks.
Some existing issues fixed and everyone feeling good.

Change input processes to capture all information related to a diagnosis. People need to work differently. Issues arise and more time needs to be spent to work out what to do.

New business rules highlight issues that require training and more initial effort from the nurses.

Deploy mobile devices for data capture and to display patient notes. Implement machine-readable tags on patient brace-elets for data entry and retrieval of notes. Suddenly staff do not need to return to fixed PCs. The new work becomes part of the flow, not an additional effort.

Overcoming the Monster: Electronic Patient Data

Initial Success - - - - - - - Confrontation

Miraculous Escape

The Call

Both stories follow the same timeline with common events. Notes around the edge call out the key events we need to include in each one.

Final Ordeals

The Quest: Securing Insurance Revenue

Leadership call to change (to use the sense of urgency we define later).

The Journey - - - - - - - Arrival and Frustration

The Goal

Map existing data to new definitions. This takes time to do correctly but allows for reports to be created on current patients.

Automated daily reports to spot potential gaps in patient care records for immediate attention. High number of false errors and data gaps initially with data

Create business rules to support data validation and integration between systems. Even more reports are failing as data rules spot gaps!

Eventually data is cleansed and new data is being captured well. Automatic generation of insurance claims at regular intervals and on patient discharge is speeding up good submissions.

Tom and his team have not been able to find a good example organization that would work for a "Voyage and Return" plot, so decide to use "Overcoming the Monster" and "The Quest" for the two stories. These plots have the same first and fourth stages where we can synchronize the timeline in the stories but take different perspectives for each of them.

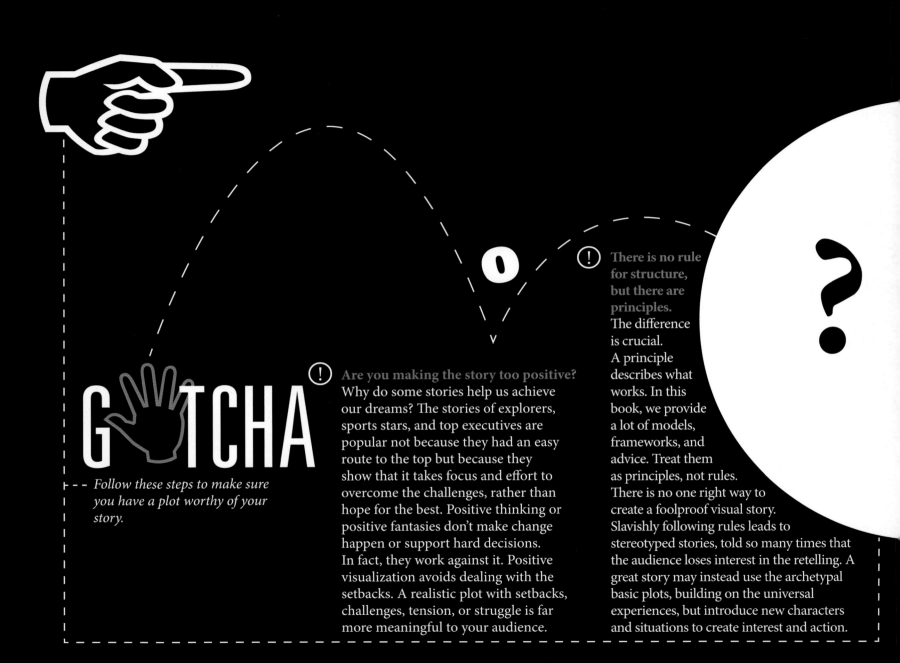

G✋TCHA

Are you making the story too positive? Why do some stories help us achieve our dreams? The stories of explorers, sports stars, and top executives are popular not because they had an easy route to the top but because they show that it takes focus and effort to overcome the challenges, rather than hope for the best. Positive thinking or positive fantasies don't make change happen or support hard decisions. In fact, they work against it. Positive visualization avoids dealing with the setbacks. A realistic plot with setbacks, challenges, tension, or struggle is far more meaningful to your audience.

There is no rule for structure, but there are principles. The difference is crucial. A principle describes what works. In this book, we provide a lot of models, frameworks, and advice. Treat them as principles, not rules. There is no one right way to create a foolproof visual story. Slavishly following rules leads to stereotyped stories, told so many times that the audience loses interest in the retelling. A great story may instead use the archetypal basic plots, building on the universal experiences, but introduce new characters and situations to create interest and action.

- ☑ Identify the basic plot (or combination) to form the basis for the visual story.

- ☑ Map the "Why," "What," and "How" to the plotline.

- ☑ Identify visual patterns to support the visualization of the story.

- ☑ Identify any subplots or nested stories to develop specific details.

- ☑ Define when NOW is in your story timeline.

- ☑ Identify the inciting incident.

- ☑ Decide when to use real or fictional content in the story.

- ☑ Check your cause and effect. Everything must be caused by the event that came before it.

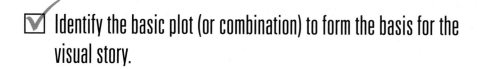

Character

11

> To create great characters, think of all your characters as part of a web in which each helps define the others.
>
> *John Truby, screenwriter, director and screenwriting teacher*

A character is no more a human being than the Venus de Milo is a real woman. A character is a work of art, a metaphor for human nature.

Robert McKee, screenwriting lecturer and author of the screenwriters' bible: Story: Substance, Structure, Style and the Principles of Screenwriting

Business thinking is full of abstractions and the turning of specific situations into generalizations. It is the way many people are taught how to work. Instead of looking at improving the process for a person, we look at the process for everyone doing a similar role. Instead of creating a small application for one person to create and record invoices, we build finance systems and document-sharing platforms for enterprises. This is how economies of scale work, and it's totally appropriate when looking at what to change and how to make investments.

But it's hard to get passionate about an abstraction, or a generalization.

The characters in a story need to be individuals who the audience can identify with, not broad generalizations. In Chapter 8, we discussed how you can create personas that represent specific roles. These personas need details that make them real and specific. They need weaknesses, personal desires, and specific issues to deal with. A persona needs to be representative of the strengths and weaknesses of the people in the group it represents.

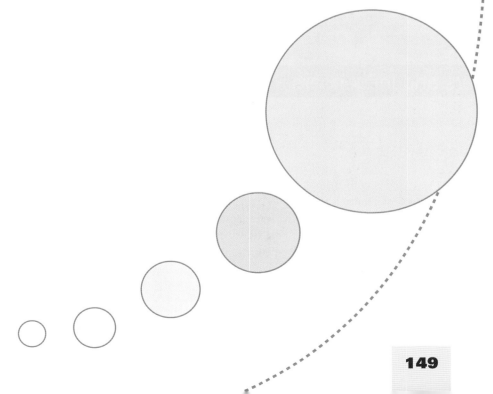

It is more often an emotional response, not a logical response that makes people act. When we see images of crowds during a famine, it can be hard to even consider where to begin, because a crowd is in many ways similar to a statistic. Although statistics of the number of children dying each day because of malnutrition are horrific, many of us don't respond by trying to help change situations based on statistics. When we see numbers, we start to become analytical, and this distracts from the flow of the story. When we understand situations from an individual perspective, we become emotionally involved.

In five minutes of television programming, a news program might start with an interview of a lady cut off by floods, and then discuss the broader issues for the flooded town. Next the program talks about an aid campaign, starting with the story of a refugee, before moving on to talk about the number of people displaced; an advertisement then shows a homeless kitten, followed by details of the number of pets in care. Are you seeing the pattern? We often see stories start with the struggles of the individual, the lives they lead, and the challenges they face. This approach builds an emotional connection, before the story moves on to tell you how many others are in the same situation. Finally, sometimes, the story tells the audience that they can make a difference.

To draw members of your audience into the world you create, you have to help them experience it. Use characters to help the audience experience the specifics of the world in the story and build an emotional connection; then form a link between the character and something you want your audience to care about.

The Hero and the Villain

Every visual story has a goal, or a desired future state. This is the ultimate objective that you want the audience to support. Giving the audience this desire to achieve the goal is key to the decision making process.

Characters take on the roles of hero and villain from the inciting incident, the point when an event begins the sequence of actions that will eventually lead to the goal of the story. Their roles come to an end when the climax of the story is resolved and the story goal is achieved.

The hero is a label we give to the character the audience believes is striving for the story goal. *The villain* is competing with the hero in order to bring about a different goal. Objectively, the story is about the conflict between these characters to achieve the goal. Every other character in the visual story is there to support or influence the progress of the hero or the villain.

Some people talk about these roles as *protagonist* and *antagonist*. The protagonist is in essence the lead character in a story, and the antagonist is in opposition to the protagonist. Like it or loathe it, the word 'hero' is perceived as being positive and 'villain' as negative. We don't expect the hero and villain in a visual story about business change to represent good and evil as that extreme is not usually very helpful, but we do want them to represent sufficiently different perspectives that the audience would rather choose to support the hero.

We made a difficult choice with CAST to use the labels hero and villain for the two key roles, rather than the more generic terms of protagonist and antagonist, because we have found that the perceptions and emotive words help the people creating visual stories (you) to develop more focused conflicts. You never need to tell the audience that your characters are heroes or villains, but knowing clearly who they are in your own mind will help you to describe the conflict in the story with greater clarity and passion.

For our purposes, the hero is striving for the goal that you, the storyteller, want the audience to support. The villain is striving for a different story goal. There is no implied good or evil, right or wrong. There is no requirement for one character to be, by default, stronger or smarter. Both hero and villain could be paragons of virtue; they just have different belief systems and different motivations. The simple truth is that we need characters in conflict, one for our goal, and one against.

Over the years, and especially for the standard film script, the hero has, by default, become the good guy and the villain the bad guy. This helps to get the audience to champion for the hero, to create a positive emotional attachment. Unfortunately, because we put film stars in these roles, many stories have become about the character himself rather than about the goal. The impression is that the hero must be a somewhat reluctant participant when the inciting incident happens and the villain must at first appear stronger or smarter than the hero, making success for the hero more difficult.

All of the basic plots in Chapter 10 have a conflict between a hero and a villain. In your visual story, you will often find it easy to identify the hero character who makes the change happen, but the villain might be harder to describe. This may be because the villain is a person in the organization, and you simply cannot politically call this out without putting your job on the line; or perhaps in the corporate culture, bureaucracy is preventing the change from happening. You still need to have the villain, or there is no conflict, and therefore little to keep the audience's attention or desire to know the outcome.

Stories need a hero and a villain to act out the arguments for and against the story goal. The audience will believe in the goal only if all the important points for and against have been covered. When you see the character roles this way, it becomes possible to take the content developed from the "Why," "What," "How," and "What If" chapters to construct a series of for-and-against positions about which the characters can compete.

An example of a conflict that would be relevant to a visual story would have a hero propose a new product to take their company in a new direction; the villain counters that this would cause a loss of focus on the existing profitable services. The hero then defines the future benefits; the villain lists the risks and the cost to mitigate them. You don't need epic battles to have conflict. This is also a good example of where the villain could be just playing devil's advocate and may not necessarily be a 'bad' character.

Sometimes the villain might win.

For 90 percent of your story, the audience might be cheering for the hero who is striving for a story goal that everyone in the audience believes in. But at the climax, the villain wins. In the resolution, you would need to have a believable and clear reason to take the audience with you, but the twist can make the story stick in their minds.

Sometimes the villain might win.

Sometimes the villain might win.

Every hero needs a villain

Character Associations

Characters are containers of information. When we use the label *hero* or a character's name, the audience has a mental model for all the information they receive about the character, including values, actions, relationships, and influence.

When you want to convince an audience of something, you must consider two simple facts. First, if members of the audience must think too hard about your message, they will not absorb it. Second, often audiences are required to understand a lot of factors in order to accept the case for change. These two facts appear to be in conflict, which is precisely why characters are important. As you build up the information about a character, you're developing the information to support the conclusion, and you can keep relating back to this growing body of knowledge through the simple name of the character. What do we know about Luke Skywalker of the Rebel Alliance, Frodo Baggins of Middle Earth, or Joey from the television show *Friends*? Quite a bit.

Throughout the story, you can build complexity into the character through your description. By the words you use to describe the character and the way he or she responds to the environment, you can channel all this complexity straight into the mind of the audience, and avoid many of the filters of perception we automatically put in the way of absorbing complex information. When you get to the end of the story and the point of climax between the hero and villain, you have a struggle that brings together all the qualities that you have managed to associate with these characters in the minds of the audience.

When Martin started learning how to dance three years ago, it took him an hour to learn a few steps. Eventually, whole sequences became automatic, and he could put them together to make quite complex dances. His dancing teacher will tell you he still has a long way to go to develop grace and poise, but he's no longer overloaded by the individual steps — she simply calls out the sequence. The same concept is true for your characters. Build the story to associate a character with a set of details, and the name of the character will trigger the appropriate associations in the minds of your audience.

Start your description of the hero with information that positions the hero in the shared experience of the audience; then build out the description as the story progresses to develop a position the audience can support.

What does the hero know about, and what does he or she not know?

What are the hero's needs and desires?

What influences the hero?

What is holding the hero back?

What is the hero committed to?

What is the hero's attitude toward other people?

Believability

Storytellers often speak about the suspension of disbelief. But we don't want members of the audience to set their attitudes aside and suspend disbelief; we want them to engage with the character. We want the audience to believe the story. If you bring something into the story that doesn't already exist or that the audience hasn't experienced, you need to describe it and make sure it's consistent within the context of the story.

In the late 1990s many organizations were introducing Enterprise Resource Planning (ERP) systems, with significant changes to their business processes. If you were developing a story about the introduction of ERP today your hero could be positioned as a veteran of ERP implementations in other companies. If instead you were creating the same story in 1995, your hero would have little knowledge of the problems to come with ERP implementations. To the contrary, putting an expert hero into a story about introducing a new technology, or a novice into a story where there is plenty of experience, reduces the believability of the characters, and the story.

When an audience stops believing, it stops caring. Characters must be positioned and behave consistently in order for the audience to believe in them.

If something is not believable — then it doesn't belong.

If you need a character to act in an unbelievable way, you will need to find a good reason for the audience to understand why. You can do this when information is added that the audience didn't have before and you want to make a specific point. The unbelievable action is supported by the previous unknown knowledge. In films, this kind of information might be included in a flashback to some part of the background not previously shown. In a visual story, it might be supported by a callout on the visual presentation or by a small side story in the dialogue.

Every character must be believable within the context of the story and in his or her relationships to the other characters.

Are the characters' behaviors true to their cultural and ethnic backgrounds? This applies to social and organizational cultures.

Characters change and develop as the story progresses. Are the changes justified and believable? They may be rational or irrational (based on fear or prejudice) but must still have a clearly understood cause.

Do the characters take action in response to the situations in the story? Passive characters don't carry the audience with them. Do the actions move the story toward the climax?

Are the characters relevant to the shared experience of the audience? The further they are from the life experience of your audience, the more you will need to develop the backgrounds and motivations for the audience to believe in the characters.

A simple trick is to make a character just slightly smarter, or a little more capable of taking on the big challenge, than the audience. Just enough to inspire the audience to emulate the character, but not so different that it's beyond their ability to see themselves take on the same role.

The Cast of Characters

In the 1920s, a Russian scholar named Vladimir Propp analyzed 100 Russian fairy tales and identified seven typical characters, shown in the image opposite. They are the *Hero, Villain, Princess, False Hero, Donor, Helper,* and *Dispatcher.* These findings are relevant far beyond his original work and can be seen in many of the great stories. For visual stories, the concepts and ideas translate well into different roles because the simplicity of character definition and interaction means it's easy to follow the story.

A character can, in fact, take on a number of roles. For example, one character could take on the roles of donor, dispatcher, and helper over the sequence of the story. The two core roles are for the hero and villain, and unless you have a Jekyll and Hyde character, these will be two different characters in the story. It's not necessary to include all of them in a story, and in fact, many good stories are perfectly complete with just the hero and villain roles. The functions of the remaining roles play important parts in developing the conflict between the hero and the villain.

The roles can also move between characters. The hero may overcome the villain in the early part of the story and be celebrating success, only to find that the villain had a much more powerful figure behind the scenes, which takes the story into the false hope milestone, and the resulting conflict with the second villain taking the story to the climax. For example, the hero and villain may initially both be well-intentioned, just with different beliefs about the best way to deliver new services for customers. Once the hero succeeds in getting his approach accepted internally, the next villain could be the external environment, where regulatory limitations and customer perceptions about security are much harder to overcome.

Propp had a very limited set of stories to work from, and you may well identify other roles necessary for your visual story. In some stories, the helper might evolve into a mentor and train the hero; in others, there may be a senior executive who plays no part in the conflict but who has power over the characters to change the situation and context as he or she sees fit. Anyone who has seen the original series of *Star Trek* knows that the unknown character in a red shirt who joins the landing party is unlikely to return to the ship. This character serves to demonstrate the power of the villain without harming the main characters.

You might also consider extending Propp's roles to create supporting roles for villains. They, too, can have a donor, helper, or dispatcher. The false hero is an interesting role that could represent competing teams in an organization, or a villain in disguise, where everyone is distracted from the real work of the hero and allows someone else to take the credit and then follows the false hero to an alternative story goal.

In the worked examples, we develop a mix of the different roles to show how to apply them. But, before you move on, take a moment to consider whose point of view you will use for the story. The presumption is often to write and tell the story from the perspective of an external observer, but telling the story from the perspective of the hero, villain, or helper may bring the audience into the story a little more.

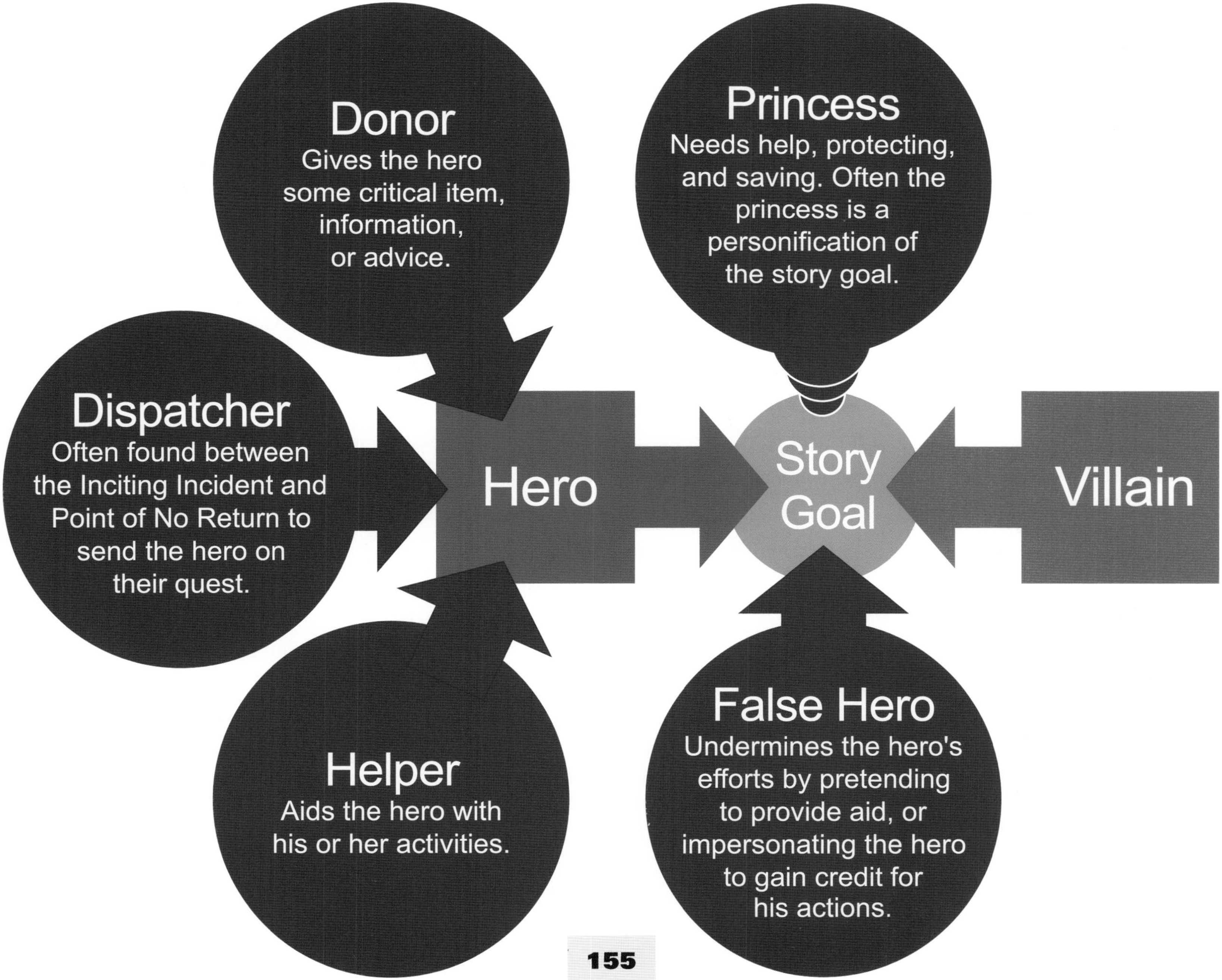

Donor
Gives the hero some critical item, information, or advice.

Princess
Needs help, protecting, and saving. Often the princess is a personification of the story goal.

Dispatcher
Often found between the Inciting Incident and Point of No Return to send the hero on their quest.

Hero

Story Goal

Villain

Helper
Aids the hero with his or her activities.

False Hero
Undermines the hero's efforts by pretending to provide aid, or impersonating the hero to gain credit for his actions.

Personification

More than half the visual stories we've been involved with have included at least one character that is a personification of a problem people face: a force of nature, corporate culture, business processes, or government regulation. Usually, this character is the villain, but in some cases, it has also been the hero. Where we want to show the conflict between two forces, such as the drivers for centralization or federation of a business, we've created these opposing forces as hero and villain, and influenced the audience to support changes required for a change in direction.

In 1967, Komatsu was a fairly small Japanese manufacturer of earth-moving vehicles, with a vision to transform itself into a global business. A major global player called Caterpillar already dominated the industry and was targeting the same market. Komatsu created a corporate story based on the "Overcoming the Monster" basic plot and portrayed Caterpillar clearly as the monster or villain. They created a story and a slogan, "Maru-C," which means *Surround Caterpillar*, to remind their employees of their strategy to capture territory in markets where Caterpillar had not yet become established. Today, Komatsu is the second largest manufacturer in the industry.

We often hear that we should not judge a book by its cover. This phrase exists because that's exactly what we do most of the time. A study in 2012 by Dr. Simon Laham at the University of Melbourne identified that people are more likely to favor people with more pronounceable names. Think about this when you create characters for personifications. If you can make the process of comprehending information easier, your audience will more likely accept it. The cover or character that you create for the information needs to be as simple and familiar as possible.

A villain can also be a problem in need of a solution. This is how Apple set up the story for the introduction of the iPhone in 2007. The launch presentation showed the problems the mobile phone users had with the phones of the day and then set up the iPhone as the hero to save time and to bring in a new world of apps to make the phone more useful.

The information you might associate with a character and the overall believability of the character that apply to "human" characters also apply to personifications. The difference is that you must identify these characteristics, rather than assume your audience will have experienced them. Sometimes you may have to exaggerate the claims to build a villain into a potential monster. For example, in 1984, Apple cast IBM as the villain in a dramatic series of advertisements. Most analysts would agree that Apple's characterization showed IBM in a much stronger position than it really was; nevertheless, the creation of a "great evil" defined an enemy that the Apple sales teams could attack with almost religious zeal. Importantly, although exaggerated, the claims were still within the bounds of the audience's ability to believe.

In the continuation of the Hospital and Personal Trainer worked examples later in this chapter, you will see that both define the villain as a personification of part of the current situation.

You are creating the visual story to influence the audience to act, to support a change, or to make a decision. They are the ones who will be doing the hard work. They should be able to identify with the characters in the story, and at least some of them will see in themselves the role of the hero.

YOU are NOT the HERO

Princess

Countless potential clients who need personal training but cannot get the expertise and support they need at a large gym.

Helper

Penny

Penny is a client of Randall's who sees how hard he is working. She tells him about the services her company uses, and suggests that there may be businesses that help studio owners.

Hero

Randall

Randall is a great personal trainer who would like his own business, but has not been successful so far as he prefers to avoid dealing with a problem rather than face it head on.

Villian

The villain has the heavy burden of performing routine business tasks, from handling complaints to preparing tax returns.

Donor

Optimal Balance (Marina)

By providing the business service and handling the training that Randall needs, he is finally free to help the clients (princesses) to reach their goals.

False Hero

Burnout personified – Frank

Frank is a fellow trainer whom Randall met at a class. Frank is always keen to explain all the systems he has created over the years to help him run his business. In the Apparent Triumph stage, Randall thinks he will be successful if only he can copy Frank.

Marina thought about the characters she might use. She decided she didn't need all the character types, so she removed some to make the story simpler and easier to follow.

Randall
Hero

Randall is a self-reliant and independent 28 year old studio owner with an associate's degree in personal fitness. He loves interacting with clients and feels satisfaction from helping them to achieve their goals. He avoids conflict and doesn't like to push supplements or other health products. He worked at a large gym for five years before starting his studio.

Penny
Helper

Penny is a long-time client of Randall's and is very tolerant of his business mistakes because she loves getting personal training. She is a smart and savvy business woman with a college degree in marketing. She likes to talk while working out, sharing details of her challenging work, at a large recruiting firm.

Frank
False Hero

Frank owns a small studio in another town. He was Randall's inspiration for opening a studio in the first place, but what Randall doesn't know is that Frank works 16 hours a day to do it. Frank has his own routines that are very cumbersome, but because he works all hours he has been able to keep his business running in spite of the way he does it.

In order to make the characters believable, Marina creates descriptions for each one based on people that she has met in the fitness business.

Overcoming the Monster:
Electronic Patient Data

Donor

IT Support Technician who gets one of the first mobile devices for Sharon. This completely changes her ability to capture and access information on the ward and helps her achieve the goal.

Princess

Patient Care
The data is the important aspect of our story, but the goal for Sharon is to ensure the quality of care for the patients, which is why the Villain is strong.

Dispatcher

Luc on behalf of Bernd

Hero

Sharon
Nurse Persona.
Character Flaws – occasionally drops back to handwriting notes when time is critical, and then with Don's help gets back on track.

Villian

Current practices
Nurses and doctors taking the easy route and just using the existing working practices, with personal paper notes to be sure they always have the information they need.

Helpers

IT Support Technician who helps Sharon with tips on using the new system. Sharon's nursing team who form a learning circle to share what they are doing to make the new systems work.

False Hero

New IT System
Not sure if this is needed. But, we could make it sound like it was the success of the IT system in the final ordeals, only to have it shown that it was the effort of the nurses that really made the difference.

The characters for the story are in part based on real people, including one persona to represent the nurses, and a characterization of existing practices and attitudes. Tom continues working with his team on the two plots they have agreed on, building up ideas for the characters and their relationships.

The Quest:
Securing Insurance Revenue

Donor

Data analyst who spots issues in patient data reports and seeks out Sharon to get help understanding why there are issues, and in return helps Sharon work out how to use the reports to improve the working of the ward.

Princess

Patient Care
The data is the important aspect of our story, but the goal for Sharon is to ensure the quality of care for the patients, which is why the Villain is strong. Loss of revenue can imply other cuts, which would put patient care at risk.

Dispatcher

Luc on behalf of Bernd and senior team.

Hero

Sharon
Nurse Persona
Character Flaws – occasionally drops back to handwriting notes when time is critical, and then with Don's help gets back on track.

Villian

Current practices
Nurses and doctors taking the easy route and just using the existing working practices, with personal paper notes to be sure they always have the information they need.

Helpers

IT Support Technician who helps Sharon with tips on using the new system.
Sharon's nursing team who form a learning circle to share what they are doing to make the new systems work.

False Hero

New IT System / Automated Reports
Not sure if this is needed. But we could make it sound like it was the success of the IT system in the final ordeals, only to have it shown that it was the effort of the nurses that really made the difference.

To test how well they will be able to create two interlinked stories, the team works on characters for the second plot to see if they are identical or would introduce some differences for the second plot. Tom highlighted in yellow the differences, which he believes are very few, for the core characters. This should make it easy to have visuals and a strong core story in common.

G TCHA

Follow these steps to make sure that your characters have body and life.

(!) Avoid the perfect hero. No hero is perfect; they have weaknesses, sometimes personal relationships that misdirect their decisions, sometimes moral failings. If your hero is too perfect, the challenges in the story will not seem believable, or challenging! Your audience will support and identify with a hero who has the ability to overcome the challenges they aspire to and who deals with the issues and flaws they know everyone has to deal with. **Ensure the hero is relevant.** The type and degree of challenge the hero has faced has to be relevant and similar to the change or decision the audience has to make. It's appropriate to use a real person as the hero in a story, when it is a true story, and the actions of the hero can be seen to relate to the challenges in the story. Olympic athletes can inspire people to reach for excellence, but telling people about the training the Olympic athlete endures will not help a personal trainer motivate someone new to exercise.

(!) Don't tell the audience the roles. We have talked a lot about the different roles, but when you tell the story, you never tell the audience explicitly who is the hero and who is the villain. The audience should be able to recognize the roles the characters are playing by their actions.

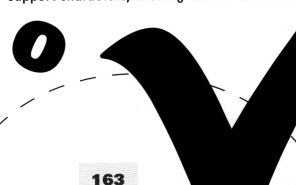

☑ Define the character whom the audience will be supporting to the desired conclusion — usually the role we consider as the hero.

☑ Define the character who will oppose the desired outcome — usually the role we consider as the villain.

☑ Identify the supporting roles necessary for the hero and villain to participate in a believable struggle.

☑ Work out the key characteristics you need to include in each character. What will change in the characters, if anything, as a result of the visual story?

☑ Develop the interactions so that the audience gradually develops feelings for the lead and support characters, wishing them to succeed?

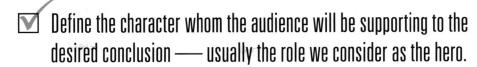

CHECKLIST

Sense of Urgency

12

At the very beginning of an effort to make changes of any magnitude, if a sense of urgency is not high enough and complacency is not low enough, everything else becomes so much more difficult.

John P. Kotter, Harvard Business School Professor and international bestseller on the subjects of leadership and change

I have been impressed with the urgency of doing. Knowing is not enough; we must apply. Being willing is not enough; we must do.

Leonardo da Vinci, Italian Renaissance painter, sculptor, architect, scientist, inventor, anatomist, and writer

The Enemies of Change: Complacency and Distraction

Your audience may accept that change will have to happen down the road but may not feel a sense of urgency to change. Why change now? Why not wait and avoid immediate pain? So, your question is what will motivate a leader to take a break from his or her daily routine long enough to listen to your story?

The first level of complacency to overcome is a belief among the members of your audience that they don't need to change. At least not right now. To break through this complacency and inspire your audience to take action right now, you need to create a sense of urgency that relates to the reasons identified when you developed the "Whys" in Chapter 4.

The second level of complacency begins the minute the decision is made and the first actions are taken. The process has started, and everyone becomes satisfied that simply having a plan in place will guarantee success. The fact that a decision has been made makes it seem like the problem has been addressed, which dilutes the sense of urgency and reduces the chance that the next steps are successfully taken. The compelling sense of urgency is important to break through the initial complacency and to maintain the effort once started.

Your audience is distracted. With the best of intentions, they will be distracted while the story is delivered, deciding how to handle what they are hearing, and by the hundreds of other demands on their attention to stay committed to decisions they may make.

I'm sorry, what did you say?
Can we discuss this next week?

Whether in meetings at work, at home, or simply at the coffee machine, most of your audience will today be multitasking, with at least one screen to look at. Whether on their smartphone, tablet, or laptop, your audience may be checking e-mails, tweeting, or updating their social status. Remember that almost daily more and more applications and opportunities for distraction are thrust in front of your audience.

Before and after your visual story is delivered, your audience is likely to be overwhelmed by advertisements, messages, spam, conflicting recommendations, and other requests for attention. Much of this information is irrelevant to your audience, so their response is to ignore it. Nevertheless, each irrelevant message takes a moment to process, and distracts your audience a little further from the message you want them hear.

How do you deal with this distraction and get past the background static? Start with the knowledge that before your audience will value the story you tell, they've got to want it. *Your story must meet an urgent need.* Many people believe that you can't do anything about these distractions, and that your audience will multitask if they want to. Certainly it is difficult to stop this behavior directly, especially if your audience consists of senior managers. However, we have seen time after time that a story with a good sense of urgency cuts through the trivial distractions of e-mail addiction, and even captures attention away from other significant business decisions.

Obsolescence

This can apply to physical products, services, practices, or personal skills, whatever is no longer wanted, even though it may be still working. Often the obsolete is being superseded by something else, and you may be seeing an early indication by its gradual decline in popularity.

This kind of situation can create a strong sense of urgency if you are the retailer, manufacturer, or person with the skill or service becoming obsolete. Obsolete products may no longer fit the way we work (for example, typewriters and fax machines) or are simply being replaced by improved versions, such as the annual cycle of smartphone improvements.

Government regulations

Whether for safety, regulating markets, or competitive advantage, governments enact legislation that requires people and organizations to adapt. Carbon taxes have been used to change the travel behavior of people, legislation for disability access and equal rights has changed the workplace for employers and employees, and forcing the use of seatbelts in cars has saved thousands of lives around the world. In business, possibly the most urgent rules are those aimed at corporate compliance — for example, those related to recording financial transactions or to documenting evidence in pharmaceutical companies that can stop you trading if not complied with.

Seasonality

Seasonality could relate to the timing needed to be ready for annual sales peaks during holiday shopping seasons, or to getting new designs ready for seasonal fashion shows, or to color schemes and materials for household decorations. Another source of urgency may come from adapting in a timely way to seasonal changes or to keeping up with changing trends.

Management direction

Whenever people hold positions of such significant power that their decisions cannot be challenged, the source of urgency can be as simple as compliance with their intentions. This issue applies to families, businesses, and government.

In 1995, Bill Gates wrote an internal memo at Microsoft about the Internet tidal wave and how Microsoft had to respond. Responding wasn't a choice for product teams. The direction was laid out and the urgency made clear: focus on the Internet, or lose the business.

The following section highlights some of the most common motivators for inspiring commitment and action.

sense of

URGENCY

New (business or technology) opportunities

New opportunities rarely last long before other competitors jump in and seize the advantage. Examples in business include the adoption of new business models like the rise of Internet businesses such as Amazon or the creation of totally new concepts such as online social media giants like Facebook. This issue also applies at an individual level where new employment opportunities might motivate a person to change. Changing technology is the opposite of obsolescence and is also often tied to new business opportunities. The obsolescence of a product may be seen by some audience members as a source of urgency, and by others as an opportunity to adopt new technology.

Lost business / opportunity

Losing existing opportunities or business to a competitor or losing the chance for a dream job can be a significant blow, but also a wake-up call that something needs to change. In this case, a sense of urgency builds on the desire not to feel that way again, not to be on the losing side.

Changing social/political expectations

Changes in the culture or political structure of societies can be powerful motivators for other changes. The abolition of slavery in the U.S. in 1863, the fall of the Berlin Wall in 1989, and the Arab Spring of 2011 all served as major turning points for the societies and also as drivers for change.

Deadlines

Most people would acknowledge that they suddenly get a boost in productivity a few days before assignments are due, products are to be released, or big events occur. Time pressure is, although the last on this list, by no means the least important. In fact, we deliberately chose to put it last because it's too often picked by default. Many of the other factors listed here can be simplified to a time pressure, but this simplification can reduce the long-term impact of the sense of urgency.

The first step to building a sense of urgency into your visual story is to recognize that it is necessary, and must come from the reasons "Why" identified in Chapter 4 at the very start of the CAST process. You aren't likely to use all the reasons you developed, but at least one of them must address a major source of complacency that needs to be overcome.

The sense of urgency may vary among the people in your audience. You may tailor your presentations to specific segments of your audience to focus on the most relevant sense of urgency. We cover this further in Chapter 13.

The sense of urgency is a tool the storyteller can use to keep the audience interested throughout the delivery. Sometimes it's much better to get members of the audience to identify their sense of urgency, instead of declaring it yourself. As a storyteller, you can identify the sense of urgency for your audience, or you can build questions into your delivery that encourage the audience to develop their own sense of urgency.

Instead of this: *Our product sales are dropping rapidly. Our products are becoming obsolete. We have a limited time to respond.*
Use this: *What is happening to our product sales? Why is this happening? How do we respond?*

Success Is a Decision

The ideal result from a visual story is that the audience, whether one person or many, makes a decision. But people often procrastinate on making the call to go forward. If there is no obvious reason to make an immediate decision, they may put it off and consider that they're keeping their options open. The work done in the Content section of the CAST process identified many reasons to make a decision. The weight of evidence is not usually the key factor to swing a decision. Often having too many data points will serve to confuse or lead to a request for further analysis to gain clarity.

Top lawyers don't recap all the evidence in a case when summing up; they focus on a few key messages to close the decision. The delivery plan you create in the next chapter might use the sense of urgency to set up the story and to close it.

Success Is a Commitment

Decisions can be changed. Keeping the decision at 'Yes' and helping your audience avoid distractions to make the change happen means using the visual story to keep the sense of purpose alive. Visual stories can evolve. Once the decision has been made and action is in progress, we often see new versions of the visual story, updated to reflect the changing situation.

When these updates are done well, they maintain the sense of urgency and also show how progress is being made toward resolving the situation defined in the visual story. Updating a visual story simply means repeating the process, but starting from the well-structured content you have from the first story. A visual story created for a major bank transformation in 2005 was updated every three months for two years to keep all the staff focused on the final goal as new services were introduced. Each update moved the story to include the recently added services, and described the changes to come in the next six months.

On the following pages we continue the examples. You will see how both Marina and Tom build on the reasoning identified in their analysis of the "Whys," but use their analysis of the audience and the story to identify the sense of urgency. Tom in particular maps out his two potential stories to the different variations for urgency identified in this chapter.

Sense of urgency
1

Loss of motivation

For personal trainers, overcoming physical obstacles can be far easier than overcoming the mental challenges that make it difficult to keep doing routine business tasks when they really don't enjoy them. This situation cannot last for long. It 's just a matter of time before they quit.

Sense of urgency
2

Lost business opportunities

The personal trainer is spending so much time on business concerns that the clients are not getting the personal attention they desire.

Existing clients may not renew their membership and will not recommend the studio to others.

Sorting through all the possible sources of urgency, Marina decides to focus on two: the motivational burnout felt by many personal trainers, and lost business opportunities.

	Electronic Patient Data	Securing Insurance Revenue
Obsolescence	Not relevant – nothing becoming obsolete.	
Government regulation	It's on the government agenda but nothing is published yet, so not urgent.	Government funding cuts are making the story important, but these are not an urgent issue.
Seasonality	Not relevant – no seasonality related to the changes.	
Management direction	Claus has said he wants to see change. But the important change is the expansion and transformation plan. This is just a part of that.	
New opportunities	Better analytics of patient issues are possible with the standardized data.	Not relevant.
Lost business/ opportunity	A few patient mistreatments have resulted from patient notes errors that would not have happened with the new approach.	We know that every day without the change means lost revenue.
Changing technology	New mobile devices are a big part of making this work on the wards. Not urgent though.	Automated data integration and billing process make this possible. Not urgent though.
Changing social/political expectations	Expectation is for hospitals to have electronic patient notes.	Public expects the hospitals to run well and bill insurance companies.
Deadline	We have a limited window to put these changes in place while the transformation plan is running.	

Tom is now convinced he really has two related stories for his different audiences. To define the sense of urgency for both of them, he starts with the examples from the chapter to understand what to consider. His problem, though, is that there are a number that could work but none of them are really urgent, except the internally imposed deadline.

Pain Chain

Claus- CEO
The three-year transformation plan is dependent on tight cost control. Errors in insurance claims cause financial losses equivalent to the total savings we must make in the next three years.

Bernd - COO
IT systems cost money to fix, but the errors caused by data issues cause financial problems for the hospital and damage its reputation.

Allan – Financial Controller
Difficult to assemble claim forms for health insurance companies from the data in our systems. Many claims are queried or rejected.

Luc – Patient Data Controller
Patient care targets are being missed because of data quality issues. But efforts to improve data quality have met with complaints about the time and effort required.

Nurses
Re-entry of patient data in multiple systems leads to errors which the nurses are held responsible for.

Nurses
Too many different places to record data makes it hard to find information in an emergency.

Failure to capture the revenue we are due from insurance companies will put the transformation program at risk. Every failed claim is another step toward having to make budget cuts.

Our reputation is based on our quality of care. Another significant issue could result in a public inquiry that would seriously damage the reputation of everyone in the hospital.

Tom returns to the pain chain and looks instead to build the sense of urgency from the specific individual pain felt by the different members of the audience. Tom works to pull these together into two statements that drive to the heart of issues people are keen to avoid: budget cuts and professional reputation.

Follow these steps to make sure you are expressing a sense of urgency your audience can believe in.

(?) **Don't end the presentation with a "key points" list.** Often we see templates or guidelines for presenters to include a slide at the end with three key takeaways for the audience. If you have to list the messages the audience should take away in such a fashion, the content of your story is probably not good enough. Finish instead with a reminder of the sense of urgency and a one-line action-oriented statement that describes what your audience should do about it. **Emphasize how the audience will benefit from your proposal.** Many presentations are delivered because the presenter wants something from the audience, and it shows. They may be selling a new product or service, and the presentation is focused on the features or very generic benefits the audience might get from it. But why is the audience there? If you've identified their sense of urgency, then you have their motivation, and you have the power to capture their attention. Focus all the content of your story on solving their problem, even if they didn't acknowledge they had the problem when you started.

(?) Remember that you are not the audience. It's worth repeating the last point from a different perspective. Sometimes the sense of urgency in a story belongs to the storyteller but isn't very relevant to the audience. The storyteller may be facing a deadline or the obsolescence of their services. Whatever the reason, if the audience doesn't share the sense of urgency, they will not feel the necessity to make a decision now.

☑ Identify the sources of complacency and distraction to work out how you will address them.

☑ Build the sense of urgency from the content identified in the first step of the CAST process, the reasons "Why." This will ensure consistency with the content developed for the body of the visual story.

☑ Accept that different members of your audience may feel different levels of urgency. Don't assume that they all have the same attitude.

☑ The sense of urgency should be describable at the start of the visual story and retain its power as the story progresses. Is the sense of urgency clearly a driving force for the hero of the story to take action?

Delivery Plan

13

Planning is bringing the future into the present so that you can do something about it now.

Alan Lakein, author on time management

You can tell any story 20 different ways. The trick is to pick one and go with it.

Clint Eastwood, American actor, director, producer, and politician

There seems to be a belief in many businesses that it is possible to take a message and create a single presentation that can be used in every situation. We often see sales teams with a standard presentation deck for their product that simply has the new customer's name and logo placed on the corner of every slide. The same concept happens internally in many organizations, with a standard presentation used many times, regardless of the audience. Sometimes a message has to be carefully controlled, and this is a good way to do that. However, many times this kind of reuse happens because it's simply more efficient for a presenter to reuse the same materials over and over.

A typical presenter will quickly adapt a standard presentation's content, removing irrelevant slides, and varying the time spent on each slide for the specific audience. Unfortunately, the result is a presentation designed for the convenience of the presenter. It ignores the specific learning and decision styles of the audience and likely focuses on generic reasons for making the proposed decision, rather than a specific sense of urgency.

A great presenter goes deeper. He or she will start every delivery by considering the audience, and working out the best way to tell the story to produce the desired effect. *The great presenter considers the audience's needs first* and adjusts the standard content to fit. We create a visual story to help an audience reach a decision, with a plan for delivery that may involve many different presentations, in different formats, sometimes even including some of the audience in the creation of the story. Each delivery, in whatever format, should be designed for a specific audience, and to move one step closer to the required decision.

Efficiency is not the only reason to reuse core content; it's also important because individuals can consistently relate the different parts of the story to different formats and presentations. However, each delivery needs to focus on the needs of the learning and decision styles of its unique audience and the personal sense of urgency necessary to gain their commitment.

The important concept here is to plan for a *sequence of deliveries* to the audience. You may have only one main presentation to deliver, but if you look back at the power map you created in Chapter 8, there are likely to be many different people in your audience who all need influencing. Some might appreciate a handout with more details, some a chance to have a discussion and work through the story step by step. Gaining and keeping the commitment you want from the audience means thinking through these requirements and planning to address the different needs.

You never get a second chance to make a first impression. Plan to make it right.

In my work, I am called upon to find the root causes for difficult business problems and create a vision for solving them. In one such case, I created a visual story that showed how the company could evolve from the problems of today to a more sophisticated solution in the future.

There were four stages to the change. To each stage, I attached an image of a vehicle. The first was a horse-drawn carriage, followed by an image of an early car, then a 1960s-era Volkswagen beetle, and lastly a modern luxury sedan (of a brand commonly owned by the executives of the company). We made the presentation many times, at many levels of the company. In each of the handouts, PowerPoint decks, and videos, we used these four images. It was an effective way to tie together the various presentations and to talk about the stages. We still refer to the stages of change as "the Model-T stage" and "the Volkswagen stage."

175

Decisions Take Time

In Chapter 9, we discussed the learning and decision styles of the audience. These have an impact on the structure of the visual story content, and also on the way in which you will deliver it. There is another dimension to the decision process you will need to cover when planning the delivery and that is to understand how much time your audience will take to come to a decision.

It might help to think of the delivery plan as a three-step process:

1. Include the information necessary to ensure that the audience understands what is being proposed.

2. Lead to a decision via content structured in such a way that the audience will best accept it.

3. Deliver the story in a way that convinces the audience to make the decision quickly.

The third step involves understanding why your audience may not make a decision immediately. It is one of the main reasons why we recommend creating a delivery plan, and considering different formats for your story. There are four different factors that contribute to the duration of a decision process: gut feel, repetition, elapsed time, and reevaluation.

GUT FEEL Some people will just jump to a conclusion and make a decision. Although it can appear rash, the decision is often based on experience and can develop from a small amount of data and a lot of assumptions. Here, to avoid any false assumptions, you need to understand the experience of the audience members and place the story in a context they can clearly understand.

REPETITION Some people will feel comfortable making a decision only when they have seen the evidence or heard the argument a number of times. This does not necessarily mean they simply need to hear the same story multiple times. They may need the experience of a presentation, hear about the story from a peer, review materials in their own time, and discuss the options at a whiteboard. Variety in the format, location, and people for delivery can have a big impact.

ELAPSED TIME Some people just need time. Trying to rush them will just get you quickly to a negative answer. This does not mean you tell them the story once and then wait. You need to think about how to give them the content and then return to remind them. The familiarity born of time can ultimately lead to a decision.

REEVALUATION Some people just never completely decide. They make a decision but keep revisiting it and may change their mind if either the circumstances or evidence change, or if influenced by another person.

A range of studies have provided data to indicate how many people fall into each of these categories. We're not going to repeat those here because ultimately that data doesn't help to get the decision made.

It is unlikely that all of your key decision makers will jump to accept your decision on the first hearing. You will usually need to accommodate over half your audience with some form of repetition and with time to consider the decision, so assume you need to do it for everyone and build this into your plan from the start.

Early in my career, I was responsible for creating project proposals. These usually had to be presented to a board for approval. I would turn up with all the data but rarely get through the approval process the first time. Sometimes it took three passes, but in reality hardly anything was changing in the proposal in each pass. Sometimes I would hear phrases like "inoculate the stakeholders," "run it up the flagpole and see who salutes," or "pivot the analysis on a broader set of options." If you've worked in a big organization, you've probably come across this kind of management-speak. I was fortunate. A manager took me to one side and explained that the two key decision makers on the board always needed time to reflect on proposals that they had not initiated. He told me to send them the analysis the week before to review and to check in with them a few days before the review board so that at the review these decision makers would be seeing the analysis for the third time — making their approval more likely. Every project from that point on sailed through.

Planning for Scale

How many people are you going to influence with your story? One person? A company? A nation? In Chapter 8, we talk about the CAST process being used at many different scales. The different scales require some very different approaches, not least because there is a physical time limit to how much personal interaction you can have.

PERSONAL STORIES are often designed to have a strong impact on individuals and their behaviors. The delivery plan also needs to be very personal, both to the individual and to the people supporting them in their change. For example, if the visual story is designed to help people improve customer service, you might include a power phrase (*if you've not heard of this before, we explain what a power phrase is on the next page*) to help them remember the message, an elevator pitch to explain why they are doing it, a poster to go up in the workplace, and a story to tell their colleagues to encourage their continued support.

In contrast to interest groups, the delivery plan for **BUSINESS AND GOVERNMENT ORGANIZATIONS** often has to consider the visible and invisible lines of power to the decision maker, who is often the most senior manager or executive in the audience. Developing support and commitment at lower levels in the organization may be critical to gaining access to the key decision maker or to supporting decision styles that rely on the input from others. Delivery plans for organizations are often based on a series of meetings or presentations to reach the final delivery.

INTEREST GROUPS are characterized by having a shared, common purpose. Visual stories that attempt to influence an interest group often need to consider individual group members as important as the group's leaders. The stories need to build on their common purpose. Effective stories for small groups often rely on individuals seeing their peers accept the story as a key element of the storytelling process. Peer acceptance of the story can be a far more important factor to gaining commitment than authority figures or expert acceptance. A delivery plan here is more often built on social acceptance than on hierarchical positioning and should include time for members of the audience to share their own stories and voice agreement with the core message.

Whether you are trying to change a nation or even **THE WORLD**, you need a mix of the three scales just described. You may need to influence the individual to change and to develop sufficient momentum that interest groups form to take the story forward. You may have to convince national or global authorities that there's a need for change, and these groups often need to see that there's large popular appeal for the political support to make the change. A delivery plan on this scale often focuses on awareness first, and can use online video sites and social networking sites to spread awareness, allowing the growth of audiences of hundreds of thousands in a matter of days.

For a great example of an organization that has shown repeated success at changing the world take a look at http://wearewhatwedo.org, a not-for-profit behavior change company.

A 30-minute video called "Kony 2012," created to raise awareness of a Ugandan warlord, was shown on YouTube in 2012. It had 26 million views in a week and 89 million in two months. The issue was not new, but the awareness needed to address it finally arrived, courtesy of a well-told story.

Hook, Line, and Sinker

For all scales of the audience, in different deliveries, you may need to tell the full story, the edited highlights, or cut straight to the ask. Sometimes you will also get an unexpected opportunity to quickly deliver the story to some part of your audience. This can be an impromptu encounter at the coffee machine, a chance meeting on the way to an event, or a request to drop in and talk about the ideas. These are the opportunities you can't build into the plan but that you nevertheless need to be ready for.

When we started in our careers, we used to talk about the *elevator pitch*. This was conceived as a short summary that could be delivered in 30 seconds to two minutes, just enough time to get from the ground floor to the executive suite. This summary needs to provide the unique character of your story and sufficient interest to get the listener to ask to hear the full story.

With the popularity of Twitter, today you might also consider what message you can fit into the 140 characters of a tweet. At first, this sounds like a nonsense idea; after all, how much of your story can you put into 140 characters? The answer is just enough of a sound bite to generate enough interest to follow a short link and read the rest of the story. This concept of a tweet-level message is common in media and marketing teams, where it might be called a *sound bite or power phrase*. These simple, powerful phrases are often designed to convey a key message and can be included in all deliveries to provide a consistency and link among them. These are the *hooks* to grab the audience.

In fishing terms, the *sinker* is a weight that ensures the hook is at the right depth in the water for the fish. To apply this analogy to the process of visual story development and catch your audience's attention, you work on the wording to create the hook that aligns with the audience by considering a sense of urgency and the use of details and language specific to your audience.

Continuing the analogy, after the hook, the *line* is the sequence you follow by telling the story in different deliveries and formats until you get commitment (land the big fish!). As you develop the delivery plan, work out what you want your hook to be, and consistently build this into the different formats and deliveries.

City University Hospital

Over the next several pages, we will use the City University Hospital example to demonstrate how to develop a delivery plan.

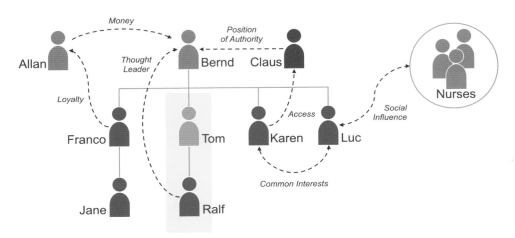

Step 1

Tom starts the process by involving Ralf, because he will provide Bernd, the key decision maker, with a first insight into the ideas and a recommendation to follow up with future conversations. Ralf is a key influencer, based on his expertise, past relationships, and position as an opinion leader. For Tom, this first delivery will be on a whiteboard to engage Ralf in the development of the story and then gain feedback and commitment because of his inclusion in the process.

TIP: Include opinion leaders and acknowledged experts early in the story delivery to leverage their contacts and credibility by association.

Ralf's qualification as an opinion leader stems from being respected by senior people in the hospital and having good connections across the organization. Ralf is not an innovator though. The difference between opinion leaders and innovators can be critical to gaining support from others. In many situations, innovators are often early to commit to support a new change. However, innovators can also be seen negatively by others, perceived as risk takers and sometimes lacking in respect for the existing way of working. Choosing an opinion leader rather than an innovator has the potential to give Tom greater credibility with the existing leadership teams.

Opinion leader = Respected + Connected (must have both)

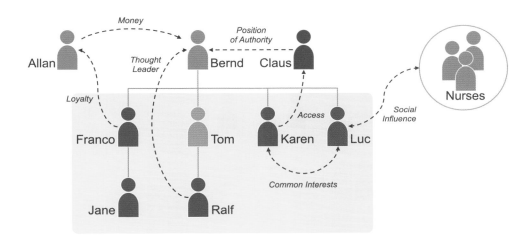

Step 2

Tom plans to offer the first presentation to his primary audience in the form of a workshop during which he will present a rough draft of the story and ask for impressions and insight. This serves as a first delivery of the story for those in the audience who need repetition or time. Tom is not going to finish the visual story presentation with a request for support, but with a question to help him determine how the audience feels about the story.

the importance of understanding the context of your audience and grounding the visual story in a shared experience. Don't treat storytelling as a broadcast system for one-way communication. In this step of the delivery plan, Tom is planning on a dialogue. In the conversation, he will be testing ideas to associate the challenge in the visual story with a challenge that the audience has faced and overcome.

TIP: *Everyone has a story. Take the time to listen to them. Meet with your audience, ask them about their experiences and then shut up and listen. Use these in your visual story.*

The use of rough-draft materials makes it explicitly clear that the audience can contribute and engage. Tom's decision not to ask for commitment at this stage deliberately avoids getting negative answers that could impact peer decisions.

One of the great skills for a storyteller is to learn how to listen to your audience, and use what you hear to build your story. In Chapter 8, we talk about

Tom will need to prepare a number of options that will align with different types of personal challenge. As he gets to the first of these options, he will pause and ask the audience who has had the relevant experience. If the answer is not helpful, he can ask about an alternative experience and build from that.

TIP: *Stories can trigger strong positive and negative emotions and perceptions linked to experiences from your audience's past. Use these to connect your story to a positive association or to link an undesirable alternative to a negative association.*

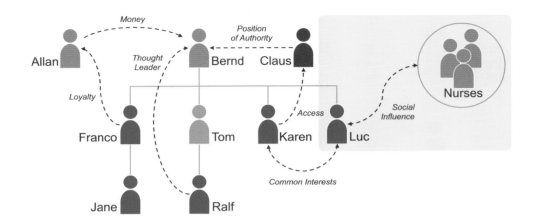

Money

Position
of Authority

Thought
Leader

Allan   Bernd   Claus

Loyalty

Nurses

Franco   Tom   Karen   Luc

Access

Social
Influence

Jane   Ralf

Common Interests

Step 3

The change Tom wants to drive at the hospital will work only if the nursing staff believe in it and understand their role. Step 3 is the presentation of the visual story to the nurses. For this, Tom has asked Luc to coordinate sharing the story with the nursing teams.

Luc, as the patient data controller, is one member of the management team who stands to benefit from the change and who can explain the change in terms of how it will also benefit the nurses. Because of shift patterns and the need to maintain patient care, it's not possible to give a single presentation to the nurses. However, for Luc to simply get to all nurse team meetings would take over two weeks, so Luc offers to brief the senior nurses and have them cascade the story.

TIP: *Sometimes the best way to present the visual story is to use a person who will benefit from the change or who is a key part of it.*

Tom plans to create a one-page handout poster that Luc can give to the senior nurses and that they in turn can hand to their nursing teams. This handout will provide the visual story in a specific variation to focus on the role of the nurses and their activities with patient data.

Commitment from the nurses will provide validation of the story to Luc and evidence to the senior team that the change can be implemented successfully. The nursing team is a good example of a situation where social proof is important. The nurses will look to their peers for commitment. As more commit, others will follow. During the series of briefings with the nurses it will be important to highlight those who have committed to the proposed changes to accelerate the commitment of others.

TIP: *Social proof is especially influential when a group of people are very similar (nurses not only have the same role, but share a standard education and reasons for choosing their profession). This is a common influencing situation for interest groups.*

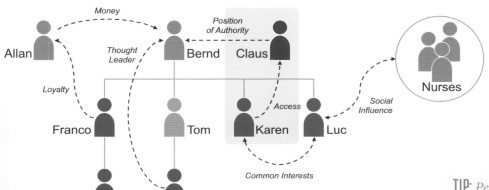

Money

Position
of Authority

Allan

Bernd   Claus

Thought
Leader

Nurses

Loyalty

Access

Social
Influence

Franco   Tom   Karen   Luc

Jane   Ralf

Common Interests

TIP: *People generally follow the direction of those in authority. For this to work, the authority needs to be recognized. Positional authority in organizations is easy to spot. If as the storyteller you are an expert on the subject matter, you should consider how you will provide your credentials. In some situations, this can be as simple as dressing and acting appropriately, in others the authority may be based on experience or earned credentials such as a doctorate. If it's not possible or appropriate for the authority to directly endorse the story or commit to it, the next best situation is to be confident the authority will not oppose it and will leave the decision to others.*

Step 4

Tom knows that Bernd is new in the role and looks to Claus for approval before making major decisions. If Claus can be influenced to support the visual story, then Bernd will be more open to listening to the story. Karen reported to Claus for two years before moving into her current role and retains a strong, friendly relationship with Claus. Tom plans a meeting with Karen to discuss her feedback on the story from the presentation in Step 2 and ask her to meet with Claus to introduce the visual story.

Tom and Karen both know that Claus prefers "What If" discussions at whiteboards to learn about new ideas and that he makes his decisions when he understands clearly how they will impact the people in the hospital. Tom leaves Karen with a copy of the handout used with the nurses in Step 3. Karen can use this as a structure to draw key parts on the whiteboard as she tells the story, and then leave it with Claus to show how the nurses will be directly affected.

TIP: *People are more likely to be influenced by people they know and like. Likeability factors include repeated positive contact, and this is the basis for Karen's relationship with Claus. Sales professionals often use praise and similarity factors to increase likeability, to appear more like their target audience, and to recognize the audience's positive attributes. This approach can go wrong if done too crudely or too obviously, but when incorporated carefully into the conversation, it can help to reduce critical and negative thoughts on the part of the audience.*

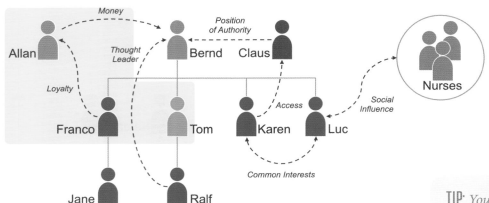

TIP: *Reciprocation is one of the most common influencing techniques, used in millions of advertisements and transactions every day. When you receive an unsolicited mailing with a free gift of a pen enclosed or a restaurant bill with mint chocolates, the person doing the giving is hoping to increase the chance of getting something in return. And it often works. Effective salespeople do this all the time to provide one small favor or concession and then ask for something in return. Nearly all levels of society, across cultures around the world, experience this from childhood and learn to follow the rule of reciprocation or suffer disapproval from others. It's not advisable to always ask for something in return or to support others only with the expectation of receiving something in return, but it is true that to receive, you usually have to give something first.*

Step 5

Bernd is more likely to make a positive decision if Allan, the financial controller, will provide his support. Franco has worked at the hospital for many years and in that time delivered a lot of projects for Allan, who is known for his close control over costs and examination of the detail in proposals. When Bernd was promoted, Franco had Allan's support to take the open position.

Tom had spent time helping Franco establish himself in the role and now intends to ask Franco to return the favor to help get Allan's support.

Sometimes you should push for a decision, sometimes for the opportunity to be introduced to the next audience, sometimes to return at a future date, and sometimes you should stop just before the conclusion, tell the audience this is where we are today and let them work it out. Don't assume the ending is always the same, but it should always end with a call to action; whether explicit or implicit, your request should be obvious.

Allan is clearly an analytical style decision maker. Tom plans to ensure that Franco can effectively deliver the visual story, and Tom also provides a package of background information and analysis that Franco can leave with Allan. Franco's delivery of the visual story will end with a request for Allan to review the details and then to attend the main presentation in Step 6.

TIP: *You don't want a presentation of your visual story to end with polite applause, or even a standing ovation, however good that may make you feel. You want it to end with the audience taking the action you have planned for them. The most important question to ask yourself before each delivery is, "What do I want the audience to do with this?"*

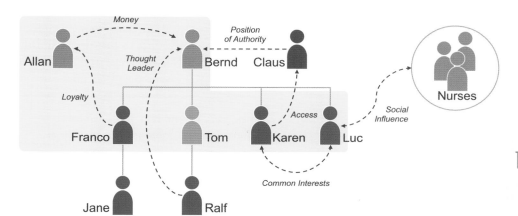

Step 6

This is the final step in Tom's plan. All of the key decision makers and the primary audience will be together for a presentation of the visual story and discussion of the proposal with the aim to have a decision by the end of the meeting. The plan will be delivered over a two-week period with most of the attendees at the presentation having had at least ten days between the first delivery of the visual story and this one.

Bernd will have received the story from Ralf and heard Claus is supportive. Allan will have had a personal presentation, time to review the details, and now is at his third delivery. Franco, Karen, and Luc will have contributed to the story and, through their personal retelling of the story, will have developed a personal support for the story. Tom plans to take the lead when presenting the visual story, but will also bring in one of the senior nurses to have them tell how the story will personally affect the work the nurses do. He will also hand out the posters the nurses received.

The combination of repetition and elapsed time should help to gain commitment, with deliveries across the six steps designed to address the different learning and decision styles. Tom also plans to build on the commitments made by some of the audience during his final presentation by thanking Franco, Karen, Ralf, and Luc for their support over the past two weeks, making visible their commitment to the story's development.

I used to deliver presentations, and then e-mail the materials to the attendees afterward. While learning about the techniques in the CAST process, I tried printing the presentation and handing it out at the end of the session. The handout usually ended up as a block of paper on the attendees' desks. I also started creating and distributing a one-page summary. When I produced these as one-page visual stories, it really made the difference. Not only did they act as a reminder of the events, I often found them stuck on office walls. A constant visual presence is much more of a reminder of a story and commitment than a pile of paper on a desk.

Martin

Delivery Tips

If I am to speak for ten minutes, I need a week for preparation; if fifteen minutes, three days; if half an hour, two days; if an hour, I am ready now.

Woodrow Wilson, 28th President of the United States

Build rehearsals and time for feedback into the delivery plan. Practice, practice, and practice some more, then throw away your notes. Rehearsals are fine for thinking about what you will say and how you will perform, but they should never be confused with the real event. Good storytellers are not just actors remembering lines; they are participants in the telling of the story. Your rehearsals should be about understanding the content of the visual story. Whether it is for a minute or an hour, rehearsals help you tell the story as though it were a treasured memory.

Audiences get bored easily. Good storytellers do not give you time to lose interest. Plan your sequence of deliveries and your sequence of events within a delivery to recapture attention every ten minutes with something different. This may mean moving between theory, practice, and example to cover learning styles, or from images to facts to video. Do whatever it takes to capture the wildly roaming attention of your audience.

Some stories have a timeless quality. The visual stories we describe are more likely to be transient by design and suitable only for the context in which they are created. You may see them referred to long after the activity they were used for as being great examples, but wonder why because they have no relevance to the current situation. Does this make them less valuable? No. The visual story that gets to a decision could be the most valuable one on the planet on the day it is used.

Robert Cialdini is a professor of psychology and author of the book *Influence: Science and Practice*. He and his team have spent many years researching the science of persuasion techniques. Cialdini lists six principles that form the foundation for successful influencing strategies. You were introduced to most of them in the City University Hospital example:

RECIPROCITY People return a favor.

COMMITMENT AND CONSISTENCY When people commit to a decision, they are more likely to take future actions consistent with the decision.

SOCIAL PROOF People do what they see other people doing.

AUTHORITY People will follow the direction of those in authority.

LIKING People are more easily persuaded by people whom they like.

SCARCITY The perception of scarcity can increase demand.

It is much easier to help someone make a decision than to change it after they've decided. Make sure you get there first.

When you deliver the visual story, always think about how to create an opportunity to return to deliver it again, if required, to get commitment.

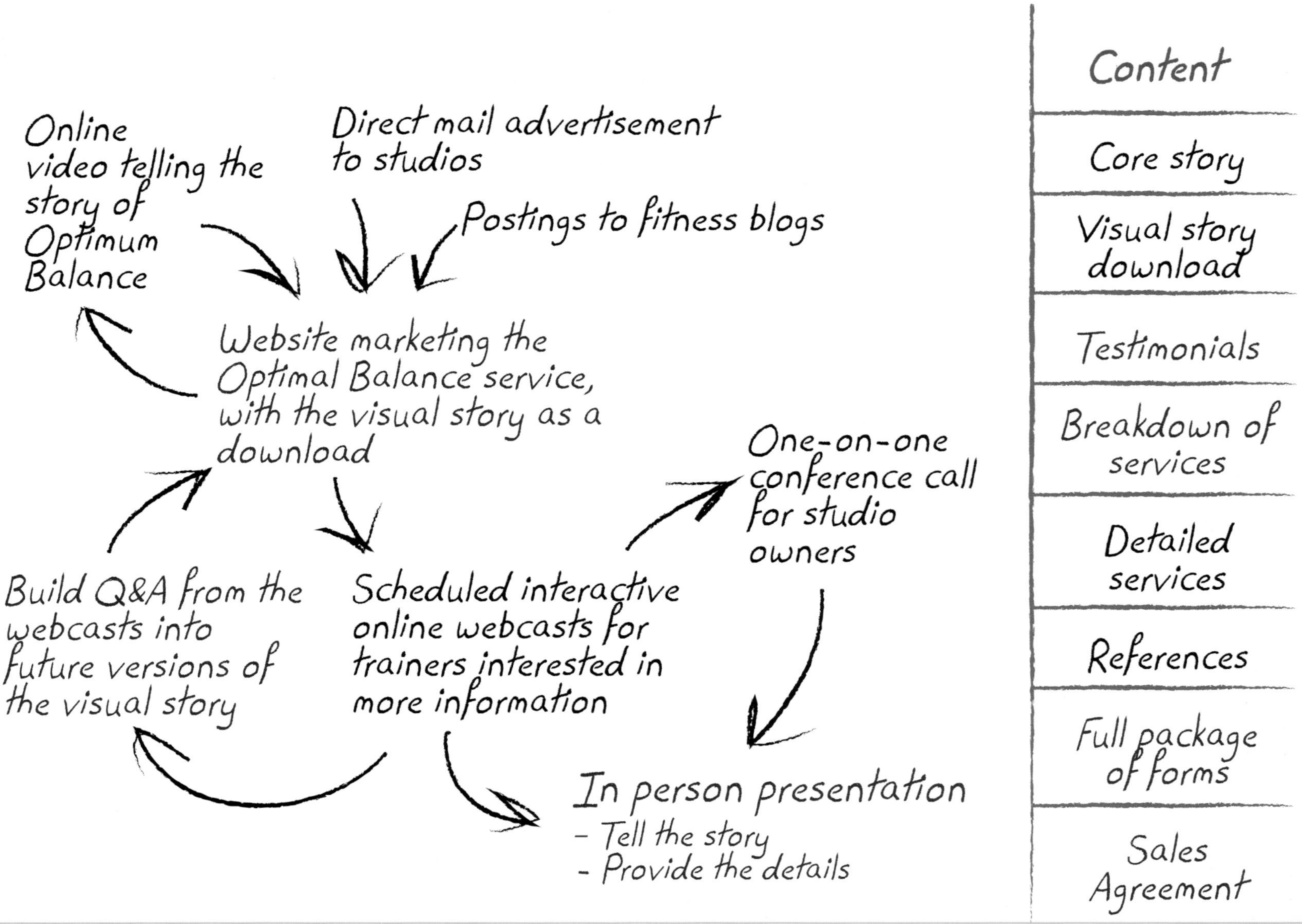

Online video telling the story of Optimum Balance

Direct mail advertisement to studios

Postings to fitness blogs

Website marketing the Optimal Balance service, with the visual story as a download

Build Q&A from the webcasts into future versions of the visual story

Scheduled interactive online webcasts for trainers interested in more information

One-on-one conference call for studio owners

In person presentation
- Tell the story
- Provide the details

Content

Core story

Visual story download

Testimonials

Breakdown of services

Detailed services

References

Full package of forms

Sales Agreement

Marina brought in her husband Nick to plan out how they would repeat the story many times to personal trainers. They sketch out on the whiteboard a mix of online and in-person activities, based around the core story and a visual story download, with a list of supporting documents and materials they need to create.

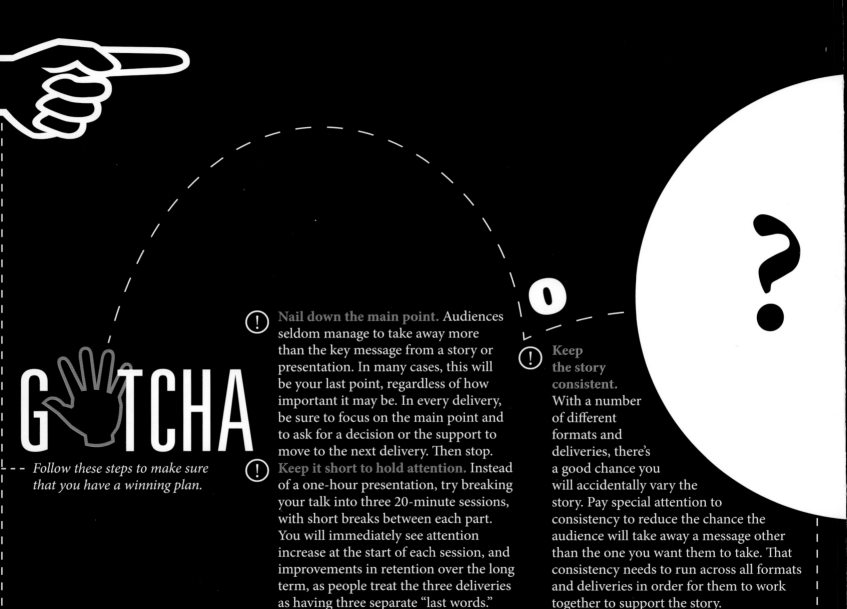

G⬤TCHA

*Follow these steps to make sure
that you have a winning plan.*

(!) **Nail down the main point.** Audiences seldom manage to take away more than the key message from a story or presentation. In many cases, this will be your last point, regardless of how important it may be. In every delivery, be sure to focus on the main point and to ask for a decision or the support to move to the next delivery. Then stop.

(!) **Keep it short to hold attention.** Instead of a one-hour presentation, try breaking your talk into three 20-minute sessions, with short breaks between each part. You will immediately see attention increase at the start of each session, and improvements in retention over the long term, as people treat the three deliveries as having three separate "last words."

(!) **Keep the story consistent.** With a number of different formats and deliveries, there's a good chance you will accidentally vary the story. Pay special attention to consistency to reduce the chance the audience will take away a message other than the one you want them to take. That consistency needs to run across all formats and deliveries in order for them to work together to support the story.

☑ Build a plan to involve the audience and focus on reaching the key decision makers.

☑ Accommodate the learning and decision styles of your audience in the delivery plan.

☑ Know the route to the people who will make the decision. If you cannot get to the decision maker directly, chart a path through others who can introduce you or tell the story for you.

☑ Consider variations of the visual story in different formats and delivery styles, including the specific sense of urgency relative to the audience in each delivery.

☑ Plan the amount of repetition and variations required to gain commitment.

☑ Good stories can be destroyed by bad presenters. Decide who gets to tell the story and make sure they know how to tell it.

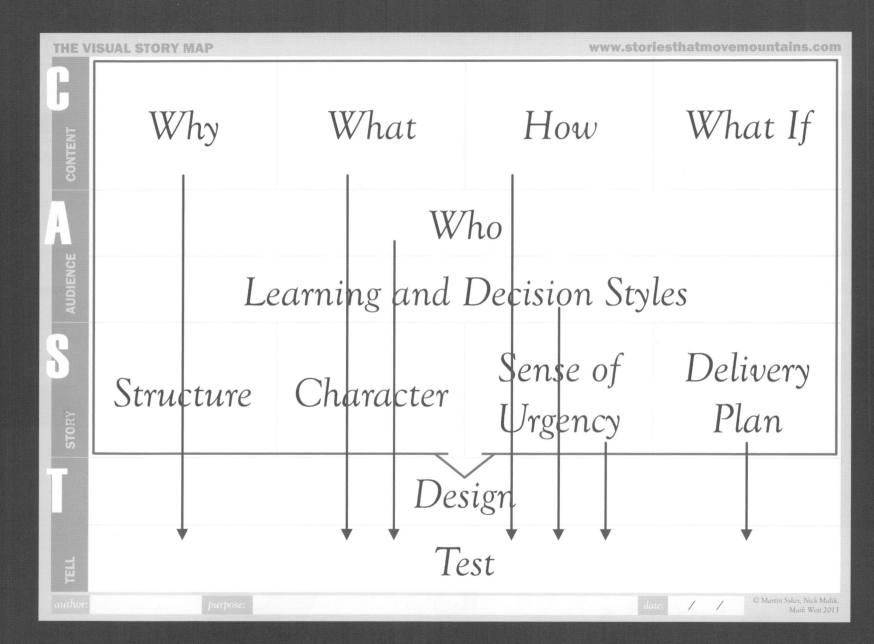

TELL

Design

14

Chartjunk flows from the premise that audiences can be charmed, distracted or fooled by means of content-free misdirection: garish colors, designer colors, corny clip-art, generic decoration, phony dimensionality.

—*Edward Tufte, writer on information design, statistician and professor emeritus of political science, statistics, and computer science at Yale University*

Every block of stone has a statue inside it, and it is the task of the sculptor to discover it.

—*Michelangelo, Italian Renaissance sculptor, painter, and architect*

Death to the drop shadow! May software tools and pre-built effects only be secondary to concepts, ideas, data and ultimately… information.

—*Mark D. West, M.A.*

Intentional Design

It's now time to start using the content to build the visual story. As the arrows in the Visual Story Map image indicate, everything you've been through so far leads to the design process. In this chapter, we show you how to create visual elements and combine them in compelling ways so that they can be viewed and understood in a variety of formats. In previous chapters, we asked you to apply laser-focus on the critical elements; that will not change now. In this chapter, we want you to understand that every line, color, and word should be chosen with equal care, and nothing should be put into the visual or written content that doesn't directly and *intentionally* contribute to the understanding of the story.

A two-hour movie without many special effects will today consume a budget of tens of millions of dollars. The lowest-cost reality TV show, with no expensive actors or scriptwriters will cost fifty thousand dollars per episode. They keep the attention of the audience for an hour or two, but the price is high. Most business presentations have a fairly minimal budget, yet have the same challenge. So what are you going to do to keep the audience's attention for the typical 30- or 60-minute presentation?

We have mentioned Steve Jobs a number of times. He became a master of the art of presentation, using heroes and villains, great visuals, and strong narrative. Science has proven what the great presenters like Steve Jobs know intuitively, that people get bored easily. Steve's presentations mixed up different formats, with left- and right-brain stimulation to keep the audience's interest. Whether you're designing for a poster, a presentation, or a whiteboard discussion, it's now time to consider the many different ways in which you can give your story a rich and varied life. Assuming you have solid content and a good visual story, you have no limit on the number of ways you can use it.

Do not expect to be working while reading this chapter. We recommend you read it thoroughly first because some topics specifically reinforce others. Unless you are a designer you might want to read it twice before you start to design.

To make things simpler, we break the design process into five steps:

1. FORMAT Visual Stories can be presented in many different formats. They can appear as a poster, a one-page visualization, a slide deck, a video, or in a number of other formats. We focus on the one-page visualization because it is a root from which many other formats can be quickly derived, but you can choose to start with any format that fits your delivery plan.

2. IDEATION Here you will rapidly move from the blank page to some content you can evaluate, edit, and filter. You will create many ideas and put them side by side to find the ones that work.

3. COMPOSITION Composing on a page in a particular format means deciding which content to include, and which to leave out to convey your message. Content that is not included visually may still be relevant, but may not be the most effective approach for a particular format. Each format has limitations that mean some content should be included and some should be left out. Just because the content is not included visually doesn't mean it's missing from the story; it's just not a part of that particular format.

4. CONTENT CODING Icons, colors, and positioning all convey some meaning. Choices here can subconsciously lead your audience to a decision, or create a mental roadblock the audience must break through to receive your message.

5. WRITING Visual stories are not just about the visuals. For any format, you must create the right language to accompany the visuals, and decide whether it's to be conveyed aloud or as text to be read by the audience.

Most people really appreciate only the final version (but be proud of your first draft — it was necessary). The final draft is, after all, what we want the audience to see. All of the hard work that went into getting to the end result will be carefully hidden from them. But the effort is necessary, and you'll see the difference in the result. Every day we are bombarded with visually polished, but poorly thought through messages. When the audience finds a story with polish *and* content, the response is noticeably stronger.

This chapter is about the visual aspects of your story and its presentation. In some situations, it may make sense to hire a designer to help you at this step. Do not shy away from this possibility, but always provide them with a story to work with, not just a pile of data! Data must ultimately become actionable information for the decision maker in your audience.

Mark

One of the most profound experiences I've had as a designer was in helping to create this book from the *beginning*. When passing the job along to someone else, the designer has most likely not had this advantage. Making a story "pretty" is one thing, but making a story more profound and better understood through visuals is another. Even at this stage in the process, your story can change for the better, through how the visuals communicate your vision. Why is your story more profound? Because the visuals play a major role in ensuring that your audience will *care* about your message.

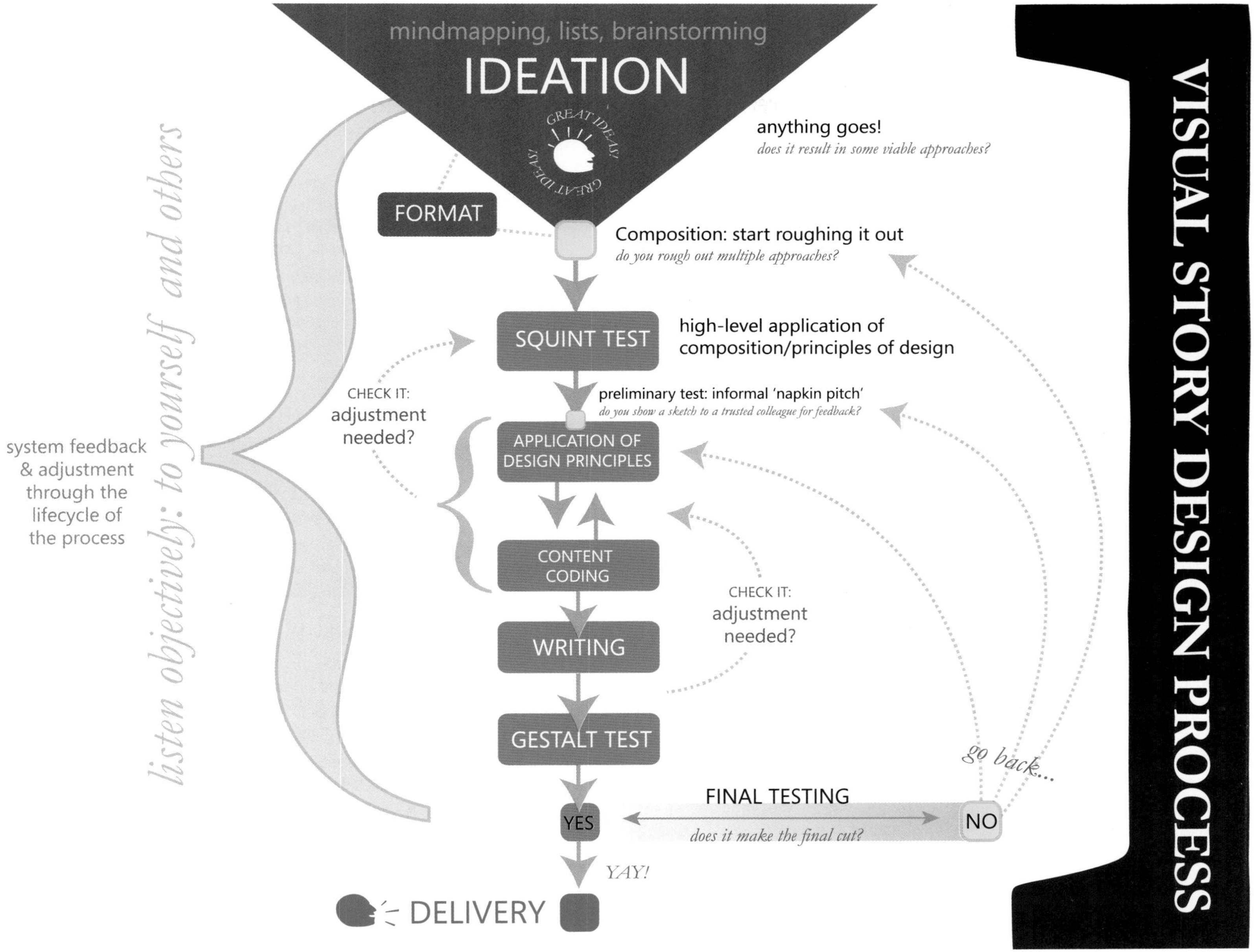

mindmapping, lists, brainstorming
IDEATION
GREAT IDEAS!
GREAT IDEAS!
anything goes!
does it result in some viable approaches?
FORMAT
Composition: start roughing it out
do you rough out multiple approaches?
SQUINT TEST
high-level application of composition/principles of design
preliminary test: informal 'napkin pitch'
do you show a sketch to a trusted colleague for feedback?
CHECK IT: adjustment needed?
APPLICATION OF DESIGN PRINCIPLES
CONTENT CODING
CHECK IT: adjustment needed?
WRITING
GESTALT TEST
go back...
FINAL TESTING
YES
NO
does it make the final cut?
YAY!
DELIVERY
system feedback & adjustment through the lifecycle of the process
listen objectively: to yourself and others
VISUAL STORY DESIGN PROCESS

Many Formats, One Root

You can use many different formats to present a visual story. We discussed these in Chapter 13 on delivery planning, and you've already identified at least one format you need to create for your story.

No matter which formats you're going to create to present your story, and you may have many, START BY CREATING A ONE-PAGE VISUAL STORY AS A RICH PICTURE, combining images and text in a concise presentation. Consider this your resource or *tree* that has all the fruit you'll need to pick at various times. The table on the right presents a summary of the format types and explains how each is related to the one-page visual story format.

Each format has a different balance between the spoken, written, and visual content. You may also vary the balance of data to emotional content, or abstract your ideas to simple single themes to fit the different audiences that will receive each format. Your choice of formats may impact your ability to deliver the story, or you can have it read or delivered by another person. For example, a poster or an infographic can go viral through social media, whereas a presentation needs someone to deliver it.

ONE ROOT

Design the one-page visual story well, and the rest will follow. The compositions, content coding, and wording from the one-page visual story can provide consistency across all the formats you choose to create. In the City University Hospital example at the end of this chapter we show the decisions Tom made when selecting the formats for his story.

Poster	One large visual, very similar to the one-page visual story. This combines images and text, often in a structure that reflects the plot of the story, based around the core characters. More text may be required than you would normally include on a one-page visual story to allow the audience to follow all the details.
Infographic	A one-page view similar to a poster, but oriented around a visualization of one or more data sets in the story and with less emotive content. This is more suitable for the directive and analytical decision styles or the conceptual learning style.
Presentation slides	A series of slides, usually projected to an audience, with limited pictures, text, charts, and graphics on each slide, structured for a logical flow through the story. This is derived from the one-page visual story by taking small logical groups and structuring onto slides.
Storyboard / Comic	A series of images, with a minimum of words, usually designed to flow from image to image in a time sequence. This is derived from the one-page visual story by taking small sequences from the storyline. It also can introduce an element of humor and style to the visual approach to widen opportunities for storytelling.
Animation / Video	An extension of the storyboard concept, but with animation or live action to convey the content. Usually with spoken rather than written content.
Article / Report	Composed mainly of written sections, with charts and images drawn from the one-page visual story as support. Start with the one-page visual story to structure the composition into sections to follow the flow of the story and logical relationships.
Whiteboard	This may start with a blank whiteboard (flipchart or even a napkin), but that doesn't mean there's no preparation. You can slowly re-create the one-page visual story on the whiteboard, telling the story as you draw the visualization.
Spoken word	There may not be any visual or written components, but as with the whiteboard, the one-page visual story provides the structure for you to tell the story. Many times, we've seen presenters use a one-page visual story as the prompt to allow them to simply talk through the story.

The Infographic

Today, the use of infographics has become widespread in order to make factual information more attractive to readers and easier to digest. We shouldn't be led to believe that the infographic is a new idea, regardless of how fashionable it has become. The graphic below, drawn by Charles Joseph Minard in 1861, depicts Napoleon's disastrous march to and from Russia in 1812–1813. The light colored line shows Napoleon's march to Moscow, and the black line shows the army's return, with the dramatically narrowing thickness showing the diminishing size of his army as it moved from place to place. In 1999, Martin was creating complex visualizations and came across this image. The simple way this graphic communicates so many dimensions of information and supports the telling of a great story created the seed from which the ideas in this book grew.

The techniques for the design of a visual story have a lot in common with the techniques used for modern infographics. The primary difference is that *we are focused on creating a story to influence an audience to change,* not just an educational or informative representation of data. Modern infographics give the audience a chance to enter the story at different places, and develop their own meaning as they review the information.

It is worth studying infographics to gain sources of inspiration, to spot patterns and designs that can be reused, and for the creation of the one-page visual story. A number of compilations of infographics are available on the Internet. Constantly updating collections can be found at http://visual.ly and http://flowingdata.com. Just remember that most of these infographics are created to present data, not to communicate a visual story, and not to lead the audience into making a decision.

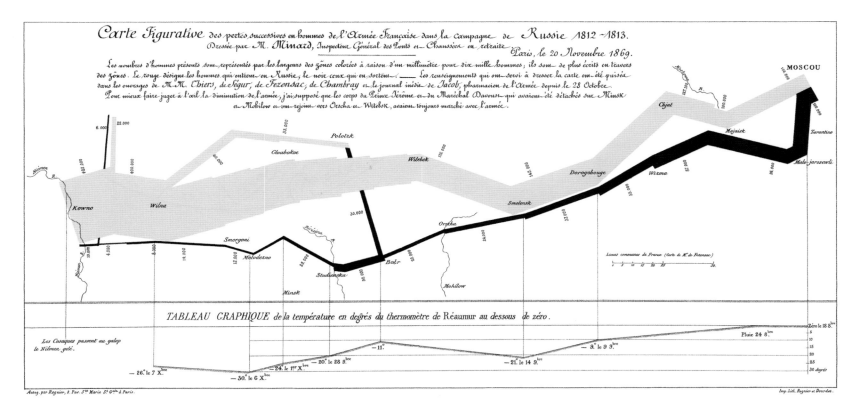

Ideation

Ideation is the process of forming ideas. It represents the brainstorming of the individual or group, in a "no-holds-barred" stream of creative consciousness to consider all that is possible. The blank page is the mind-killer. Very little else comes so close to halting the creative process. Some design teachers will suggest you draw a first line on the page simply to break the spell and get started.

You have a lot of content to start the ideation process. Many people will start with the story structure identified in Chapter 10 to decide on an overall layout. For example, if you chose *The Quest*, you might start laying out a journey and a set of ordeals on the page (refer to Chapter 10 to review the main stages in the story structure for ideas). You might also work with the characters you identified in Chapter 11 to create focal points on the page for the character interactions.

The best way to avoid being stuck in front of a blank page is by releasing all judgment on visual ideas. The core of productive ideation expands outward through the urgency of free association. Mindmapping is one way people like designers generate many ideas quickly. Mindmapping qualifies your intentions and makes the story real as you document all that's possible in an organic and very "human" way. *Remember that the only reason you're mindmapping is to "map" your content to corresponding visuals and see what's possible.*

it might get messy!

In the Ideation phase, **document** your ideas for visual approaches. It's like musicians humming an idea for a song into a recorder the moment they awaken from a dream, before it vanishes into the ether, never to be heard again.

Jot down everything that comes to mind without analysis. Here you will have the chance to draw relationships across concepts as untapped ideas are revealed. Often this approach also works well with small teams working together on the same map collaboratively.

Start by **defining** a central word or concept. Think quickly as you draw a series of bubbles with words inside them. Then **draw relationships.** Write down and connect concepts based on what those words and relationships inspire in you intuitively. Keep moving. Think fast. Break boundaries, but stay objective, and avoid judging your ideas.

As the map grows, move toward slightly deeper analysis looking for patterns, repetition, and relationships across words and concepts. Be observant, making marks and color coding items if helpful to differentiate priorities. Try to have fun and make this process your own.

And here's the tension of the push and pull: Ideally, you need to feel

like you *shorten* your time during the ideation process in some places, but *lengthen* the process in other places. Both before and after your mapping session, allow some time in your schedule to let ideas percolate and eventually come to the surface. Not only can we write songs in our dreams, but we also can develop existing ideas subconsciously while doing other things, such as living our lives.

As you do more and more designing, you'll get better at developing concepts and ideas.

Alex F. Osborn, in his book *Applied Imagination: Principles and Procedures of Creative Problem-Solving,* broke the process into the following:

- **Orientation:** Poking at the visual problem.

- **Preparation:** Gathering pertinent data.

- **Analysis:** Breaking down the relevant material.

- **Ideation:** Piling up alternatives by way of ideas.

- **Incubation/percolation:** Walk away for a while and go about your day, often inviting illumination.

- **Synthesis:** Putting the pieces together by looking through the resultant list and absorbing the ideas into your subconscious mind.

- **Evaluation:** Judging the resultant ideas; using your judgment and intuition to funnel the ideas down to a favored few. Some people seek feedback only at this point, from a few trusted others.

Where are we going with this?

Over time, you will develop a method for your ideation that will most likely have to stay flexible but that will nonetheless exist to drive the visual approach for your story. Create some order for the creative chaos that needs to exist in this part of your process.

ITERATION ⟷ ITERATION

As you build up the layout on the page, the core of your content will come from the information, relationships, and timeline defined in the Why-What-How timeline from Chapter 6. Remember to also include the options and alternatives you identified in Chapter 7.

In Chapter 9, you identified the balance needed in your story between learning and decision styles. Use this now to help allocate proportions for educational content and recommendations. Drill deeper into the specific learning and decision styles to consider the balance between material that is abstract or concrete, data driven or emotive, following a single logical flow or multiple threads.

Now it's time to jump into some design lessons!

Note: Most of the lessons can be applied equally well to all visualizations, not just the one-page visual story.

Know that when it comes to composition and design, the variables are sometimes difficult to separate, but you do need to get beyond bullet points in your presentation. You will start to see how the big picture concepts relate to the details, creating a bit of a "push and pull" as you jump between these when you examine your layout. It's a strong skill to cultivate — so make the jump often. After reviewing this chapter, you may find yourself frequently moving between the Squint Test, Content Coding, and the Gestalt Test, all of which you will learn about shortly. When it comes to visual stories, apply the "less is more" concept as often as possible, especially since every inch of visual space will often be spoken for when considering something as short as a one-page visual story format.

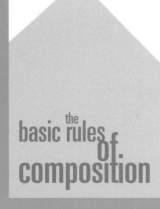

LESSON

1

the
basic rules
of
composition

A *drawing should have no unnecessary lines and a machine no unnecessary parts.*
William Strunk Jr., Professor of English at Cornell University and author of
The Elements of Style

Develop an approach of "less is more." It's paradoxical how it takes more time to strip things away and end up with less, than to create it in the first place. Doing this is hard, but well worth the time to focus your message. Like Michelangelo revealing beauty from a block of stone: The essence of your message is waiting to be revealed.

Let the format help to dictate what content you pull from your relatively full bag of ideas. Don't clutter the focus of your communication with too many points. Pick the content to fit the format. There is no standard for the amount of content or level of detail, but question every piece you include. It's your judgment call, based on what you know about your audience.

Insert textual content here

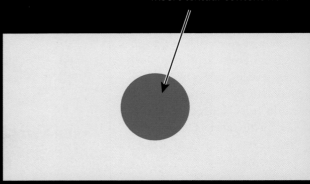

Without more formalized content around it, the emptiness (less) creates a focus on what's important (more)... mind you, this is an exaggeration.

Use the **"rule of three."** Three is a powerful concept, in writing, photography, typefaces on a page, and even gardening. Four men rarely walk into a bar, it's usually three. Two people in a relationship are common; three make for a more interesting dynamic. If you have ten points to communicate, it's unlikely the audience will remember them. Work on three they will remember and leave the rest to further reading.

Rhythm and flow are established through some sort of underlying structure, like an organizational grid — the *scaffolding* or foundation of your layout. This will allow you a basic way to align elements to other elements, balancing the compositional elements by organizing the page as though it were a series of shapes, or at least rows and margins and columns. Use tools like columns, grids, and rulers in your software program of choice, and adjust (or break) from the grid as needed to make sure things intuitively "feel" balanced.

Timothy Samara in his book *Design Elements: A Graphic Style Manual* described **symmetry** as the ultimate evil. Unless you have a strong argument for making the arrangements of design elements equal in all directions, go with a more dynamic approach that inspires movement and navigation across your visuals. Is it possible for the dynamic changes you are depicting to be perfectly balanced? Maybe, but not likely, because processes are often unpredictable, dynamic, and include unintended consequences. They evolve and grow in not-so-ordered and organic ways. Your arrangement of elements should reflect that.

Now that you've gathered all your content, you're at a pivotal moment — it's time to do what I'm doing right now as I write this:

Edit.

Edit.

EDIT!

Convince your decision-makers with focused evidence.

The **Squint Test** is about getting the overall *shape of the data* nailed down right at the beginning. By literally squinting your eyes and taking an objective step back, you reduce the detail and should be able to get a clearer look at how the data is moving across the page. It helps to identify and reveal higher-level relationships that unify your one-page visual story. The Squint Test is most effective for icons, colors, shapes, and text on printed pages, as a deeper level of recognition is required for moving or static representations like comics, films or animation. You must tie variables like the data, people, tools, concepts, and ideas together with processes so they are coherent and visible. Basically, you need to ask: Where are they going, what are they doing, and what's happening here? Sketch it out on a napkin or sketchpad . . . let things get messy. It's not meant to be too refined yet.

Establish the **visual priority.** What's your visual goal and what do you want your audience to see first? Literally, squint your eyes and ask these questions. From a priority standpoint, do content priorities and visual priorities match? Do you see the start of a process or description in your sketch? What's worthy of audience attention and in what order? Emphasis can be created through the size of elements, their relation to the amount of negative space (that is, a small circle in a sea of whitespace), and also to the amount and position of color (large amounts of maroon in the upper part of a composition might create some tension).

conduct squint tests

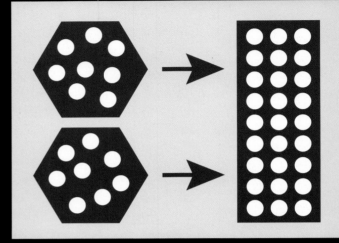

from chaotic groups to alignment

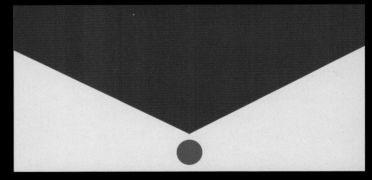

tension point reaching a solution?

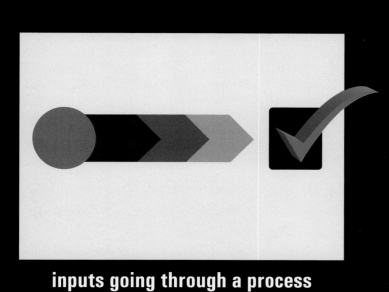

inputs going through a process and creating a deliverable

As you arrange your elements, your final solution will provide something for both the presenter and the audience to talk about, set a foundational context for discussion, and can create a sense of community around the topics your graphic addresses. Lay out the high-level data and the back-story first, before diving into the details. Think of this as a layout version of how many of us were taught to write reports at school, with the sequence of introduction, body, and conclusion.

At this stage you're testing how the audience will approach the layout and start to understand it. You are aiming to allow the viewer to go beyond the typical spoon-fed presentation sequence of slide bullets, and move toward a meaningful relationship with the information. Every person in your audience should have the opportunity to enter your graphic interpretation of the data in their own way and to create meaningful associations in ways that they can individually relate to. The graphical representation must lead toward the big decisions that need to be made, and this often starts by considering the *shape* of the data on the page. Try to keep all your choices for the overall shape intentional and utilitarian, with success determined by the use of only what is needed to direct the attention through the evidence to the final decision.

Direct your audience by convincing your decision-makers with "shaped" evidence.

The following paragraphs address some of the standard devices designers employ when they create page elements and arrange those elements on the page.

Never underestimate the power of a **line**. The movement of a line, and the shapes it may surround or engulf, will create responses that help determine your sense or feeling of the relevant area of your visual story. If the Squint Test shapes the overall flow of the floor plan, the line determines the details of what's happening on the ground floor and how we compare one detail to another. The line creates feeling, flow, and movement. A single jagged line simply "feels" different than a wavy line and one line does not quite move with the same force of three parallel lines: A thick-to-thin line is much more dynamic than any single weight line.

When used together, lines create **forms** (also known as *shapes*), and even the absence of a shape can be perceived as one. Be very aware of placement, because the intimate relationship between a shape that you've created and an empty area called *negative space* can actually be perceived as a *positive space* or another shape by your audience. What's *there* is just as important as what's *not there*. This applies to individual details as well as the overall flow in the Squint Test.

Extending upon negative space, **shapes** are perceived, contrasted, and compared by not only the quality of the shape itself (a square versus a triangle), but also by the **positional relationship** of those shapes to others (five squares relatively close to each other are perceived as a "group").

Even the nature of the line (a wavy double line and a jagged single line) could indicate different meanings.

One of the most important tools you can use in your designing is showing the differences, or **contrasts**, between things. Contrasts and similarities shape our understanding and how we classify the elements on the page. Simply put, *contrast = change*. Take two squares and make the second one larger (size contrast), or round-off the edges (line contrast), or change the color (color contrast). In these cases you always start with the reference of one object and then have a similar one altered to show the change.

Design principles allow your audience to identify the minute details of your problem and to have a chance to *feel* the details, moving from the high-level flow of information to the details. Thus, you can balance the aesthetic of *form* with the utility of *function* without employing your favorite special effect or describing things in bullet points.

scale = change = difference = drama = effect

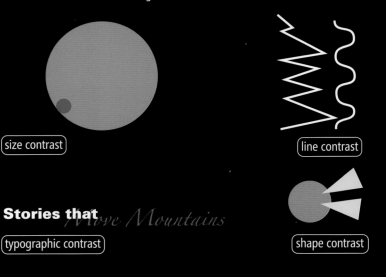

size contrast

line contrast

Stories that *Move Mountains*

typographic contrast

shape contrast

design principles

this is the difference that changes the weight & strength of a font

Typefaces feel "heavier" due to their "X-height" proportions in relation to the other letters The less difference in X-height to other letters, the heavier the font, Helvetica is a great example.

Although each row below matches point sizes, compare their different proportions, weight, stroke width, legibility, 'feel' and size differences

Helvetica   Garamond   Rockwell   **Bodoni Bd BT**

a serif!

thick-to-thin stroke contrast

Use **letterforms** thoughtfully. When you select a typeface in any software program, you have the opportunity to play with the boundaries of what is seen (shape) and what is read (character). Typography involves the art of selecting a typeface that affects the voice of your visual story, that creates association for the audience, and that creates something that is not only readable but that is also a series of perceived shapes. Sometimes you may not even want the text to be readable! There are no boundaries here. Just make it intentional, and know the basic rules you're choosing to break.

IMPACT *script*

Typefaces have many different classifications. We'll address one of the most basic classification schemes: serif and sans serif.

Serifs — those little extensions on the ends of letters — affect feeling and flow from one word to the next. Just like the shapes previously discussed, a modern serif font with squared serifs like Rockwell Extra Bold feels different (stronger, modern, sturdy) than an older italic serif font like Goudy Italic (venerable, older).

Do a little research work and experimentation with your typefaces before you do too much design work. Print a sampling of all your typefaces, noting the differences in weight and how those pesky serifs allow for easier reading from page to page. Also look for the ones without serifs — *sans* literally means without. Sans serifs are a bit more modern feeling, many with more consistent width strokes. They hold more weight from page to page, and do not flow as well in blocks of text, which explains why many textbooks and longer writings don't use them.

Select a typeface, adjust its size, typestyle (for example, bold, italic, regular), and spacing (kerning and tracking); and then contrast it to the typeface next to it by changing the choice of color, size and typeface. Put a bold sans serif next to a thin script: the two vastly different and contrasting typefaces will create a "wow" moment that makes it clear there is a change going on between those two elements. Want to create some drama and impact? Well, you could use the Impact sans serif typeface, I suppose. Regardless, choice of typefaces can create a subtle or marked difference in perception. A tremendous amount of work is out there on typography, but it's not considered as often as it should be. To summarize, typography involves the art of using typefaces as text and letterforms, allowing for ease of reading, or for style, effect, ornamentation, or illustration

SUBSTITUTION

Choose **colors** based on hue (color in the visible color spectrum), saturation (vibrancy), and value (tint or shade for lightness or darkness). Also consider that warm colors (red, orange, and yellow) tend to be seen first because they appear to advance toward you, and cool colors (blue and green) appear to recede. Different amounts of warm and cool will, of course, vary the intended effect, and color will quickly create focal points for the viewer when used to extreme, especially when opposite colors of the color wheel (complements) of equal saturation are chosen. The position of the color on the page will also direct eyes through the composition, so after fine-tuning your choice of color, the amount and position are critical to a compositional *sense of rhythm*.

Warm colors attract attention, don't assume red is always best

Explanatory text of the "problem" is separated by a "messy" uneven line

Blue is used as a "resting" point to calm the viewer. Cool greens and blues work well for this.

Warm colors also signal "alarm" or caution... "the pain."

Gray for the background, to avoid getting in the way of potential color coding. Not only do the colors used work as notated, but choose appropriately, based on the "coding" of your audience. Keep an eye on saturation.

What's going on?

insert text here
insert text here
insert text here
insert text here
insert text here
insert text here
insert text here
insert text here
insert text here

insert text here
insert text here
insert text here
insert text here
insert text here
insert text here
insert text here
insert text here
insert text here

Why it's happening

insert text here
insert text here
insert text here
insert text here
insert text here

Text gets larger, coming forward to bring movement and depth to the composition.

Also assisting the rhythm and flow of the composition is the orange line; note the variation in line weight to create a more dynamic visual. An arrow could be used here, but this can often be a more interesting approach.

BLUE
UK/US: calming, peace, masculinity, conservative, corporate, gentleness, wisdom, inspiration
CHINA: immortality, femininity
RUSSIA: loyalty, honesty, faultlessness, wisdom

PURPLE
UK/US: royalty, spirituality, wealth, fame, honor, arrogance, dignity
JAPAN: privilege, wealth
BRAZIL: death and mourning

RED
UK/US: energy, excitement, love, passion, warning, stop, anger, aggression, power, danger, strength
CHINA: good luck, celebration, ceremonial and festive color
RUSSIA: Bolsheviks and Communism

YELLOW
UK/US: imagination, energy, optimism, happiness, honor
CHINA: sacred, imperial, royalty, honor, masculinity
GREECE: sadness

Complementary
[opposite on the color wheel]

Harmonious/Analogous
[next to each other on the color wheel]

Triadic
[equally spaced on the color wheel in a triangular formation]

At the very least, it's safe to say that color is a very complex beast. Different color choices mean different things to different people at different times. People and cultures respond differently, create personal associations, and have emotional responses and feelings toward color.

Color associations include

- Object and environment association (for example, blue as water, green as grass).

- Combinations: Red and green = Christmas season; red, white, and blue = freedom and the American flag.

- Conceptual association: Red as fire or hot temperatures.

- Cultural association: The connotations of colors vary widely across countries — for example, white is seen as purity in the U.S. but as death or mourning in parts of Asia. The color infographic provides a deeper dive into the different meanings color can have.

A few years ago Mark had a student put a vibrant green pistol on a vibrant red field for a color project. It "attacked the senses" to prove a point, literally burning the retinas in a very visceral way, as it proved a point in both content and visual form! That said, in most cases, you don't want to attack the senses with lots of strong colors; rather, you may want to include smaller amounts of stronger colors in your palette for creating emphasis in your composition.

Colors often work best in *threes*, so consider using a lighter color for background and darker or more vibrant colors for the other two. Grays or lighter and darker variations of your chosen three will work well because less prominent colors will not get in the way of what you're emphasizing — with gray being the best choice if you need a solid color that's not associated with any of your color coding.

The result? Cohesion and calming, as opposed to jumbled and jarring. Stay consistent in your color use, especially if you create your story in many different formats. This keeps you within a branded approach that will reinforce your topic. Think about how companies choose the right typefaces, shapes, colors, and symbols to be consistently represented. Doing so sends the right message.

design principles

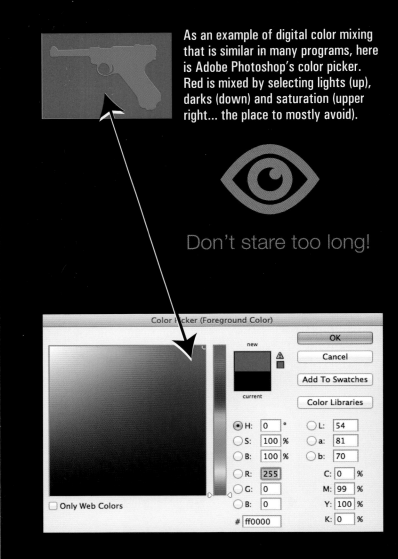

As an example of digital color mixing that is similar in many programs, here is Adobe Photoshop's color picker. Red is mixed by selecting lights (up), darks (down) and saturation (upper right... the place to mostly avoid).

Don't stare too long!

The difference between green and blue, or even between green and red, can be indistinguishable to some people. You can try to find out if some members of your audience are colorblind, or just assume that some of your audience may be and avoid using colors that can be confused by the audience to have different meanings. We could write page after page about the importance of choosing color carefully, but we'll save you from that with this real-world example: Martin is color blind. One day while writing the book, his wife, Jules, stopped him to point out his socks were different. To Martin they are identical. Now, imagine what would happen if you were to use colors like this to mean very different things in your visual layout? How many people in your audience would not get the point?

Convince your decision-makers with color choices that clarify and support your evidence.

Content Coding

Now it's time to focus on time for you to visually communicating the data in the best way possible — what devices, such as photos or cartoons, will you use? (If publishing, always make sure you have permission to use any sourced content.) How can you visually represent the various "players" in your story? Chances are, you're showing some combination of people, processes, and deliverables — or inputs, outputs, and what happens in between.

For example, if you have a process, how will you communicate an outcome at the end of the process? Use the visual device checklist on the following pages to clarify how to get your *visual voice* heard.

What is the best way for your audience to understand what you are trying to say? Content coding and formatting of your layout will solidify your message. Presenting certain kinds of information may not be possible in limited spaces, so consider that fact carefully as you determine your choices, based on your understanding of your audience.

LESSON
4

All of these coding elements will create a type of *coding system.* When taken together, they will not only solidify your message, but when used correctly, they will give your audience multiple ways to understand the depth of the information being communicated, as well as the data it comes from: Data creates *information,* which is the meaning that can bring the audience to action.

Semiotics, the study of signs and symbols, is a fascinating area. In talking about icons, you could use the word *fire* or a picture or illustration of fire. Or you could do something less obvious — for example, by signifying or subtly suggesting *fire* by the use of *smoke.* What will engage your audience the most while also making the coding clear to them?

choosing the code

☐ LIMITED USE OF BULLET POINTS. Have you attempted to avoid the typical use of bullets in your presentation? Is the audience listening to you first and then using your presentation to deepen their understanding? Remember that to you, your presentation is an index card to keep your story on track, but to your audience, it's a way to connect with you and your message. Make it interactive and respond to your audience in real time, without an overscripted plan.

☐ INTENTIONAL ICON AND SYMBOL CHOICES. Are your graphics achieving optimal effect in front of your audience? Icons can be explicit and/or pictorial or implicit and/or metaphorical. Whether it's a more obvious visual or an implicit but thought-provoking one, an icon stands for something, such as a stakeholder or decision-maker — and a lot of what it stands for has to do with what has already been accepted by your target audience or the world at large.

☐ PHOTOGRAPHS, FOR CONTENT AND COLOR. A black and white (or colored) picture says a thousand words, but it also provides a different way for learning than reading does. When appropriate, select images to tell a story by first *showing* the experience and then describing it in words.

VISUAL DEVICE CHECKLIST

[?] **USE OF A VISUAL HOOK.** A visual hook enables you to use a central graphic that acts as the foundational core for all your elements. This approach eliminates the need for text and/or additional support graphics that might be needed for a data-heavy graphic. The hook is like the chorus in your favorite song that won't leave your brain, and it's what makes the viewer exclaim, "Aha!" Make this hook the focal point of your design whenever possible. You can grab attention and improve memorability by placing the hook either at the center or at the very end of the infographic

[?] **HARNESS THE EXPLODED OR DIMENSIONAL VIEW WHEN APPROPRIATE.** This is a way to call out the detail in a high-level process and a way to show what's going on in there. Icons may accomplish this purpose fine, but sometimes zoomed-in detail or a different angle or a 3D approach brings the data to light.

[?] **LEAD THE EYES WITH MOVEMENT DEVICES.** How can you be explicit about depicting processes or movement? Use arrows, lines, clustering, and color to pull your audience across the graphic.

[?] **BRING HUMOR AND STYLE THROUGH CARTOONS, ILLUSTRATIONS, AND LINE DRAWINGS.** Use these special techniques to create something memorable through humor and the style of the artist.

It's time to accessorize: Use your running shoes to quickly move far away and your microscope to zoom in fast. Before you know it, you're back at the beginning, at the perception of the whole! This is what we refer to as the Gestalt Test. We started with the Squint Test and the higher-level flow, and we end up coming back to those concepts. Designers, painters, sculptors, artisans, and photographers are all constantly shifting visual gears, moving from the parts to the whole. As you create your design you must do the same.

Gestalt and visual psychology principles have numerous applications, many of which we've addressed in various direct or indirect ways in this chapter. A key takeaway of the approach is how you perceive the *totality of elements* on a page. They can't always be measured objectively, but they can always be experienced subjectively. While the Squint Test looks at the flow of the information, the closely related "Gestalt of it all" is how the pieces come together to create the whole.

Objectively and systemically, evaluate the effects of the whole layout as much as possible, but don't spend too much time tweaking. Get your work into the testing phase quickly. You will probably have more changes to make after testing so test early, before you become too fixed on your ideas.

putting it all together with the Gestalt test

Gestalt is how all the relevant pieces of the content come together to equal or create something much more than the simple sum of the parts . . . your intended message. The space between the pieces is as important as the combination of the parts. It's rare to use all the visual devices in a single design. If you have used too much information your message may be cluttered. Are you trying to use too many elements and say the same thing too many times, in too many different ways? Sometimes using both a symbol and a corresponding word is too much; other times without both, it's not enough.

When objectively reviewing your design, attempt to first make design changes from the level of how the whole is perceived. Editing can occur at any point in the process, and the process here is not always linear — it's curved, organic, systemic, and iterative. This means that any part of the process can feed into important design changes and layout adjustments.

Keep the items on this list in mind as you complete this lesson. At the root of the remaining topics in the list is the need to "cut out" as much visual content as possible to avoid anything getting between the audience and the point you are making. Just keep saying to yourself "less is more," and challenge every pixel or drop of ink to make a deliberate and intentional contribution to the message.

putting it all together with the Gestalt test

VISUAL DEVICE CHECKLIST

[?] **DIRECTLY DESIGNATE COLORS IN YOUR LAYOUT.**
Be direct and to the point with your audience. Instead of using a legend or key to indicate what colors mean, use colors as direct references in the design, creating meaning that is in context — for example, you might use one color for the text of a label, the fill in a chart, and the color of an icon when they all have the same meaning, and be careful not to use that color for any other meaning.

[?] **INTELLIGENCE.** In general, cater to the intelligence of your audience and know that you will also be discussing your visuals with them. Sometimes too much explanation in a visual can seem like talking down to your audience. Assume that they are intelligent and during your presentation, be prepared to explain when needed.

[?] **USE THE HUMAN FACE FOR PERSONALIZED CONNECTION.**
Just how important is the human connection? Humans have grown quite adept at spotting the faces of other humans and animals, so using a human face can be a great way to create memorability. We can extract facial detail more than almost anything else from clutter, and we can even see faces where there are none!

VISUAL DEVICE CHECKLIST

☐? **DRAW OUT KEY WORDS.** What words will stick in the minds of your audience? Use callouts and enlarged key words to pull out important data and evoke responses in your audience.

Stories that Move Mountains have...

Visual *influence*
Characters
Intentional design
A call to **action**
Clarity
A beginning, a middle and an end
of the
A PLAN for delivery
A plot with **strong** relationships
message
Focus on the audience
A proven track
record of success

☐? **A SPECIFIC TYPEFACE.** Remember what we've mentioned about typefaces. Is the repetition of a certain typestyle critical for the memorability of any of the players in your map?

☐? **A CERTAIN SHAPE OR LINE.** Shapes and lines can be critical to the indication of movement, process, or grouping so plan accordingly.

☐? **A UNIQUE COMBINATION OF APPROACHES.** Have you been attentive to the unique needs of your audience? In Chapter 9 we looked at the learning and decision styles to understand that different people and audiences respond in different ways. In the visual design you also need to consider how to combine different elements to address the different styles.

This is the time to check the success of your design with a test audience. This audience should be as close as possible to the characteristics ofdifferent styles. how to n combine different elements to address fill in a chart, and the color of an icon when they all ha your target audience.

To test your audience's understanding of your design, watch how they read it, and ask how they create meaning from it. Ask questions after you give your presentation, and have someone else take notes for you if possible. Then go back and make any necessary adjustments, referring to comments and revisiting composition and content coding choices.

If at all possible, execute this process in *installments*. That means drafting a design with an initial sense of shape, form, color, and so on, and then doing an alpha test with a sample audience to see what they think, or simply with a trusted co-worker in a relatively informal setting.

Ask open-ended and close-ended questions, bridging wide and specific topics. Does the layout need some shifting? Do you need to change a color because of perceived associations?

Who are the most important decision-makers — people who like drawings, illustrations, or icons or people who like more three-dimensionality? Does your method and choice of all compositional items fit not only the *message* but also the *audience?*

These are all important checkpoints to consider, but most importantly, try to remain objective and know your presentation is still a work in progress. Hopefully, a full reboot will not be necessary after testing, but that's why this initial alpha test is important. In the decade it has taken to develop CAST we have created many visual stories. Sometimes we got the first design very wrong. We know that one of the hardest things to do is to be objective and recognize your design is not right, throw it away, and start again.

Writing

You can find many great books that cover writing styles. In just a few pages, we can barely scratch the surface, and in reality, if you are against the clock to create your first visual story, you don't have time to change much of your personal style. Here, we focus on three recommendations that have proven time after time to make a big difference: keep it simple, speak directly to your audience, and make it personal.

The balance of words and pictures varies between formats. ***It's not automatically good or bad to use words or pictures or both.*** The goal is to use the right mix for the situation and to use words and pictures to convey ideas, direct content, and supporting information as appropriate. If questions arise about something being clear, use more than one visual device for a concept to give the audience more than one chance to absorb the information.

Good textual content is vital for posters and infographics. Callouts, panels, and headings lead the reader around the content. One-page designs are often used as posters where there is no presenter to tell the audience how to read it so the words have to do a lot of work.

Keep It Simple

Great communicators keep it simple. But you've probably heard the old expression, "I'm sorry this is such a long letter, I didn't have time to write you a short one." Simple is hard to do. It often takes willpower and courage, because *simple* is the opposite of how most communication is done in big organizations, academia, and government. The words people use are often selected to project an image or hide poorly thought out ideas, rather than clearly inform.

Write your story beneath your audience's ability to comprehend it. The most common word processing packages include built-in tools to test your readability level using a measure called the Flesch-Kincaid readability score. Aim for a score greater than 60, which makes the text easily understood by 13- to 15-year-old students. Higher scores are better, with the Readers Digest typically scoring in the 60s, Time Magazine in the 50s, and Harvard Law Review in the 30s. This chapter, for example, scores 60.6.

This is not about dumbing down your work. It's about aiming for a level where your message slides smoothly into minds your readers, without them having to put too much energy into understanding the text. This is the level you find in the best written works by Pulitzer Prize winners.

You should expect to spend more time rewriting than you do on the original writing. Every word should be able to support itself and be unique in the sentence. When you think you are finished, try removing the last line. Often, we go further than we need to and, thus, weaken the ending. Try the same thing at the start to capture attention.

Business language is full of phrases like "best of breed synergies" and "comprehensive capabilities." Be aware of when you're taking refuge in jargon, and stop. Writers invoke jargon because they think it has magical power, or is a sign of legitimacy. Maybe. But more often, it's tossed into the verbal salad with little concern for whether it adds to the plate. SIMPLE DOES NOT MEAN BORING. Work a little on finding and using great action verbs. They can add energy to your language and perhaps evoke a fresh perspective. If you've used "divide" already, try *carve* or *splinter* or *slice.* Too much use of the thesaurus can grow cartoonish, but a little of it is great seasoning.

Always favor a plain, direct word over a long, vague one. Don't implement promises, but keep them. Don't say superexcited when excited will do; otherwise, when there really is something amazing, you'll have no words left to describe it.

Speak to Your Audience

Use words that complement the audience's learning and decision styles. If your audience is analytical or directive, it's likely that a lot of what you write will describe logical arguments or processes. You cannot stack points out of order. Just like flat-pack furniture instructions, when you stack points out of order, referring to a concept you haven't yet introduced, your language just serves to confuse.

The key to influencing decisions is to make people care. This means engaging feelings with descriptive words that grab attention. Your task is to help the audience visualize what you're describing, not to tell them how to feel. If the visualization is good, the feeling will follow. If working conditions are bad, describe them; don't just say they're terrible. You need the audience to understand the feelings, to be able to relate to them, not just to hear the result.

Using words that help your audience visualize data is important as well. To most people, statistics with large numbers become too abstract. We see the response to this in documentaries that compare the size of things to a London bus or to the weight of elephants. Work with something that people can relate to, but try to avoid the clichéd comparisons.

In 2005, the UK government admitted that it had given permission for four percent of new houses to be built in areas that had previously been designated as green belt areas or on land that was to have remained undeveloped. These new houses covered an area of 2400 acres per year. Do you know how much that is? Most people don't, so how would you describe this information so that it will have the appropriately understood impact?

In the UK, you might expect to put eight houses per acre on valuable greenbelt land. A common technique to help visualize data like this is to reduce it to a scale a person can relate to. Here a little calculation tells us this is 19,200 houses in 8760 hours, or **one house every 30 minutes**. Imagine that!

Make It Personal

Specific content engages the audience. **THE MORE SPECIFIC YOU ARE, THE STRONGER THE CONNECTION.** Imagine a fictional visual story about truck drivers in the U.S. starting like this:

Sixty eight percent of professional freight drivers spend more than three nights per week sleeping in their trucks. There's an estimated shortfall of 28,400 truck-parking spaces in the U.S. This means that the average truck driver may spend 40 minutes each day finding parking for the night and services for toilet, hygiene, and food.

Imagine, instead, it starting like this:

Let me tell you about Bill. He's been an owner operator of a big rig for nine years. Bill has a wife and two children back home in Denver. The job means that three nights a week, he is away from home sleeping in his cab. Two nights he generally finds a parking bay in a safe service area, but one night each week, he's parked in a roadside layby. Bill is taking risks with his choice of location that neither he nor his family really want.

Which do you relate to? The difference in empathy and relationship in the second story about Bill is huge for most audiences. Whether this is a persona, representing the typical truck driver, or a real example, it has a personal quality that enables your audience to relate to it. Look back to Chapter 8 and the discussion on shared context for your audience. The personal examples you use must fit into the shared context. Here, we may not know much about truck drivers, but we do understand family, and taking risks with personal safety.

In the Personal Trainer example later in this chapter you will see how Marina created a one-page poster with a lot of words, and also developed a page of notes to support the delivery of her story.

The tips on writing given here were picked up from Tom Farmer, who worked on improving a lot of content for Martin some years ago. Tom was executive producer for Larry King Live *for many years and is an excellent journalist, editor, and author.*

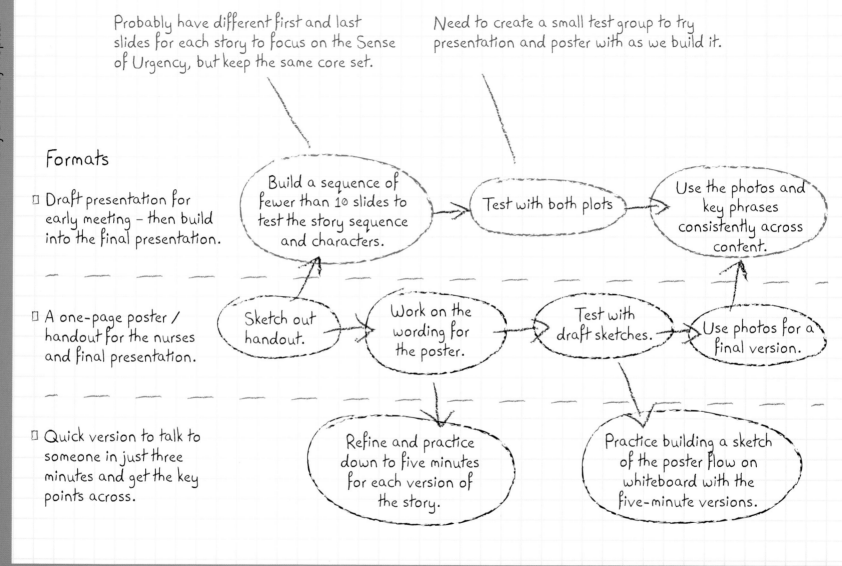

Probably have different first and last slides for each story to focus on the Sense of Urgency, but keep the same core set.

Need to create a small test group to try presentation and poster with as we build it.

Formats

☐ Draft presentation for early meeting – then build into the final presentation.

☐ A one-page poster / handout for the nurses and final presentation.

☐ Quick version to talk to someone in just three minutes and get the key points across.

Build a sequence of fewer than 10 slides to test the story sequence and characters.

Test with both plots

Use the photos and key phrases consistently across content.

Sketch out handout.

Work on the wording for the poster.

Test with draft sketches.

Use photos for a final version.

Refine and practice down to five minutes for each version of the story.

Practice building a sketch of the poster flow on whiteboard with the five-minute versions.

Tom begins by listing the different formats he needs for his delivery plan. The draft presentation will need to be done early, but before that he plans to work with Ralf some more on the story and get his big picture thinking on the one-page poster.

Need a sharp title to go here!

Sense of Urgency goes here.

Text here to note some of the current issues – such as handwriting of patient notes on printouts.

Text here to note some of the future opportunities, including capturing handwriting electronically.

Closing message. This change depends on the nurses.

Reception nurse taking details from a patient on arrival.

PATIENT NOTES
updated at 3pm
172/96 3:15pm
Samples to lab at 6pm.

Text here to talk about the migration of existing data.

PATIENT NOTES

Explain how the patient data improvements allow for better patient care and fewer insurance claim rejections.

Introduce Sharon taking notes while a patient has a scan.

Put in some details here about the challenges the nurses and doctors will face with the changes.

Sharon talking with a specialist to modify the care plan for a patient.
Updating the patient details as they talk.

Patient alarm on automatic monitoring equipment sounds late at night. Fortunately a false alarm, but the nurse had all the patient details immediately and the incident logged automatically.

Tom spent a few hours with Ralf trying out different visual layouts to support the story. They ended up with the concept shown here. Neither thinks they can draw well, but they will use photographs staged like the rough sketches, and work with the team on the words. The poster is mainly for the nurses, but it still has at least one reference to the insurance claims to help link the stories.

The **Optimal Balance** system helps fitness studios *thrive*, and lets personal trainers get back to doing what they *love*.

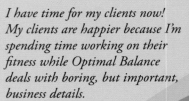

I have time for my clients now! My clients are happier because I'm spending time working on their fitness while Optimal Balance deals with boring, but important, business details.

I love helping people get fit and lose weight. I have spent a lot of time training to be a personal fitness trainer. I know that if I do a good job of training people, they will come to my new studio.

Randall's Gym

success

arghhh!

It is hard getting enough new members to make money, and my existing members are leaving. Large gyms are cutting into my business. Billing issues are wearing me down. Running a business shouldn't be this difficult.

I rely on my trainer, but he needs help to run this business!

I am spending all my time dealing with business issues. I don't have time to create training plans or train clients. This is not the job I wanted to have.

Optimal Balance can help you deal with your business issues.

You can do it!

SERVICES TO CHOOSE FROM
We serve the needs of fitness studios, clubs, and spas, including:

- Automatic billing
- Friendly phone service
- Legal forms
- Web marketing
- Pay for training network clients
- Insurance claims
- Supplements
- Physician referrals

SCIENCE-BASED PROGRAMS
While you are free to create your own programs, you can also take advantage of our programs developed from years of behavioral science research.
Our programs:

- Avoid up-front fees
- Encourage tracking
- Allow trainers to assign programs electronically

COMPETITION
from large gyms can be a challenge. Optimal Balance helps you compete. Your clients can train at any studio in the network, and if a client from another studio trains with you, you are reimbursed. In addition, your studio can collect medical insurance, sell supplements and accessories, and work with local physicians to get client referrals, revenue channels that only the largest clubs can otherwise take advantage of.

HOW MUCH DOES OPTIMAL BALANCE COST?
Optimal balance charges a small transaction fee on membership dues and on transfer reimbursements. Simple monthly reports detail all charges, while your net membership dues are automatically deposited into your business account. It couldn't be simpler.

JOINING IS EASY
Once your studio joins the Optimal Balance network, a project coordinator will create a plan to address four changes.

- Free staff training
- New paperwork forms
- New membership cards and card scanner
- Updates to your studio's website

Marina and Nick develop the story presentation and create a draft layout for the visual story. The story is designed to be printed on a large sheet of paper to be handed out during one-on-one presentations, and available for download from the website.

Delivering the Optimal Balance Story

 **Dark Power** → **Temporary Success** → **Living Death**

The story starts with some background on the current state of the fitness studio industry. The data includes how many studios fail each year, and the reasons why they fail.

Introduce the theme that many personal trainers suffer from a lack of time to give attention to individual clients because of the time required to manage the business.

Introduce Randall, a personal trainer who thinks that he can successfully run his own business, based on his experience as a trainer in another gym.

He begins well with existing clients from his old gym, and some friends and family. They are very forgiving of early missteps, and the business seems to be a success.

Contract problems and billing mistakes are reducing customer satisfaction, which in turn reduces his referrals and new clients. It takes more effort to run a business than Randall thought.

 **Apparent Triumph** → **Miraculous Redemption** → **The End**

Introduce Penny, who tells Randall about the services her company uses, and helps him find out about Optimal Balance.

Introduce Frank as a fellow trainer and studio owner. Randall is convinced that he doesn't need outside help as Frank explains the systems he has created over the years to run his business.

Randall thinks he will be successful if only he can copy Frank, and begins to spend every evening at the gym, working late, trying to catch up on paperwork.

Penny plays Randall the Optimal Balance video and shows him the visual story. Randall arranges a one-to-one meeting and finally understands the benefits and how it will change his life.

Randall buys Optimal Balance services and soon has time to dedicate to training clients and getting people excited about their own health.

Finish with a sense of urgency based on the stress and effort that studio owners are facing. For personal trainers, overcoming physical obstacles can be far easier than overcoming the mental challenges that make it difficult to keep doing routine business tasks when they really don't enjoy them. It's just a matter of time before they quit.

Marina and Nick use the visual story in presentations. They also create a one-page reminder of the story to help with the first deliveries.

G TCHA

Follow these steps to make sure that you're creating a design instilled with pride and the opportunity to influence the audience.

(!) **"But I can't draw!"** Chris Bangle, who once led design for BMW and was one of the most influential designers in the world, regularly presented with stick figures and a few written words. He didn't change this approach, whether he was with executives or in a factory. The stick figures ensured that the visuals remained at a level everyone could understand, and that he would be forced to prepare his content.

Are you including some things in order to remember to talk about them? Use the one-page visual story as your prompt. When you put up slides full of bullet points, you might as well just shut up and let the audience read. Visuals should support understanding, not replace the need for the speaker. If you want your audience to listen to you and respond to your message, every part of the visual story must be focused on their needs.

(!) **Should you pass the job to someone else?** Too often, we see people hand a pile of content (their vision) over to graphics designers, or subordinates who have some skill with presentation software, and expect them to create great visualizations. Unless you delegate the work to specialists in the development of stories, and they have a process to work with you to develop an insight into the message of the story, often what you get back will be a very pretty picture, but not a story to influence the audience. However, you can take the Visual Story Map, your supporting data, and your rough one-page visual story to a designer and get a great result. The difference is substantial; it will be your story.

- ☑ Choose the formats to support your delivery plan.

- ☑ Mindmap or brainstorm relevant creative approaches (with several people if possible).

- ☑ Create a one-page visual story around your story framework and core characters.

- ☑ Run through the Visual Device Checklist to determine the best way to code the content (this can be done together with creating the one-page visual story).

- ☑ Create a rough draft of your presentation and put it in front of your test audience before your ideas become too set.

- ☑ Refine the visual approach, add a little writing, test again, and keep repeating this cycle.

15

Experience is what you get when you didn't get what you wanted.

Charles Saatchi, co-founder of global advertising agency Saatchi and Saatchi

Great stories happen to those who can tell them.

Ira Glass, radio host of "This American Life", with a regular audience of 1.7 million listeners

Testing and Rehearsals

If this is the first review of your visual story using the test criteria defined in this chapter, then there is one guarantee, it will not be the last time. This is the last step in the CAST process, but the point where you are likely to jump back to a previous step to fix a problem with your visual story. This isn't a problem. It's a necessary part of the process.

Think about how a musician creates a new composition. Songs and arrangements don't appear fully formed. The musician plays the tune and listens to it, gets feedback, tries alternative variations, and gradually works toward the completed piece. In the same way, testing and iteration are core to the creation of great visual stories. We often tell people that one of the secrets to CAST is to do it quickly to get a rough draft, and then repeat, repeat, repeat. . . .

So many factors come together to create a winning presentation or a brilliant one-page handout that to spend too long on any one factor without considering the impact of the others just leads to problems later.

So create a draft, test it, listen to feedback, and iterate. Stories evolve. Hearing what others take from your story gives greater insight into the message that is really being delivered. Testing is about listening and observing. Hear what your test subjects have to say about your story, but also take time to observe how they physically react to it. Did they get distracted to check e-mail? Did they look shocked? Or bored?

Be deliberate in who you get feedback from. Plan this as carefully as you plan the delivery. They could be key members of your audience or people totally uninvolved and therefore with no attachment to the outcome or alternative agenda.

You have to tell stories to get stories.
Ken Metzler, author of "Creative Interviewing: The Writer's Guide to Gathering Information by Asking Questions"

When hearing a story, people will often contribute their own anecdotes and variations of what has happened to them. This sharing of stories seems to be human nature across many cultures. Some may help to add specificity, emotion, or key examples to your story. Capture these where they support a key point and reuse them — and quote the source to acknowledge their contribution and broaden the credibility of your overall delivery.

Rehearsals are just another form of testing, usually to help fine-tune the oral presentation. Rehearsals are tests best made in company. Sure, you can rehearse on your own, but the feedback is a little one-sided. A great approach for rehearsals is to deliver to people who don't know the subject area, such as your spouse, partner, grandmother, or children (replacing the bedtime story with your latest visual story is not recommended though). With a rehearsal, you're concerned about the content and about the style of delivery, so that you can tell the story with emotion and passion.

You can still use a rehearsal if you're creating one-page posters or other visuals that will be delivered without an oral presentation. Give a copy to members of your test audience and ask them to read it while you wait. Don't talk about it when they finish; talk about something completely different for at least three minutes. Now, remove the copy they were looking at and ask them to recount the story to you and to tell you how they feel about it. If you've managed to get the visual story on paper, the retention will be fairly high, but listen carefully for the content they don't recall — and no prompting!

Opening, Closing, and Timing

Most presentation coaches focus on the opening and the closing. Rightly so, as this is where the oral delivery can be lost in seconds. If the delivery starts or ends badly, everything else is just wasted time. How long are we talking about? No more than a minute, often much less than that. Your audience is making their decision to listen or to read the rest of the delivery in the first few seconds.

So how should you start? You can find hundreds of pages on the Internet and books on delivering presentations to cover the oral presentation, with a variety of guidance about introducing yourself, avoiding jokes, smiling, and so on. But let's be clear; the people sitting in front of you have come to hear your story, and the first thing they need to understand is why it matters to them. You can share a key fact or ask a question that begs the audience to identify the sense of urgency. You might simply start with "Let me tell you a story."

TIP: To leave your audience with a positive feeling — finish early! Delivering a 30 minute session in 25 minutes means your audience can leave calmly without having to rush away to their next scheduled event. This is such a little thing to plan for, but very powerful.

How a story ends matters more than how it starts. A happy ending is very powerful. If you end on a negative note, you can ruin the follow-through. The visual stories we create with CAST are about influencing change and decisions. You might end with a call to action, a request, or just short of stating the choice to be made (leaving that to your audience to deduce). In all cases, end with an opportunity for your audience to take a specific and positive step.

If you are delivering your visual story as a presentation with slides, consider the guidance given by Vinad Khosla, a venture capitalist who has seen many presentations. He shows a slide for **five seconds** then removes it and asks the viewer to describe it. This should remind you of the Squint Test in Chapter 14 (and the effect on the eyes of the red and green example). A text heavy, bullet-point list fails this test. A dense slide fails the test and undermines the reason for having a presentation deck, which is to increase the impact of the

presentation. While the audience is reading the slide, they aren't listening to you. If you have to provide data or a chart that takes more than five seconds to absorb, then shut up and let them read it. The flow of the presentation has moved from you to the screen. Definitely take the flow back after they've read the content and move on. Don't read the bullets. Don't try to work down the slide.

If you want to see how professionals tell stories with graphics, watch the news! Do you see any bullet lists? Actually, check how long visuals stay on the screen. Try to imagine yourself in a news reader's chair, and pace your story in a similar fashion.

Repetition

When we discussed the delivery plan in Chapter 13, we made a big point about planned repetition of the story. If you want to influence behavior, you must keep telling the story using different approaches, different media, and at different times, long after you might have thought you would be finished. Advertisers know this. To get a message to stick so people take action requires repetition. This probably sounds obvious to you, but again and again we see senior managers say something a few times, send a follow-up email, and then wonder why people do something other than what they clearly said should be done!

Many parents would recognize that repetition can sometimes lead to the recipient tuning out the message. You avoid this, firstly, by using as many different approaches and variations as possible, and secondly, by always asking the audience to do something at the end of every telling of the story.

When you've gone through the CAST process to work out what you want to do, the story will seem pretty clear to you. But when your audience hears or reads the story, they're doing so without the benefit of all that time you had to process it, and they must handle other distractions at the same time. To you the story is important. Your audience must take it in and believe in the sense of urgency you portray. There's a big difference between you saying something and your audience actually hearing it.

So when you think the repetition is getting excessive, hold that thought, and tell the story just one more time.

Retention

Do you have a lot of material in your story? How will your audience remember it? There are limits on the number of things we can hold in our very short-term memory. This limit depends on the person, but it's usually between five and ten different things. When people are taught the techniques for improving recall and the ability to remember long lists, part of the training is learning to create visual sequences, build stories from the content, and cluster content into groups they can then name.

The same techniques apply for your visual story. Whether in a presentation that's delivered totally orally or on a poster, you will create structures that group information to make it easier to remember.

> **TIP:** While drafting your story, it may even be useful at some point to enumerate your top five messages to help you stay focused, keep them numbered in your presentation until the last minute, but drop the numbers from the final versions, unless you want the audience to treat the items sequentially.

In Chapter 11 we explained that a character in your story acts as a container for motivations, actions, and characteristics. So be sure that all your characters have names to provide the consistent link to the information about them. As you test your story, check to be sure you have associated your content to the characters to help your audience remember. It's no accident that the CAST process is split into four main sections, each with two or four activities, and each activity with a number of techniques. This grouping aids the ability to recall the process.

Audiences seldom take away more than one or two main points from a story or presentation, and in many cases, the point taken away is the last one delivered. You can increase the amount of information retained by considering how to structure the information. If you divide your story into clear sections with well-defined start and end points, you can increase what the audience takes away.

The Six Key Tests

Genius is one percent inspiration, ninety-nine percent perspiration.

Thomas A. Edison, prolific inventor and entrepreneur

When we designed this book, we deliberately included a checklist at the end of most chapters to help keep you focused on the key activities. If you've been following those, you may realize that this chapter is not about the content from any specific step in the CAST process, but about ensuring that the whole visual story comes together successfully.

A lot of effort can go into a good visual story, effort that's not always apparent to the audience, because if you've done it well, you will have removed everything that could confuse or lead to a wrong decision. Your audience may even say a visual story looks simple.

Getting to *simple* is hard work, but to help you out, we've identified six key tests that ensure you have the necessary focus.

Perfection is achieved, not when there is nothing left to add, but when there is nothing left to take away.

Antoine de Saint Exupery, French writer, poet, and aviator

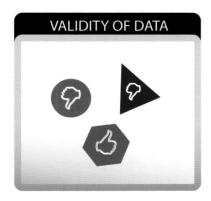

VALIDITY OF DATA

You need to ensure that no one in your audience can credibly dispute any of the data behind your story. If they can, then you have a big problem, especially with the analytically minded in your audience who will rapidly lose confidence in a story with poor data.

If you're using anecdotal evidence, make that clear.

If you derive your data from systematic research or from first-hand stories, be specific about your sources.

Is your data from a sample large enough to be **CREDIBLE** as evidence, or are you generalizing from a small sample?

Are you using evidence from an unnamed expert or group, or are you relying on an unqualified opinion? Watch for phrases like, "Experts claim. . . ."

Are you making claims that something is true because it's a common practice or a common belief? For example, many believe that people use only ten percent of their brains, but there's no evidence to support this belief.

So, do you need to fully **REFERENCE** all data and assertions in your visual story? No! But you do need to know you can back up your claims. With easy access to online data sources, the world has changed. In a few minutes on the Internet your audience can find supporting data, and possibly contradictory data. If there can be any doubt on the accuracy of data then provide a way for your audience to look at the sources you used.

INTEGRATION OF EVIDENCE

If the individual data items in your visual story pass the first test, the next level is to consider whether they integrate properly. The integration should flow from the **RELATIONSHIPS** and filtering performed in the Content activities at the start of the CAST process. As you work through the CAST process, there's always a danger that the data isn't as clear as it could be for all members of the audience because of the way you structure it for the characters and activities in the visual story. Members of your audience with a conceptual bias will lose interest quickly if the integration is poor.

Don't assume there's only one way to integrate the evidence. Look for alternatives that might surprise the audience.

Have you cherry-picked the evidence to confirm a bias you already had?

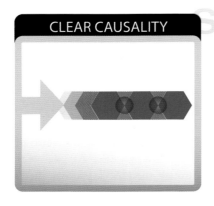

CLEAR CAUSALITY

A story usually has at its core a **SEQUENCE** of events. So, people expect to see a clear causal relationship through the events in the visual story. It doesn't take the skills of a crime scene investigator to spot inconsistencies and gaps in a story, so pay particular attention for these common errors.

Are you using a set of independent outcomes to deduce a future outcome? This is the trap gamblers fall into when assuming that a series of past throws of the dice mean a certain number should come up next. Similarly, just because something may be probable doesn't mean it will happen.

Could your audience mistakenly believe that because you have two events happening together or in sequence, there's a causal relationship?

Are there other causes for the events in your story that haven't been included?

When you start by assuming one small first step leads to a chain of events, you may be on a slippery slope. Is the assumption defensible?

PATH TO DECISION

The causality from event to event in the story ensures that the evidence flows, but does it go far enough to clearly set the ground for a decision to be made? If the audience likes the story but has no idea what to do at the end, then you have failed.

Does your visual story jump to the **CONCLUSION** without first setting out the relevant evidence?

Consider that there may be more than one path to the decision or change. Have you considered the alternatives? There are always alternatives to a decision; are you representing them fairly and clearly? You might play down the alternatives, but avoid ridiculing opposing arguments. Also check that you aren't oversimplifying the alternatives to discredit them.

Could the audience jump to the wrong conclusion partway through the story? Are you suppressing evidence or failing to use relevant information that could lead the audience to a different conclusion?

Finally, are you seeking a decision based on fear of the opposite happening? Appealing to avoid a negative can be successful in the short-term; however, it rarely conveys the sense of urgency required to see a change to completion, but merely until the negative is no longer painful enough to notice.

If the reader is lost , it is usually because the writer has not been careful enough to keep him on the path.

William Zinsser, author of key works on how to improve your writing

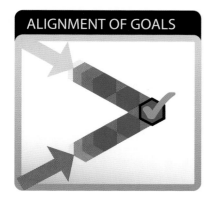

ALIGNMENT OF GOALS

In many cases, a visual story has to bring together different threads to reach a **CONSISTENT** goal in order for multiple audience members to make the change or decision happen. When bringing together the goals and agendas of different people, there's a danger you'll have to make compromises in the story to satisfy the different parties.

And it happened all the time that the compromise between two perfectly rational alternatives was something that made no sense at all.

Neal Stephenson, science fiction and cyberpunk author

Have you made compromises in order for the visual story to satisfy particular audience members that will weaken the impact for others?

Do you explain away problems instead of explaining how to resolve the issues?

Is it possible for the different members of the audience to reach different conclusions that will lead to conflict later?

UNINTENDED CONSEQUENCES

Unintended consequences arising from the activities in the visual story are simply outcomes other than the one you want, whether good or bad. The good unintended consequences are often thought of as lucky additions; the bad ones may have negative side effects, or even make the situation worse. No one can have the perfect **FORESIGHT** to avoid all potential unintended consequences, but you can regularly check throughout the story to see if the audience could take an alternative path. Here are a few examples that no one predicted:

- The sinking of ships in shallow water at the end of World World II was an easy way to dispose of the ships, and had the unintended positive outcome of creating the structure for new habitats.

- E-mail, invented in 1971, was designed to help people communicate, but no one thought about the security to prevent the spam and phishing e-mails we have today.

- Forcing helmets on cyclists saved lives but the unfashionable headgear led to a reduction in the number of young cyclists.

- Draining wetlands can provide new land for housing or agriculture, but it also often increases the risks of flash floods because the ground's ability to dissipate water is reduced.

You might identify potential unintended consequences from the ideas considered in the "What If" content of Chapter 7. Listen to your audience in the tests and rehearsals, and ask how they see the options developing.

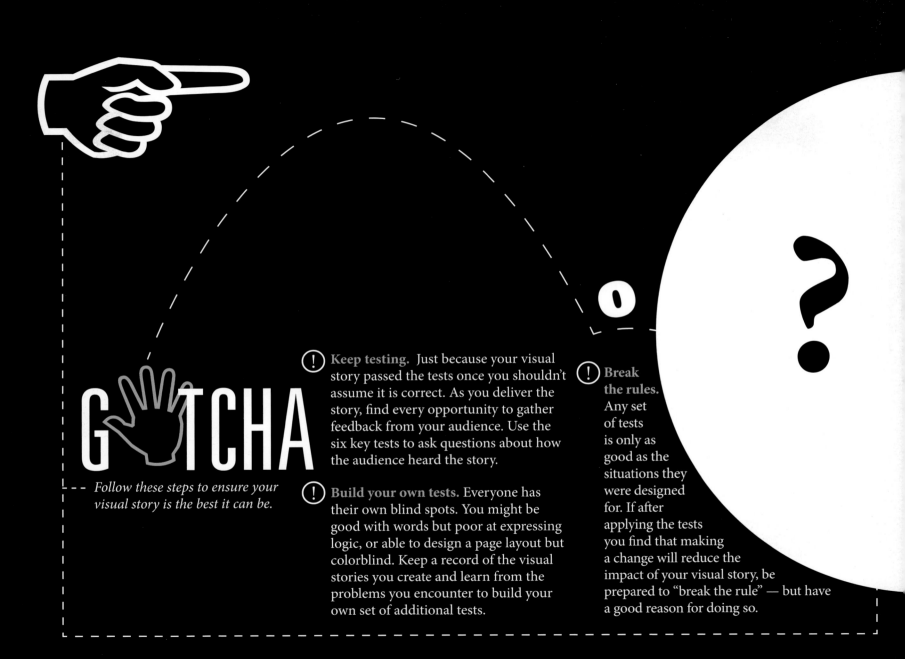

G✋TCHA

Follow these steps to ensure your visual story is the best it can be.

(!) **Keep testing.** Just because your visual story passed the tests once you shouldn't assume it is correct. As you deliver the story, find every opportunity to gather feedback from your audience. Use the six key tests to ask questions about how the audience heard the story.

(!) **Build your own tests.** Everyone has their own blind spots. You might be good with words but poor at expressing logic, or able to design a page layout but colorblind. Keep a record of the visual stories you create and learn from the problems you encounter to build your own set of additional tests.

(!) **Break the rules.** Any set of tests is only as good as the situations they were designed for. If after applying the tests you find that making a change will reduce the impact of your visual story, be prepared to "break the rule" — but have a good reason for doing so.

☑ Check the validity and credibility of your data.

☑ Be clear on the relationships and integration of your data.

☑ Be sure you have a clearly defined causal relationship from each part of your story to the next part.

☑ Check that your visual story leads to a clearly defined decision or request for the audience to act.

☑ Look for compromises or messages for specific audience members that may lead to different outcomes.

☑ Consider the potential unintended consequences of the change or decision you are proposing.

CAST Example:
What a Difference a Day Can Make

Example is not the main thing in influencing others. It is the only thing.

Albert Schweitzer, theologian, philosopher, and Nobel Peace Prize winner

The things we have to learn before we do them, we learn by doing them.

Aristotle, Greek philosopher and author of Poetics, possibly the earliest description of the principles of storytelling

The two-page visual story in Chapter 1 was really a story about creating a story. The intent was to lead you, the reader, quickly into some of the key reasons for creating a visual story and the activities involved. The objective was simple: to set up a situation you're familiar with, to tell a visual story to show how to get to resolution, and to leave you with the desire to find out more.

If you have read through the book to get here, rather than skipping ahead, you probably realize that we used many of the techniques from CAST to create that story. In the following eight pages we look in more detail at the experiences Bob and his team went through on Thursday and Friday as they prepared for their big presentation.

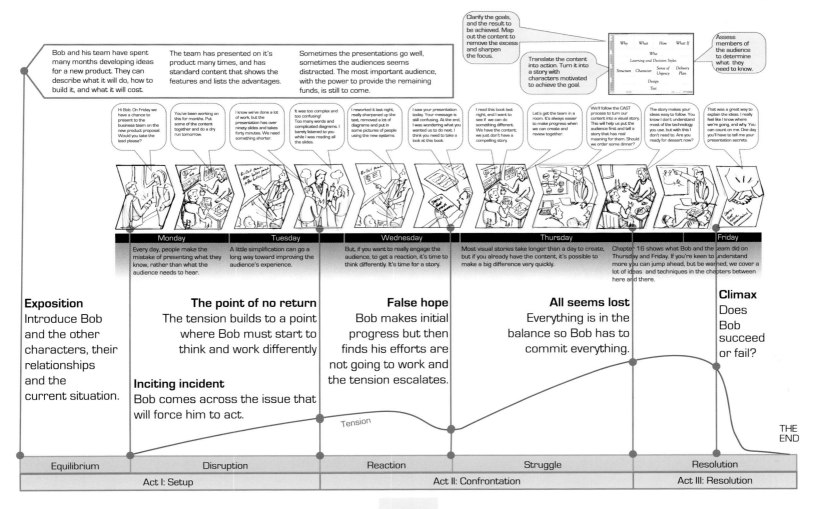

Thursday starts with Bob calling the team together to explain that he wants to try a new approach for the presentation on Friday. This approach is going to take the team a day, with all the work they've already done as the starting point.

Bob's team has been developing a proposal for new device and online services they can provide to their customers based on the latest technology. The product is a new mobile device to help people with their weight loss and diet plans.

You don't really need to understand anything about the new product ideas Bob's team wants to propose to appreciate that the team has done some very detailed analysis, and has a lot of data to show how its ideas will work.

The team has market surveys and analysis, competitor-cost breakdowns, product designs, production plans, and a great business case to support the proposal.

Bob still faces a major challenge. The presentation on Friday will be made to a review group well known for derailing presentations on the second slide, jumping ahead to ask questions, and rejecting proposals for missing details.

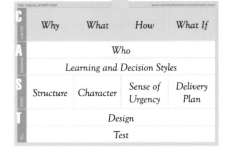

YOU ARE HERE

THE VISUAL STORY MAP				www.storiesthatmovemountains.com
C	Why	What	How	What If
A	Who			
S	Learning and Decision Styles			
T	Structure	Character	Sense of Urgency	Delivery Plan
	Design			
	Test			

The first step to follow in the CAST process is to review the content and work out what is really important to focus on.

Bob already knows who will be in the audience for the presentation, so he can start the Content mapping process with a clear idea of how much each person already knows about the new product proposals.

0800

THURSDAY

Most visual stories take longer than a day to create, but if you already have the content, it's possible to make a big difference very quickly.

A common situation is a last-minute presentation to an influential group by a team or individual who has been doing a lot of work, and already has a lot of material.

The CAST process starts by asking you to decide on the content that is important for a specific audience, before you start creating slides, or open presentation software.

Bob starts by using the outcome mapping technique to clarify the reasons why the proposal is important. This is a great technique when you already have plenty of content. The team then uses the Five Whys to be sure they really have the reasoning clearly stated.

Bob leads a discussion of the detailed project plan to look for clusters. Each cluster has some incident or complication, followed by action to achieve a resolution. The team then sequences the clusters and looks for evidence or anecdotes to support each one.

The project includes activities to build an online store for new content.

Complication: People want to personalize their devices. How can we do this?

Resolution: Provide the ability to link to their existing content and to buy new content, making their device very personal.

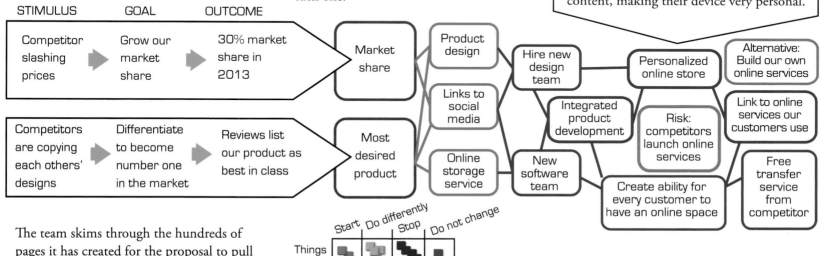

STIMULUS | GOAL | OUTCOME

Competitor slashing prices → Grow our market share → 30% market share in 2013

Competitors are copying each others' designs → Differentiate to become number one in the market → Reviews list our product as best in class

Market share

Most desired product

Product design

Links to social media

Online storage service

Hire new design team

Integrated product development

New software team

Personalized online store

Risk: competitors launch online services

Create ability for every customer to have an online space

Alternative: Build our own online services

Link to online services our customers use

Free transfer service from competitor

The team skims through the hundreds of pages it has created for the proposal to pull out the important changes for the new product to be a success. All of these changes will contribute to the information needed for the actions of the characters.

	Start	Do differently	Stop	Do not change
Things				
People				
Process				

As the team reviews its content, it also pulls out the project risks and the alternatives it considered. These items point to key issues the audience is likely to ask about, and are linked to the clusters where the issue may be raised.

1000 THURSDAY

The techniques to review and filter content were presented in Chapters 4 through 7. If you have only a day to get it right, use a subset of these in a few hours to develop your focus.

On these short timescales, remember that you're working with existing content. This is not the time to start a new analysis or create new materials.

Usually the starting materials are not structured in a Why-What-How sequence, so expect to iterate over the models, and have a final hard review to filter the content.

Using the analysis of learning and decision styles, the team ascertains that it needs to have a strong focus on the conceptual, with clarity regarding the data for the analytical people. The focus is on the decision styles, as most of the audience already knows of the technologies, and this meeting is focused on the reasoning for a decision.

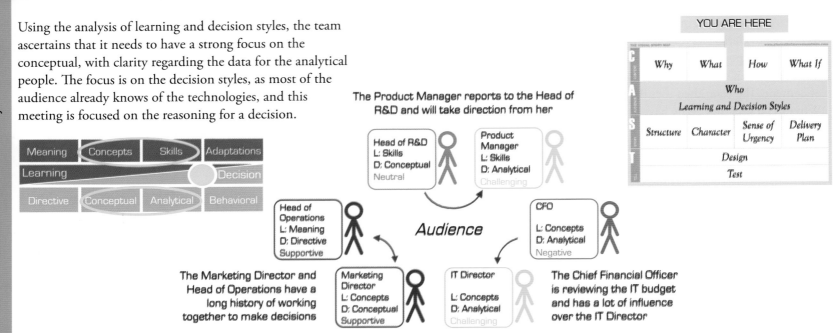

The Product Manager reports to the Head of R&D and will take direction from her

Head of R&D
L: Skills
D: Conceptual
Neutral

Product Manager
L: Skills
D: Analytical
Challenging

Head of Operations
L: Meaning
D: Directive
Supportive

CFO
L: Concepts
D: Analytical
Negative

Audience

Marketing Director
L: Concepts
D: Conceptual
Supportive

IT Director
L: Concepts
D: Analytical
Challenging

The Marketing Director and Head of Operations have a long history of working together to make decisions

The Chief Financial Officer is reviewing the IT budget and has a lot of influence over the IT Director

YOU ARE HERE

Bob and his team know the six attendees who will be the audience for the review presentation. All the key people to take the new product proposals forward will be in one room. The most difficult discussion of the morning is about the merit of telling stories to this group of people. They're used to getting data-oriented, detailed

presentations for projects, and the team knows they can be difficult to present to. The benefits of a story-based approach will be to put the data into a personal context, and to keep the audience's attention throughout the presentation.

Along with understanding the personal styles of the audience members and the influence relationships among them, the team also talks about the interactions it's had with the audience in the past to assess how supportive they might initially be to the new product ideas.

1200   THURSDAY

You have a great starting point when creating presentations like this for important audiences. You know who the audience will be. Don't waste the opportunity to use this information to focus the story.

The influence map is far more important than any organizational chart. Your audience will talk to each other and influence each other. Use this to your advantage.

Think of the learning and decision styles as a quick indicator of the considerations you need to make with the delivery. Don't try to overanalyze the situation.

Overcoming the Monster	The Quest	Voyage and Return	Comedy
Tragedy	Rebirth	Rags to Riches	

Everyone on the team took turns trying to position the content into one of the seven basic plots. After a few minutes considering each plot, it was clear some would work much better than others. The Quest seems to be the best fit for the creation of their new product, but the Rebirth story would work well to show how their product has been overtaken by a competitor and now they must fight back. The team keeps the Rebirth story idea as it might be useful for a different audience to include the history of the decline of their old product into the story.

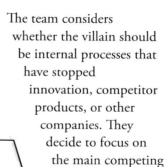

The team considers whether the villain should be internal processes that have stopped innovation, competitor products, or other companies. They decide to focus on the main competing product as a very tangible villain, with features and characteristics everyone can understand. The team decides their new product will be the hero. In fact the hero will start as the old product, looking tired and defeated, but as it heads out on the quest the situations will provide the transformation necessary for it to grow into a market-beating product. The new software and design teams will act as Helper characters, and a social networking site will act as a Donor, bringing in new features.

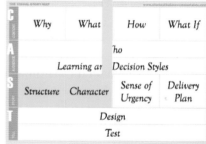
YOU ARE HERE

The Call		The Journey		Arrival and Frustration			The Final Ordeals	The Goal
Describe the current market and our desire to be a market leader	Hire new design team	New software team	Integrated product development	Create ability for every customer to have an online space	Personalized online store		Link to online services our customers use	Free transfer service from competitor
Equilibrium		Disruption		Reaction	Struggle		Resolution	
Act I: Set Up				Act II: Confrontation			Act III: Resolution	

14:00 — THURSDAY

When you already have a lot of content to include, you can quickly test the basic plots for consistency with your theme and content, and then pick two to test against each other.

As content clusters are mapped to the plot structure, use the complication and resolution for each one to test that the sequence makes sense and develops the story.

The characters can be introduced as the story progresses. The hero arrives early so that the audience is clear about whom it's supporting, with the villain becoming apparent by the end of Act I.

Bob starts the conversation on the Sense of Urgency with a Venn diagram on the whiteboard. He tells the team that to create a great sense of urgency, a reason why the audience will support their project now, they need to find a combination of words that draws on three different perspectives: the reasons for the proposal his team identified, the checklist of categories from Chapter 12, and what they know about the audience's personal and business agendas.

"Isn't the Sense of Urgency just one of the reasons we identified at the start?"

"Yes and No"

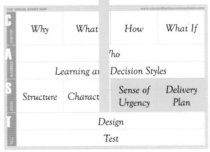

YOU ARE HERE

C	Why	What		How	What If
A			Who		
		Learning a	Decision Styles		
S	Structure	Charact		Sense of Urgency	Delivery Plan
T			Design		
			Test		

THE VISUAL STORY MAP   www.storiesthatmoveinstatms.com

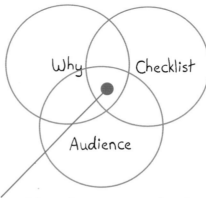

Why   Checklist

Audience

After a long debate, the team agrees that the strongest sense of urgency will be based on the current product becoming obsolete in just the last month with the release of a much better competitor product, leading to a rapid market decline.

Bob decides to use the projector only for the product images, and to create a one-page visual story handout with all the key details for costs, market analysis, and the development program on a timeline for The Quest.

Bob knows that to reach a decision some audience members have to be convinced a lot more than others. The CFO is likely to be the hardest to convince, and he's a key influencer on the IT Director, so during the presentation Bob plans to build an agreement with the CFO that they don't want to lose the revenue from product sales, and then try to build consistency with that position to support the new product.

To prepare the audience he will mail them the most recent market analysis report, which shows the rapidly declining market share. This should have enhance the sense of urgency in their minds.

THURSDAY   161600

The sense of urgency is closely tied to the initial reasons for the visual story and the audience's personal pain. Make sure you are solving a problem the audience has.

The audience has to also want to solve the problem today. Your sense of urgency needs to be phrased so that it motivates the audience members personally to act now.

Every presentation can benefit from a delivery plan, to arrange pre-meeting information and to provide takeaway content to reinforce the decision.

	Why	What	How	What If
C				
A		Video		
		Learning and Decision Styles		
S	Structure	Character	Sense of Urgency	Delivery Plan
T				

Design

Test

Format

In this case, the formats are defined by the delivery plan. However, over dinner with his wife Bob finds he is drawing a few sketches on a napkin to explain the overall flow. The sketching process adds interactivity to the delivery, so he adds a whiteboard sketch as a part of his presentation.

Ideation

The team members each sketch very rough pictures on the whiteboard to word associate with a quest. By common agreement, they keep it to a simple timeline.

Composition

Bob sketches a timeline on the whiteboard. The team sticks up all the notes from the content analysis and shuffles them around until they match the flow of the story.

Content Coding

Images from the company brand library help to set the right tone. Then every color and line is selected to add to the visual story, and to be consistent with the rest of the page.

Writing

There will be a lot of content on the page, but it needs to be simple and clear. It's mostly taken directly from the existing materials, but the team edits to get the content to avoid confusion or distraction caused by complex wording or technical language.

It's been a long day, but Bob is still buzzing with the visual story, and over dinner with his wife he runs through the story.

The team has already been through the content to check that all the data is correct, well integrated, and flows in a logical sequence to the decision. Bob's wife is a very detail-oriented accountant, with a great feel for other people's reactions. This makes for a great test audience because her style is almost the opposite of Bob's. Gently but firmly, she points out all the reasons why the CFO might reject the ideas. She also identifies one unintended consequence of the current story: the new product's features could make another one of their products obsolete.

It's not too late to fix the story. Bob stays up late to rework the storyline and practice the sketch he is going to make on the whiteboard. Meanwhile, his team has put the finishing touches on the one-page visual story and has the printouts ready for the morning.

1800 THURSDAY **2000**

For your first visual story, it's often best to keep the layout and visual components as simple as possible and focus on the sequence of the actions in the story.

Remember to practice. Rehearsal time is vital. With each rehearsal you'll refocus the words, adjust the timing, and consider where to place the emphasis.

To understand just how much top presenters rehearse their content, try to watch the same presentation twice. You will notice that the seemingly spontaneous sections are really very well planned.

As the review group entered the room, Bob wondered, Am I doing the right thing? He had done many presentations in his career, but few in the past decade had taken so much preparation, or had him so nervous before he started. The only thing he was sure of was that he knew his content. All the rehearsals had made sure of that! As the last of the audience sat down, Bob started to speak.

"Good morning. Today we are going to share with you a proposal for a new product. Our market share is declining fast on our current weight loss aid, and from the market research we can see this is due to the competition pushing prices down."

Bob hands out the visual story, turns on the projector to show an image of the current product and the top competitor, and continues.

"We have provided the key information for today's presentation on the handout. Let me talk you through our vision of the product roadmap and what it means for our company."

Bob talked for the next 15 minutes, setting the context with the audience for the current market conditions and the reasons why the competition has been able to force prices down.

To respond, Bob talks about the new software and design teams he is recommending. These teams will work together on a solution linked closely to the social web. At first the new teams appear to be a great start, until Bob explains the challenges the teams will face bringing together all the different company resources. This sets up the next complication, where the resolution is an integrated product development approach.

Bob continues in this way, taking a few minutes to set out each complication and follow through with the resolution as he works his way to the goal.

To bring the story to a close, Bob walks up to the whiteboard to draw the model he worked out last night. It shows the process for linking the new device to online services the customers use and transferring any content they have from previous devices, including competitor products.

0900   FRIDAY

If you want to grab the attention of an audience you can start with a controversial statement. If you want to build consensus and agreement, start with agreed facts.

A 15-minute visual story is ideal for working through a series of complications and resolutions to get to the final goal, and for linking the story to the physical one-page document.

Using the whiteboard for simple models during a presentation can increase interaction and show that you clearly understand the content, and it demonstrates credibility.

Fifteen minutes into the presentation and Bob closes by saying: "This isn't an easy path, but it will put us into a leadership position. We've asked you here today to review this proposal and to agree to proceed with the first stage, to bring in the new software and design teams."

As Bob said this he realized he had not been interrupted. Not once. But now the questions started. What was interesting this time, compared to previous experiences with this audience, was the impact of the one-page visual story. This time, the audience has the data in front of them to help them make the decision.

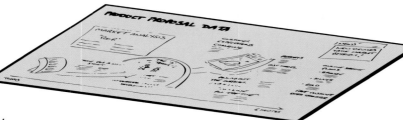

In answering their questions, Bob was able to start with content in the visual story. It didn't take long before the audience caught onto this and started discussing between themselves the details of the proposal among themselves.

Did Bob get a decision to proceed? He got a conditional yes from the CFO who was very positive, but who wanted to confirm the numbers in detail himself. Later that day the CFO called Bob and asked if the finance team could have a presentation of the proposal, with more insight into the reasons why the current product was failing.

Bob went back to the visual story map and decided to quickly rework the content to use a Rebirth plot for a ten-minute introduction, setting the first half of the story in the initial success, and then recent demise, of their current product. The Quest storyline then starts the miraculous redemption stage of the Rebirth, and tells the story of the fight back against the competition.

Stories that Move Mountains

At that point Bob realized that he was starting to understand how to use visual stories.

FRIDAY   121200

A key step in reaching agreement for a group is the interaction and discussion. Always think about finishing your story with a discussion.

A visual story handout aligned with the verbal story provides all the data for discussion and key reference points that link back to the story that's been presented.

Always remember to ask for the outcome you want to achieve. If you don't ask, the audience has to decide themselves what the outcome should be.

Afterword:
Improving Your Visual Storytelling

> If people only knew how hard I work to gain my mastery, it wouldn't seem so wonderful at all.
>
> *Michelangelo*

17

There is no magic wand to wave over an idea to create a great visual story. Real work is required, and quite a bit of creativity. Master storytellers get to the top of their craft because they have absorbed a wide range of approaches to structure a story in a way that is relevant to the situation and their audience.

Practice Makes Perfect

Most people's idea of how to improve their storytelling skills is that they have to give more presentations. However, that is a mistake they should avoid. Delivering a dozen bad presentations doesn't mean the next one will be great. If you get a little better each time, you're still damaging your reputation and losing the chance to influence an audience.

If you want to gain real improvement, practice daily. Zig Ziglar (American author, salesman, and motivational speaker) jokes, "People often say that motivation doesn't last. Well, neither does bathing — that's why we recommend it daily." There are many different techniques used in CAST, and you don't need to use them all together to get value from any of them. Take one activity at a time and build it into something you are doing each day, monitor your performance, look for improvement in your effectiveness, and put the feedback into your approach. The repetition of practice and objective feedback is key.

Mark

As an artist and musician, what has helped shape the storyteller in me today has everything to do with the exposure I've had to the work of others. I absorb what's already out there to develop the inspiration required to lead with my own unique voice.

Whatever kind of presenter you may be, the best storytellers know how to connect established conventions and new ones. This is where change happens — where people are moved by your work. Take a proactive approach to absorb what's happening around you, and integrate that into your own unique approach.

Use Your Tools

Take every opportunity to try creating visual stories. Become a collector of stories. Keep a notebook with you and record the anecdotes and stories you hear. You can use these to add points and interest to your future work.

Keep a copy of the Visual Story Map handy. It was designed to help you.

When you're creating a story, the Visual Story Map helps you to remember the key activities and to record the main points. You've seen the detail required to build a visual story, and that cannot all go on one page, but you can capture the key points for quick reference in the development process.

The Visual Story Map can be used as a learning aid to review other people's stories. Simply listen to a story and analyze it to identify the messages, the audience, how it has been structured, and the characters. Ask yourself if the sense of urgency is well defined. Do the visuals support the story or reduce its effectiveness? If you're watching a presentation that is a series of bullet point slides, try to capture them and see how you can restructure it.

While CAST was originally developed for creating stories to promote organizational change, we also discovered it is useful for creating stories about personal change, including losing weight and stopping smoking, and even for creating the cover letter and curriculum vitae for job hunters. CAST is not a silver bullet for every problem, but it's amazing to use the power of a story to grab attention and get results. Certainly, these situations will help you to practice the techniques.

Watch the best, and copy what they do.

Since you're going to tell a story, you might as well get good at it, focus on it and tell it in a way that you're proud of.

Seth Godin, American serial entrepreneur and author

HOW DO YOU GET TO CARNEGIE HALL? PRACTICE, PRACTICE, PRACTICE.

243

Know the rules well, so you can break them effectively.

Dalai Lama XIV, Nobel peace prize winner and leader of the Gelugpa lineage of Tibetan Buddhism

CAST is a process built on what we've learned from the experts, but it can also be extended to incorporate new and alternative ideas and techniques. When working on your own visual stories, think about the techniques you've used in the past and don't be afraid to incorporate them with CAST.

Lastly, the most important lesson we wish to communicate is that everything we've included in this book is simply a guide — and it shouldn't be followed blindly. As authors, we learned a lot about storytelling while developing the content we included in this book. Even though, we humans have been telling stories for thousands of years, there is still much to learn. When designing on a grid, break the grid often and push the boundaries when you decide it's the right time. Tell the best story possible by knowing when to break those boundaries, trying things and learning through the feedback that results.

We will continue to explore the science and art of visual storytelling and the specific role it can play in influencing decisions and making change happen. You can follow our personal stories as they develop and receive updates on new techniques and ideas by going to our website at **http://www.storiesthatmovemountains.com**.

You are the storyteller of your own life, and you can create your own legend or not.

Isabel Allende, Chilean American writer and educator

References

Check out these books and websites.
They're really good.
We promise.
Or at least Martin does.

*The essence of a good story requires **creativity**.*

You cannot reduce the craft of storytelling to a few simple formulas or mandatory story elements.

You can build on frameworks and techniques that have been proven over time.

Some books go to great lengths to list every possible reference source. This section highlights only those titles that can provide greater insight into the techniques and frameworks used in CAST.

> *We are like dwarfs sitting on the shoulders of giants. We see more, and things that are more distant, than they did, not because our sight is superior or because we are taller than they, but because they raise us up, and by their great stature add to ours.*
>
> John of Salisbury, 12th Century theologian

Why	What	How	What If
Who			
Learning and Decision Styles			
Structure	Character	Sense of Urgency	Delivery Plan
Design			
Test			

Why	What	How	What If
Who			
Learning and Decision Styles			
Structure	Character	Sense of Urgency	Delivery Plan
Design			
Test			

Why	What	How	What If
Who			
Learning and Decision Styles			
Structure	Character	Sense of Urgency	Delivery Plan
Design			
Test			

Advanced Presentations by Design: Creating Communication That Drives Action

Andrew Abela
Pfeiffer, 2008

Resonate: Present Visual Stories that Transform Audiences

Nancy Duarte
Wiley, 2010

Teaching Around the 4MAT® Cycle: Designing Instruction for Diverse Learners With Diverse Learning Styles

Bernice McCarthy, Dennis McCarthy
Corwin Press, 2005

Story: Substance, Structure, Style and The Principles of Screenwriting

Robert McKee
Regan Books, 1997

This book draws heavily on wide-ranging research to understand the different approaches to presentations. Although it takes a different approach to the CAST method, many of the concepts and techniques overlap or are complementary.

Again primarily focused on presentations, this book covers many techniques based on a story-based approach that you can use to make a strong connection with your audience and motivate them to action.

Learning styles are linked to preferences in the ways people perceive and process experience. With more than 25 years of testing and usage by educators around the world, this approach helps to understand the way to structure information as well as how to assess learning styles. You can learn more about the 4MAT® Cycle at www.aboutlearning.com.

McKee writes for the scriptwriter, for the stage, and for the big screen. This is after all where we find the best examples of stories. This book helps us to understand why people need stories, what makes them work, and what can go wrong.

Why	What	How	What If
Who			
Learning and Decision Styles			
Structure	Character	Sense of Urgency	Delivery Plan
Design			
Test			

Why	What	How	What If
Who			
Learning and Decision Styles			
Structure	Character	Sense of Urgency	Delivery Plan
Design			
Test			

Why	What	How	What If
Who			
Learning and Decision Styles			
Structure	Character	Sense of Urgency	Delivery Plan
Design			
Test			

Why	What	How	What If
Who			
Learning and Decision Styles			
Structure	Character	Sense of Urgency	Delivery Plan
Design			
Test			

Universal Principles of Design: 100 Ways to Enhance Usability, Influence Perception, Increase Appeal, Make Better Design Decisions and Teach Through Design

William Lidwell, Kritina Holden, Jill Butler
Rockport Publishers, 2nd Edition, 2010

This book is an encyclopedia of design concepts. It breaks away from other design books that simply show many pages of designs, to clearly describing a concept and showing an example. When considering how to lay out a visual story, the concepts described here can help everyone, from a novice to a professional, find something to use or improve upon.

Beautiful Evidence

Edward R. Tufte
Graphics Press, 2006

This is just one in a series of books by Edward Tufte, all of which have become classics in their own right. *Beautiful Evidence* is especially relevant to the work of visual storytellers because of its comprehensive range of design principles that together improve the effectiveness and quality of stories. For a visual story there is often a justifiable reason to include content that Tufte would exclude, but that decision should be careful considered and a part of the intentional design process.

Made to Stick: Why Some Ideas Survive and Others Die

Chip Heath, Dan Heath
Random House, 2007

After you understand what needs to be in a story, this is one of best books on how to make sure the message sticks.

Influence: Science and Practice

Robert B. Cialdini
Prentice Hall, 2008

Cialdini's work is based on a significant amount of research into human behavior. In the six principles described in this book, he provides clear descriptions of the different techniques that can be used with the delivery of a story to create an actionable outcome.

The Best of the Rest

The Leader's Guide to Storytelling: Mastering the Art and Discipline of Business Narrative

Stephen Denning
Jossey-Bass, 2005

This book focuses on the art of storytelling in business and the importance of story as a tool for leaders and influencers. This is the business person's version of Robert McKee's book, *Story.*

Presenting Magically: Transforming Your Stage Presence With NLP

Tad James, David Shephard
Crown House Publishing, 2001

As well as invaluable advice on how to deliver a presentation, which also works for delivering a story, this book builds on the 4MAT approach to explain how to structure information for effective delivery.

Benefits Management: Delivering Value from IS & IT Investments

John Ward, Elizabeth Daniel
Wiley, 2006

A book about delivering the value of IT investments seems a strange contributor to the subject of visual stories. Benefits management is another way of looking at the first part of the CAST story. The method described in this book for linking organizational and personal benefits to change is one of the greatest models I've ever used and easily extends to all parts of business and personal change.

Business Model Generation: A Handbook for Visionaries, Game Changers, and Challengers

Alexander Osterwalder, Yves Pigneur
Wiley, 2010

This is one of the books that shows how to effectively mix content and design for a business audience. If your story involves a major change to your business model, the information in this book can give you a great way to structure the business issues and then have the right content for your message.

The Anatomy of Story: 22 Steps to Becoming a Master Storyteller

John Truby
Faber and Faber, 2007

This book is strongly focused on story design for TV and film, with a 22-step story structure that defines the sequence of events in a film and a 7-step process for creating the core characters and content for the story. The content in early chapters helps when creating the sort of stories you might use for change with techniques to identify the key characters, their reasons for action, and the options they face.

PechaKucha

http://www.pecha-kucha.org

PechaKucha 20x20: show 20 images, each for 20 seconds. What started in 2003 in Tokyo by Astrid Klein and Mark Dytham has now spanned the world and, with it, a drive to make presentations fast-moving and focused, often based on a core story. We have a colleague who has taken the style and now fills 70 minutes with hundreds of images. He is closer to live comic strip animation than presentation, but never fails to fill the room and tell a great story. However extreme you want go, PechaKucha shows a different way to think about delivery.

A Periodic Table of Visualization Methods

http://www.visual-literacy.org/periodic_table/periodic_table.html

When you're looking for the one right structure to present your core message and a seed to get you started, use this website to find just the spark you need.

The Goal: A Process of Ongoing Improvement

Eliyahu M. Goldratt, Jeff Cox
North River Press, 2004

How do you take an introduction to the management theory of constraints and make it into a book people rave about? Build the content into a story. The explanations, told as fictional events, demonstrate the principles with effective metaphors from family experiences being used to explain complexity in manufacturing processes. This book demonstrates how even the driest of management theory can gather an army of raving fans when told the right way.

The Seven Basic Plots: Why we tell stories

Christopher Booker
Continuum, 2006

With over 700 pages and 34 years in the making,

this book isn't a light read. In fact, I've never read it from cover to cover. This is a reference book about stories, and one that can probably be described as the most comprehensive on the market. It is what I reach for first whenever I need examples of the different basic plots or how they mix together.

Understanding Comics: The Invisible Art

Scott McCloud
William Morrow Paperbacks, 2004

Comics appeal to all ages and cultures, but why? Scott McCloud gives a great insight into the nature of comics and how the comic strip actually works. This book slips a great many concepts and techniques directly into the brain to improve the way you think about presenting your story. After reading this book, I can guarantee you will want to try a comic strip approach on your next story.

Visual.ly

http://visual.ly/

Here you can find hundreds of examples of infographics with more added every day. When the creative juices are blocked, this site is always worth a visit for inspiration.

Storycraft: The Complete Guide to Writing Narrative Nonfiction

Jack Hart
University Of Chicago Press, 2011

Jack Hart comes to story writing with a journalist's perspective. You can find many nuggets of wisdom ranging from how to write content for case studies to white papers (and books). The focus is much more on the written story than the visual, but it's a great contribution to the skill set of a master storyteller.

Hope Is Not a Strategy: The 6 Keys to Winning the Complex Sale

Rick Page
McGraw-Hill, 2003

The delivery chapter explains why a sales mindset is important when structuring the delivery of your story. There are hundreds of books on sales techniques that could have made the grade, but this one is a clear introduction to an effective process.

Managerial Decision Making: A Guide to Successful Business Decisions

Alan J. Rowe, James D. Boulgarides
Macmillan Collins, 1992

There are many books that reference and build on the decision styles created by Rowe and Boulgarides,

but this is the first one that brings together the materials we used in Chapter 9.

Screenplay: The Foundations of Screenwriting

Syd Field
Delta, 2005

Where Robert McKee has a focus on the character and the story, Syd Field starts with the three-act structure, and includes much more guidance on the structure and visual elements of screenplays, that can be very useful for visual stories.

INDEX